Mole

Also by William Hood

Spy Wednesday (1987)
Cry Spy (1990)

Other Volumes in the Brassey's Intelligence & National Security Library

Roy Godson, series editor

Adda B. Bozeman • *Strategic Intelligence & Statecraft: Selected Essays*

Alain Jaubert • *Making People Disappear: An Amazing Chronicle of Photographic Deception*

Abram N. Shulsky • *Silent Warfare: Understanding the World of Intelligence, 2d Edition, Revised*

Werner Stiller with Jefferson Adams • *Beyond the Wall: Memoirs of an East and West German Spy*

Mole

William Hood

Foreword by
Roy Godson

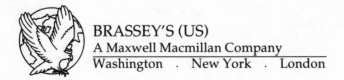

BRASSEY'S (US)
A Maxwell Macmillan Company
Washington . New York . London

For Robert Gray and Edward Foster

"The *peasantry* is the Achilles heel of Soviet Communism."*

MERLE FAINSOD

*Merle Fainsod, *How Russia is Ruled* (Cambridge: Harvard University Press, 1959), p. 442.

Brassey's (US)

Editorial Offices
Brassey's (US)
8000 Westpark Drive
First Floor
McLean, Virginia 22102

Order Department
Brassey's Book Orders
c/o Macmillan Publishing Co.
100 Front Street, Box 500
Riverside, New Jersey 08075

Brassey's (US) is a Maxwell Macmillan Company. Brassey's books are available at special discounts for bulk purchases for sales promotions, premiums, fund-raising, or educational use through the Special Sales Director, Macmillan Publishing Company, 866 Third Avenue, New York, New York 10022.

Library of Congress Cataloging–in–Publication Data
Hood, William, 1920–
    Mole/William Hood: foreword by Roy Godson.—1st Brassey's ed. p. cm.
    Originally published: New York : Norton, 1982.
    Includes bibliographical references.
    ISBN 0-02-881079-1 (paper)
  1. Popov, Pyotr. 2. United States. Central Intelligence Agency—Officials and employees—Biography. 3. Espionage, American—Soviet Union. 4. Espionage, Soviet. 5. Soviet Union. Komitet gosudarstvennoi bezopasnosti, 6. Spies— Soviet Union—Biography. 7. Spies—United States—Biography. I. Title.
JK468.I6H66 1993
327.1'2'092—dc20
[B]   93-4459
                                                                                                                      CIP

Designed by Bedrock Design
10 9 8 7 6 5 4 3 2 1
Printed in the United States of America

CONTENTS

FOREWORD

William Hood's *Mole* is a classic.

When first published in 1982, *Mole* was acclaimed as a significant contribution to intelligence literature—and with good reason. It combines history with mystery and does so with the style of a gifted writer and the expert eye of a seasoned intelligence practitioner. Hood began his intelligence career during World War II with the OSS in X-2 Counterespionage, worked in a variety of positive intelligence assignments, and retired in 1975 while serving as the executive officer of the Counterintelligence Staff of the CIA.

At the time Bill Hood wrote *Mole*, he was unable to acknowledge his personal participation in the recruitment and handling of Pyotr Popov in the introduction to the book. Thus, *Mole* appears to be fiction, but it is the actual story of Popov and the CIA operatives who handled him. Popov, a Lieutenant Colonel in Soviet military intelligence, spied on the West, but at the same time he also came to spy for the CIA for six highly productive years. In fact, Popov appears to have been the first significant penetration by the agency of the Soviet Union in the Cold War era.

This account of Popov's career, by a real-life participant in the story, is a very useful resource on the history of U.S. intelligence. When Popov first approached the Americans in Vienna in 1952, Hood (in the book, Amos Booth) was chief of operations in the CIA's Austrian station and, as such, was directly involved in the management of the case. *Mole*, then, is not a journalistic "reconstruction" or, conversely, fictionalized history. While in places a fictional gloss was employed by Hood to protect certain sensitive aspects of the operation, the story is essentially a firsthand account.

But the value of *Mole* goes well beyond the particulars of the Popov case itself. In remarkably few pages, Bill Hood provides his readers with a primer on human intelligence operations. The world of double agents, illegals, walk-ins, dead drops, brush contacts, surveillance, countersurveillance, and more is surveyed, explained, and equally important, tied to the operational realities of running an agent. Yet *Mole* is not a dry catalog of the world of espionage. Far from it. Watching Popov's CIA case officer, the rumpled but highly effective George Kisevalter (in *Mole*, Gregory Domnin) go about his work is alone worth the price of admission to this show.

Brassey's (US) **Intelligence and National Security Library** is intended to provide students, scholars, and national security experts with books on intelligence that make a unique or significant contribution to its study. Probably there is no single volume better than *Mole* at providing a scintillating overview of the complexity and reality of running an agent-in-place, especially one who is also an officer of a hostile intelligence service. It is a wonderful addition to the **Library's** collection.

ROY GODSON
Series Editor
Brassey's (US) Intelligence
and National Security Library

INTRODUCTION

Like war, spying is a dirty business. Shed of its alleged glory, a soldier's job is to kill. Peel away the claptrap of espionage and the spy's job is to betray trust. The only justification a soldier or a spy can have is the moral worth of the cause he represents.

Many spies run desperate risks but are mercenaries at heart—like well-paid stuntmen, they are only of passing interest. Other agents with impeccable motives have so little influence that their activities are soon forgotten. But when an ordinary man puts his life at stake for a political cause and has an impact on history, the story is worth telling.

This book is a memoir, the recollection of an intelligence operation based on the memories of the people who were involved in it. It had not occurred to me to write it until, after retiring from CIA, I noticed a reference to a highly secret operation in a book* by a retired CIA officer and approved by the agency for publication. The agent, referred to as "Major B," was described as the most productive spy the agency had run in the 1950s. In 1978 a writer probing the background of Lee Harvey Oswald published even more information on the case.† He named the agent, gave some details of his activity, and even noted the possibility that the agent had been betrayed by a spy the KGB had recruited within CIA.

These disclosures prompted me to look around for any other references I might find. As the facts had supposedly been clapped tight to the CIA bosom, I was puzzled at the amount of information that had

---

*Harry Rositzke, *The CIA's Secret Operations; Espionage, Counterespionage, and Covert Action* (New York: Reader's Digest Press/ Thomas Y. Crowell Company, 1977).
†Edward Jay Epstein, *Legend: The Secret World of Lee Harvey Oswald* (New York: Reader's Digest Press/McGraw-Hill Book Company, 1978).

been published since 1959 when the case came to term. The first reference in the American press was a *New York Times* story (20 December 1962), which announced that a Soviet army officer named Popov had been found guilty of espionage and executed in Moscow. In March 1964, *Show: The Magazine of the Arts*—a curious place to find a significant counterintelligence disclosure—published a review of Allen Dulles's *The Craft of Intelligence* by Peter Deriabin.* Deriabin had defected from the KGB in Vienna and settled in the United States. Pleased to sink a shiv into his new adversaries, Deriabin pointed out that the well-publicized Colonel Oleg Penkovsky was not the only spy CIA had recruited within Soviet intelligence. Lieutenant Colonel Popov, with whom Deriabin had served in Vienna, had also been a CIA agent.

Looking farther, I found that the Soviet press had been more outspoken about the case. The first and most comprehensive disclosure came in a two-part article in *Izvestya*, published in March 1963. There were many other accounts which, in the aggregate, pieced together the salient details of the case. These KGB-approved publications were alike in two respects. At no time was it admitted that Popov had the slightest connection with any Soviet intelligence organization; he was consistently described as a weak and corrupt "former military man" who had been blackmailed into espionage. In my opinion, this was not true.

As I was to learn, Pyotr Popov was the very model of a Soviet success story. A peasant from an impoverished backwater in Russia, he was a graduate of two of the most prestigious academies in the USSR, a field grade officer, and a member of the elite Soviet military intelligence service. There can be no doubt that the Soviet Union had given him the best it had to offer.

Like most people and all the spies I know anything about, Popov was an imperfect man. He drank too much. He was forgetful. He was bored by what he considered political nuances and he saw the world in black and white. Given the opportunity, he ran breathtaking—in retrospect, almost insane—risks. Although he loved his wife and children, he was hopelessly devoted to a randomly acquired mistress. But for six years he trundled bales of top-secret information out of the secret centers of Soviet power. In the process he shattered the Soviet military intelligence service, caused the transfer of the KGB

*Peter Deriabin, "The Difficult Intelligence Business," *Show: The Magazine of the Arts,* March 1964.

chief (a four-star general and one of the most powerful men in the USSR), and saved the United States half a billion dollars in military research.

Musing over the open references to Popov, I could see no reason why, more than twenty years after his death, his story should be left to molder in the secret files, another "dead case." Although the essential facts of the case were on the record, there was only the KGB's twisted version of Popov himself. I wondered if it would be possible to do a book that told the whole story—how he had been handled, what he had accomplished, what might have tripped him up, and, most important, what had motivated him. Because only part of the story was evident from the published accounts, I would have to rely on additional research for missing facts and other lacunae.

As a former CIA officer I had signed an undertaking to submit anything I might write on intelligence to the agency for review. I had no quarrel with this at the time and I have none now. If such an oath, or "contract" as the agency now calls it, cannot be enforced, all anyone who dreamed of a *roman vérité* need do is to sign on with CIA, take notes, resign, and head for the nearest word processor. One can argue against the propriety of spying and even against the need for a secret intelligence agency, but if an intelligence service is to operate abroad, it can only do so if its secrecy is protected at home.

Before starting I went to see one of the deputy directors of CIA, under whom the security review and legal officers labor, and said that I planned to do a book on the Popov case. No objections were raised and I set to work.

Some of those familiar with the case refused to discuss it; others spoke freely, but always with the understanding that the manuscript would be reviewed by the agency before publication. This, we all agreed, would protect any existing equities while permitting the publication of the story.

After some twenty months' work, I submitted the manuscript to McLean for review. Although the entire story was known in Moscow, and my manuscript showed the agency doing exactly what the taxpayers think it should be doing—collecting information on the USSR and thwarting Soviet espionage against the United States—it was immediately clear that CIA would prefer the Popov case to remain in the archive.

I found this bewildering. CIA had made information on the case available to one writer and had cleared what he published in 1977; the KGB had released their carefully slanted version to the Soviet press; and, from another published reference to the operation, I could only assume that at least one other writer had been quietly briefed by CIA.

As we struggled to come to terms, the agency reminded me that the director of Central Intelligence is charged by law with safeguarding the agency's "sources and methods." I pointed out that in this instance the source had been arrested in 1958 and, according to Soviet authorities, put to death in 1959. This had been published in the Soviet Union and abroad and had been acknowledged in publications approved by CIA. There remained the question of methods.

The methods—called "tradecraft"—described in this book are not unique to CIA. Except for the Soviet proclivity for murder, kidnapping, and blackmail, there is not much difference in espionage methodology East *or* West. Tradecraft may seem mysterious to outsiders, but it is little more than a compound of commonsense, experience, and certain almost universally accepted security practices. In the past eighty years newspaper accounts, informed novelists, and historians—particularly of World War II—have put considerable tradecraft into the public domain. In 1976 Senator Frank Church made an immense amount of data available to anyone willing to plow through the reports of his committee investigating CIA.

The fact is that tradecraft is like arithmetic: it has been around for centuries. The basics are easy to learn and good texts can be found in any library. Although it is easy to make mistakes under pressure, only the advanced aspects—like multiplying fractions or manipulating double agents—are particularly complex.

The only significant changes in espionage in this century have resulted from the application of advanced technology to operational problems. Radio and more sophisticated means of communication have replaced letters and the telephone. Eavesdropping has been relegated to electronic gadgets, and more intimate, over-the-transom snooping is now done by miniature TV cameras. Even binoculars—still occasionally called "spy glasses"—have given way to earth-orbiting photographic satellites.

For obvious reasons, there were some details CIA did not want published. Aside from three officers whose identities have been in the public domain for half a decade, *all* CIA personnel appear here in pseudonym. Some of the CIA officers involved in the operation are now dead. I would have liked to use their names, but this was forbidden. Two persons—one claiming to have been dragooned into espionage, the other more or less innocently associated with Popov—have also been given pseudonyms. To keep the record straight, the opening chapter—Moscow, 1959—is more speculative than the rest of the narrative, but is based on clues in the Soviet press and a yarn I heard late one wet night in Europe.

It was, of course, important that the book not disclose anything that might add to Soviet knowledge of the operation. The versions of the story published in the USSR show clearly that during the months Popov was under forced interrogation, the KGB had wrung from him every detail of his cooperation with CIA—the pseudonyms of his case officer, the addresses of safe houses, dates, places, the name of his mistress, and other operational details such as concealment devices and letter drops. Some communications between Popov and a contact man allegedly came into KGB hands and the Russians claim to have photographed at least two Moscow rendezvous. Since Popov's arrest some twenty-two years ago, the KGB has had time to conduct clandestine investigations abroad to confirm what they learned from Popov and others. The Russian file is obviously complete and nothing in this book will add a jot or tittle to what Moscow already knows.

In any really productive operation, the spy's motives are of critical importance. Popov's motives are portrayed as accurately as those who knew him best have been able to describe them. The dates, other than those quoted from the press, can only be approximately correct.

After some considerable discussion with the agency, we came to terms and in May 1981 the CIA's acting General Counsel informed me that the CIA Publications Review Board had found "no security objections to the publication" of the manuscript.

One last confession: the title may be misleading. However descriptive of a penetration agent it may be, the world *mole* was not in the intelligence lexicon in my day. John Le Carré found it—Marx had used it, but in a political sense—and popularized it. Mole is, however, so apt an expression that, for all I know, it may now be part of the professional vocabulary.

ACKNOWLEDGMENTS

Special thanks are due to those who dredged their memories to recollect events, reconstruct conversations, and to provide the flavor of these long-ago events. Although they worked without documentation, these sources proved to be remarkably consistent. Any errors of fact or interpretation must, of course, rest with me. Dorothy Olding and Peter Shepherd of Harold Ober Associates Incorporated helped to get the project off the ground and provided in-flight encouragement. At W. W. Norton, Starling Lawrence, a most perceptive and patient editor, managed to keep the narrative on the track. Josepha Gutelius and Kathleen Anderson were also most helpful. Throughout, Mary Seton's assistance was particularly valuable. Roy Doliner's advice and encouragement were as perfectly timed as his criticisms were pertinent.

W. H.

1
MOSCOW, SEPTEMBER 1959

Contact men are assigned cover names. The man who walked into the Aragvi Restaurant on Gorki Street was known as Daniel. It was an easy name to remember.

There had been a snap of fall in the air when Daniel invited the three guests he would use as cover. Perfect weather, he explained, for a dinner of the spicy Georgian food that was the Aragvi's specialty.

Menus were brought by a jovial waiter, a rarity among the sullen Moscow restaurant help. When drinks were ordered, Daniel reached across the table for a piece of the warm peasant bread, another house specialty. His shirt cuff eased back over his wristwatch. It was eight-thirteen. Excusing himself, Daniel walked slowly across the restaurant. It was exactly eight-fifteen when he pushed open the door and walked into the men's room.

Max was already there, soaping his hands at a washbasin. Beneath the closed door of a toilet cabinet in the corner of the room, Daniel could see dark trousers crumpled over the heavy Russian shoes of the man seated on the toilet.

Stepping up to a washbasin, Daniel glanced into the mirror. Max's familiar face was gaunt, almost emaciated. His heavy suit hung loosely from his thin body.

After a quick glance at the corner toilet, Max turned toward Daniel and put his finger to his lips. As Daniel bent over the washbowl and turned the faucet, Max touched his elbow. Facing Daniel, his back to the occupied toilet, the Russian pointed to his chest, indicating a slight bulge beneath his shirt. Then, lifting his hand to his ear, he made a circling motion with his index finger.

They had not rehearsed this signal, but Daniel could guess the meaning—Max was wired, wearing a miniature radio transmitter taped beneath his shirt. Daniel nodded his understanding.

With a grimace, Max tugged at a bandage covering his left thumb. It was thick as the finger of a fur-lined glove. Twisting the bandage, Max pulled it off intact. Daniel could see a jagged cut, closed with crude black stitches and matted with dried blood. What appeared to be strips of lined paper were wrapped around the middle of the wound.

Daniel watched as the Russian gingerly unwound the paper, his back still turned from the occupied toilet. The strips looked as if they had been cut from a lined note pad. Max handed the soiled paper to the contact man and forced the bandage back over his thumb. Then, with his hand close to his chest, he made a shooing motion toward Daniel and the door leading from the men's room.

Turning off the faucet in his basin, Daniel looked warily at the motionless feet in the toilet and handed Max a tightly wrapped package, about the size of a book of paper matches. With a resigned smile, the Russian slipped it into his pocket.

Daniel dried his hands, walked slowly up the stairs and across the restaurant to his table, the paper strips cached in an inside breast pocket of his suit.

He had not glimpsed the message on the paper strips, but the men's room pantomime could only mean one thing: Max had been arrested and had come to the rendezvous under KGB control.

It was nearly midnight before Daniel could free himself from his three guests and return to his rooms. His stomach was sour with the heavy meal he had scarcely been able to force down, and he wondered how he had gotten through the dinner without anyone noticing the turmoil churning within him. He took an antacid tablet from his pocket, put on his reading glasses, and spread the soiled strips—each about an inch wide—across his desk. For almost an hour he studied the meticulously penciled message.

When Daniel got up and walked across the room to a liquor cabinet, isolated phrases tumbled through his mind. "... They are treating me better now.... I tore these strips from the paper they gave me so I could write answers to some of the questions in my cell.... I made each the same width so they would not notice.... They have stopped beating me now. . . . Please try to do something for my family. . . . I managed to gash my finger in the cell. . . . Even General Gribanov was at one interrogation, sitting behind me. . . . Whatever happens do not break contact. . . . If my plan works they will let me go abroad again as a double agent . . . if not, my only hope is that your president will intercede with Khrushchev for me. . . . Relations are good now . . . perhaps they will hand me over if the president asks. . . . Disregard all intelligence reports I send, *they* are writing the messages. . . . Do what you can for my family. . . ."

Daniel poured himself a drink and walked back to the desk. As he began to read the notes again, he remembered the first time he had heard of Max. He wished they could have shaken hands, a last time.

2
THE DROP: VIENNA, 1952

It all began when Freddy Baer insisted on sitting in the front seat. Freddy was five and all the Armistice Day holiday meant to him was that his father did not have to go to the office. He liked that. But now he was tired from the shopping trip along the Kaerntnerstrasse and cranky enough to insist that on the drive home he sit up front, alone with his father. Just this once, his mother would have to sit in the back.

Peter Baer was glad to have a day off. His job in the intelligence co-ordination office of the U.S. high commissioner for Austria was not exactly what he had in mind when he joined the Foreign Service. But in occupied Austria in 1952 intelligence was important, too important, according to the high commissioner, Ambassador Walter Donnelly, to be left entirely in the hands of the dozen American intelligence agencies that had proliferated in Austria since the occupation troops had arrived in 1945. The occupation would not go on forever, and the time for cops-and-robbers activity was long over. In his dual role as high commissioner and ambassador, Donnelly had established the liaison office and given Baer the difficult job of keeping track of the work of the various intelligence agencies. He was to inform Donnelly of any activity that might embarrass the embassy. It was not an easy job. None of the intelligence outfits was accustomed to sharing its secrets with an outsider.

Baer unlocked the car, opened the rear door for his wife, and lifted Freddy onto the front seat. As he started the motor and swung out onto the Opernring, Marilyn bent to pick up something from the floor behind the front seat.

"You've dropped a letter," she said, tapping his shoulder with a white envelope. Baer glanced at it. The thick envelope was addressed *"An den Americanischer Hockkommissaer,"* Bolzmanngasse, Vienna XVIII. There was no stamp.

"What the devil is this?"

Marilyn remembered that no one had been in the back seat since they had driven to Salzburg for the weekend, almost a month ago.

"Someone must have dropped it through the window," she said.

"Whoever it was couldn't spell *Hochkommissar* and got the grammar wrong, too," Baer sniffed.

For a moment he considered stopping at the embassy to glance at the incoming cable traffic and to read the letter. But that could wait. It was a holiday and for the first time in days it was not raining. The duty officer would call him with anything important. Now that the shopping was done, he might be able to get in one last game of tennis. He stuffed the envelope into his jacket pocket, deciding to look at it when he got home.

It was late that afternoon when he finally got around to the bulky envelope in his pocket. He noted again that there was no stamp and the flap was carefully sealed with scotch tape. He tore it open. Another envelope inside, also sealed with scotch tape. There was one difference—the address on this envelope was typed in Cyrillic. Inside was a sheet of heavy bond paper. Baer's languages were French and German, no help in reading the few lines of neatly typed, double-spaced Russian text.

The embassy employed several Russian interpreters and translators, but Baer had read enough security reports to know that, as Russian émigrés, they were prime targets for Soviet intelligence. In recent months two had reported attempts at recruitment by Russian intelligence officers assigned to the Four Power Control Commission. He remembered the embassy security officer's comment that the *reported* pitches were no sweat—it was the ones you didn't hear about that mattered.

Like most embassies, Vienna got its share of crank letters. This could be one, but even if it were from someone like the old Viennese lady who regularly reported seeing Martin Bormann at the Café Mozart, Baer decided he had better ask his friend Joel Roberts, the CIA station chief in Austria, to have one of his staff make a translation. CIA, unlike some of the other intelligence outfits in Austria, had always been cooperative with Baer. He would leave the letter with Roberts on the way to the tennis courts.

The next morning Joel Roberts and Amos Booth, his deputy and chief of operations, bent over the original letter and a hastily prepared translation. It was a straightforward approach.

"I am a Russian officer attached to the Soviet Group of Forces Headquarters in Baden bei Wien. If you are interested in buying a copy of the new table of organization for a Soviet armored division, meet me on the corner of Dorotheergasse and Stallburgasse at 8:30 P.M., November 12. If you are not there I will return at the same time on November 13. The price is 3,000 Austrian schillings."

A memo from Alex Koenig, who had prepared the translation, noted that although the Russian text had no spelling errors and was grammatically correct, there were two errors in the German address on the outer envelope. At a time when all Western intelligence agencies were plagued with intelligence fabricators, this detail could be important. Most of the swindlers spoke fluent German—few Soviet officers spoke any at all.

3
BLUE-BOTTLE

Amos Booth had arrived in Austria from Washington a few months earlier with the lofty title of Deputy Chief of Station and Chief of Operations. Being deputy meant only that when Roberts, chief of station since 1947, was out of the country, Booth acted in his place. Roberts was rarely absent—Booth's real function was to direct the day-to-day operational work of the station. There was also something called "operational planning," seeing that the station kept at what were called the "hard targets." And they were *hard*.

The day Booth left Washington for Austria, Richard Helms called him into his office. At the time Helms was chief of an operational division responsible for secret operations in Austria and other areas including some of Eastern Europe. Helms said he wanted one last chance to emphasize a point he had made repeatedly during the weeks Booth had spent reading into the files on Austria.

Booth thought he knew the speech by heart, but this one started differently.

"The Austrian station has one real mission and a bucket of marginal responsibilities, many of them bilge." Helms always spoke precisely and to the point, but—Booth was now reminded—this was as close as he ever came to using a four-letter word.

"Your job is to recruit Russians. Until we've done that, we've failed. I don't care how many reports the station sends in on the Czech Communist party or Hungarian order of battle. Our basic job is to penetrate the Soviet establishment—that's the only way we'll get the answers the White House is screaming for. One penetration agent will be worth a ton of the scraps we're getting from those so-called spies—the guys on the outside looking in."

He was right. But Booth suspected that neither CIA nor any other Western espionage agency had yet been able to recruit a Russian official. As for "the guys on the outside looking in," his impatience was making Helms a bit unfair. There had been a steady flow of useful information from CIA's "outside" sources. It was just enough to goad the agency into ever more strenuous, even grotesque, efforts to break through the Soviet perimeter defenses. (In one reported incident, a case officer had importuned a startled Russian in a restaurant. Electrified by this sudden exhortation to commit treason, the Russian bolted across the dining room and into the ladies' room. Having locked the door, he completed his escape by climbing through a window.)

"All we can do from Washington is to keep some of the marginal jobs off the station and see that you get the necessary support," Helms went on. "Put in the plumbing and then concentrate on recruitment."

By "plumbing," Helms meant the operational support structure—safe houses, surveillance agents, letter drops, and a technical section trained to make quick audio installations, handle clandestine photography, and provide reliable short-range radio communications. Safe houses—usually small apartments rented under a pretext—were used by case officers to meet and question, or as jargon had it, to "debrief" agents. The usual dodge was to have a case officer pose as a businessman who, say, lived in Berlin but visited Austria often enough to need an inexpensive place to stay and meet his business contacts. Because these cover stories were not very plausible, safe houses had a common characteristic—they were not necessarily very safe.

A nervous landlord might suspect the new tenant was a black-market operator and tip the police. This was at the time of *The Third Man* and although Benno Blum, allegedly the inspiration for Graham Greene's Harry Lime, had been killed in a police raid, the Austrian black market still flourished. There was also the chance that an observant neighbor might think he had spotted something that could be sold to the Russians. Because of the risks, the station seldom used an apartment more than three months. Most apartment owners insisted on six months' rent in advance—for them the rapid turnover was a mini-Marshall Plan.

To save money and to cut down on the work involved in renting safe houses on the open market, the station also kept a few small flats in the buildings requisitioned for housing low-ranking members of the occupation forces in Austria. These were kept for meeting low-level contacts, persons of doubtful security or slight operational value to whom the station did not want to expose any of the more costly apartments.

As Helms went on talking, Booth found himself recalling the gap between the promises headquarters personnel always made to people headed for the field and what they were eventually able to deliver. Even when Booth was a junior member of the wartime OSS station in Switzerland, Allen Dulles had trouble getting what he wanted out of headquarters. It could do no harm to remind Helms that at least one bit of the necessary support was already missing.

"You know the station hasn't got a Russian-speaking case officer?" he said. In those days, few of the available Russian linguists could be spared until there was actually a case at hand that required fluent Russian.

Helms tilted back in his chair and stared at the ceiling. It was a mild form of bristling.

"Alex will be there in six weeks," he said. "Make a recruitment and you can have as many Russian-speakers as you need."

Alex Koenig was the pseudonym of a contract agent, a Russian refugee who had emigrated to the United States from Germany in 1946. He had been cleared by security but, because he had only recently been granted citizenship, he could not be given staff status in CIA and, in fact, literally was not allowed to enter any CIA office. He would work under official cover as a civilian employee of the occupation forces. This meant that he would be completely separated from the station and could only be met in a safe house. It was a clumsy arrangement but it did offer an added element of security.

"Nobody knows more about Austria than Roberts and no one is better at keeping relations with the high commissioner on an even keel," Helms said. "Roberts knows the station is up to its knees in targets and he's as anxious to score as I am."

There was no doubt about the targets—Vienna particularly was an intelligence battlefield. Like Germany, Austria had been divided into four zones of occupation in 1945. The Russians held the eastern zone, an area that included Vienna, the capital. The U.S., British, and French occupation areas stretched out to the west. Vienna, some ninety miles deep in the Soviet zone, had been chopped into five segments—one for each of the occupying powers and a fifth, the famous

First District or *Innere Stadt*, established as an international sector to be administered and policed by each of the occupation forces on a monthly, rotating basis. Unlike Berlin, where access to the Soviet sector was lightly controlled even before the wall was built, anyone could circulate freely within the Vienna city limits. But as a rule few Westerners ventured into the Soviet sector—some of the more cautious even avoided the *Innere Stadt* during the months the Russians were in charge.

On the few occasions Roberts was called on to brief a visiting congressman or junketing mandarin, he usually began by reminding him that Vienna was east of Prague. Until they checked the map on the office wall, few believed him. Its location made Vienna both a natural haven for defectors and refugees fleeing Czechoslovakia or Hungary and a jumping-off point for Western agents heading for Eastern Europe. There were some one hundred thousand Russians in Austria. And there were hundreds of Russian military, diplomatic, and intelligence personnel stationed in Vienna and at the nearby Soviet military headquarters in Baden bei Wien. They were the "hard" targets—and the slightest one of them would have been welcome as an agent. At the time, firsthand information on the USSR was so hard to come by that the lowest dogface private deserting from the Red Army was considered a valuable source and immediately flown out of Austria to a defector center in Germany.

"Remember, the station is vulnerable—the KGB* has penetrated the Austrian police and they've got informers three deep around the embassy and every other American office."

Helms was back on familiar ground. Although Soviet intelligence was primarily interested in recruiting American or British spies, it was also infiltrating agents into every element of the Austrian government that might be of interest once the occupation ended. Young agents had been slipped into the Austrian political parties, the post and telegraph systems had been penetrated, and the Russians were heavily engaged in phone-tapping operations.

---

*The Soviet secret police came into being in 1917. First known as the Cheka, it went through a number of reorganizations and name changes—GPU, OGPU, NKVD, NKGB, MGB—until in March 1954 it became the KGB. Since 1917 the Cheka and all of its successor organizations have had much the same responsibilities. To avoid confusion, KGB (Committee for State Security) will be used as a blanket term for the Soviet secret police and state security organization throughout this book.

"The KGB is looking right down our throat and they are playing for keeps—you can bet your hat and breakfast that they will double or kidnap any agent they spot."

A few months earlier the KGB had abducted "Otto" at a roadblock on the outskirts of Vienna. An Austrian with a natural flair for intelligence work, Otto had been hired by the station in 1946. Since that time he had recruited and handled a score of subagents. As soon as the station had learned he was missing, Otto's agents had been warned and offered resettlement in the U.S. zone of Austria. Few had accepted, but none was permitted to continue in any operational activity.

There had been no trace of Otto since the kidnapping, but there was one possible encouraging sign. Not one of his agents had reported any indication of KGB interest, none had admitted having been approached by the Russians. But unless Otto had contrived to commit suicide, it was hard to believe that even one so tough could have resisted Soviet pressure to talk. More likely he had been broken and had told most of what he knew. Probably Soviet counterespionage had decided to wait, hoping that, if it took no action against the blown agents, the station would rationalize Otto's disappearance and reactivate his net. But the KGB was wrong. Even the case officers known to Otto were transferred out of Austria.

"That's it, friend. When you score, remember to slug the cable 'Blue-Bottle' and send it *Eyes Only* to me. We won't want many people in on the act."

"Blue-Bottle" was an agency indicator used only on cables of the greatest secrecy. It meant that the message could be deciphered only by the chief of the communications staff on duty when it arrived. Three copies would be made, one for the director, one for the chief of the Operations Directorate, and another for Helms. They would be delivered by courier in sealed envelopes. No one else in the agency was authorized to open these messages.

Helms was more confident than Booth that the Austria station would ever have occasion to type Blue-Bottle on an outgoing cable.

4
THE WALK-IN TRADE

One of the many myths pinned on secret intelligence by imaginative journalists is that no espionage service will accept a spy who volunteers his services. In the real world of secret operations, volunteers have produced some of the greatest coups. "It's the walk-in trade that keeps the shop open" is one of the first bits of operational wisdom impressed on newcomers to the business.

Booth had an early introduction to this philosophy. In 1943 Fritz Kolbe, a career diplomat in the German foreign office, slipped into Switzerland with a sheaf of diplomatic cables in his brief case. After he had twice been put off by the British intelligence chief in Bern, he persuaded a Swiss friend to arrange a meeting with Allen Dulles. The British, unable to accept Kolbe's emotional declaration of anti-Nazi feelings, had temporized while consulting London. With his Swiss visa running out, Kolbe was ready to take his chances with the Americans.

One glance at the smudged carbons was enough to convince Dulles that the cables were authentic. If Kolbe had been sent by German intelligence as part of some elaborate deception scheme, it would become apparent in time—meanwhile Dulles would accept whatever Kolbe was offering and ask for more.

Dulles gave Kolbe the pseudonym "George Wood" and arranged for regular contact in Switzerland. Within weeks the "Wood" diplomatic cables were recognized as an important counterpart to the prized *Ultra* material—the German military and intelligence cipher traffic made available when British cryptanalysts broke the German code machine *Enigma*. By 1945 Kolbe's messages were considered to be among the most important intelligence items reported by Dulles from Switzerland.

Dulles's handling of Kolbe became a precedent for American intelligence. Estimate the risks, proceed prudently, but—above all—get on with it.

As it turned out, the intelligence services were not to be the only beneficiaries of the Dulles walk-in doctrine. When German military resistance collapsed in May 1945, the slight contact Stalin had tolerated between Soviet intelligence and the Western allies went with it. By 1946 the major espionage services were locked in a brutal clandestine conflict. The demand for intelligence was so great, and at the outset so undiscriminating, that a seller's market sprang up. Hundreds of agents found employment in one service or another—a few of the boldest attempted to work both sides of the street. In Austria, and particularly Vienna, where honest work was hard to come by and scarcely paid a living wage, part-time spying became a cottage industry.

Neck and neck with the scores of agents who at least tried to do an honest job of spying—and perhaps occasionally reading over their shoulders—ran a horde of tricksters who scratched a living by compiling imaginative reports from refugee gossip and press gleanings. Emigrés with intimate—if dated—knowledge of Eastern Europe, former Nazi intelligence officers, and con-men competed to peddle fabricated reports to any intelligence service gullible enough to buy them. The favored approach was to walk into an embassy or refugee interrogation center, claiming to represent a "friend" whose identity could not be disclosed for security reasons, but who for a price could be persuaded to part with red-hot information on one of the more obvious intelligence targets. The bait in many of these swindles was the "friend's" alleged position in one of the Soviet military or intelligence organizations.

As CIA gained experience in the postwar operational climate and learned more about its targets in the east, the most egregious fabricators—some of whom were so prolific they were called "papermills"—were identified and put out of business. But in 1952 espionage bunko games were still common. *Anyone* volunteering information was suspect until his data and sources had been identified and tested. Recently the station had spent hundreds of hours ferreting out the sources—nonexistent, as it turned out—of a former colonel in the prewar Royal Yugoslav intelligence service. The information was trash, but the wily colonel had done a brilliant job of packaging it.

It was because of this that Alex's comment on the buckslip was important. If the letter was a pitch from a fabricator, it was written by someone who at least knew Russian and had access to a typewriter with Cyrillic characters. And the misspelled German was interesting: a Russian officer would not necessarily have known much German—and few fabricators were that subtle.

5
A QUIET CORNER IN THE *INNERE STADT*

As Roberts and Booth began to rough out a meeting plan, two considerations were paramount. When an intelligence officer agrees to meet an unknown person at a place of his choice it is called "blind-dating." It is always a dicey proposition: in the Vienna *Innere Stadt*, where the KGB could operate almost as freely as in Moscow, it was downright dangerous. No CIA officer had ever been kidnapped in Austria, but there could always be a first time.

Because the letter was written in Russian, Booth had little choice but to recommend that Alex, still the only Russian speaker, make the meeting. In choosing Alex, Roberts and Booth had to reckon with the possibility that the KGB had gotten a line on him and had devised the approach to lure him to a spot where he could be grabbed. As an émigré whose new citizenship the Russians would not necessarily recognize, he was particularly vulnerable. Should he fall into their hands, the Russians could, if pressed, simply announce that Alex had seen the light and returned to his homeland. Aside from applying some diplomatic pressure—and the State Department had already shown it had little enthusiasm for bailing out secret agents—the station would be powerless to help him. Moreover if for whatever reason he should disappear, the station would be hobbled by the security precautions it would have to take on his account in future. The possibility of immobilizing a key CIA station—one uniquely situated to work against the Soviet Union—would be enticing enough to make the KGB consider a snatch.

There was a second and much more important consideration. No matter how much they might need a bit of walking-around money, Russian officers were not known for the habit of selling classified documents. The station was not particularly interested in the table of organization of a Soviet armored division. But Roberts was very much indeed interested in any Russian officer who might be willing to sell it.

"Have you ever heard of a bona fide approach as bald as this one?" Roberts had never served in CIA headquarters and Booth knew that he tended to assume that those who had knew far more than in fact they did.

"There was an NKVD man—Volkov—under diplomatic cover in Turkey. He approached the British in 1946. But he wanted to defect and he knew the English diplomat he talked to." Booth was clutching at straws.

"What happened?"

"Kim Philby was sent out from London to handle the case. By the time he got there the NKVD had wigged to it. Volkov was shipped back to Moscow on a stretcher in a Soviet air force plane."

When Booth left for Austria in 1951 Philby was still chief of the British intelligence post in Washington. One of the most highly regarded officers in the British service, he was a good bet to replace Sir Stewart Menzies, the chief of the British secret intelligence service. Neither Roberts, nor Booth, nor anyone—except possibly James Angleton, who was soon to take over CIA's counterespionage service—then suspected Philby. As it was later proved, Philby had been a Russian agent since 1935. He was eased out of the British service in 1952. When the evidence began to pile up against him, Philby levanted to Moscow in 1963. Two years later in a memoir,* Philby casually admitted having delayed his trip to Turkey long enough to tip the Russians to the would-be defector. Konstantin Volkov was drugged and shipped back to Moscow on a Soviet military aircraft—his last trip.

If this is a straight offer," Booth said, "he's not asking for much cash."

Roberts nodded.

Three thousand schillings was about one hundred twenty dollars, a lot of money in Vienna at the time, but less than a hungry fabricator would have asked for.

---

*Harold A. R. Philby, *My Secret War* (New York: Grove Press, 1965).

The decision was obvious: the approach would be treated as bona fide. If there was anything to it, the case would be off on a secure operational footing—if nothing came of it, the station would have had a good dry run.

"It's a damned quiet corner," Roberts muttered, "but at least we should be able to see if he's alone." After six years in Austria, Roberts knew every alley in Vienna's *Innere Stadt.*

"I'll send a car through first and have someone ride shotgun on the way back," Booth said. "Maybe we can have a couple of people on the street—at least they can raise a row if something comes unstuck."

"Riding shotgun" sounded fierce: all it meant was that a second car would follow Alex as he drove the walk-in to the safe house. Case officers rarely carried weapons—if a situation got so sticky that they could not talk their way out, Roberts figured the other side had more experience with guns and would carry the day anyway.

As Booth drove across the Waehringerstrasse toward the office building where one of the operational wings of the station was lightly, but, Roberts hoped, innocently, cloaked as the Plans and Review Section of the Vienna Military Command, he realized he had another problem. Any Russian officer desperate enough to approach American intelligence by tossing a letter into a parked car was bound to be jumpy. If he detected any protective surveillance on the street, he would be likely to bolt before trying to decide whether it was CIA or the KGB. It would be too risky to have any foot surveillance in the area. Alex would have to do this one on his own.

There was one consolation. Perhaps it *was* just a hoax concocted by one of the fabricators still working the Vienna intelligence bourse.

With Peter Todd, Booth checked a detailed street map of the *Innere Stadt.* Todd was chief of the station's Soviet operations branch. The son of a New York newspaperman, he had grown up around the city room of a prominent New York daily. While working as a reporter, he had married the daughter of a Russian émigré. By 1944 he had assimilated enough Russian to land a job in the press section of the U.S. Embassy in Moscow. At the end of the war he was transferred to Germany where he came to the attention of OSS. By the time his State Department contract expired, CIA had been formed and Todd was hired. Todd's training as reporter was useful—not only could he draft cables and dispatches faster than anyone in the station, he was not one to let anything stand between himself and a bit of intelligence or a recruitment.

As part of the "plumbing," Booth had procured a bulky set of Vienna street maps. Whatever other shortcomings the Austrians might have, they were superb mapmakers. Every building, street, and alley was clearly drawn and in perfect scale. As Booth studied the map, he realized Roberts had been right. The corner of Dorotheergasse and Stallburggasse was a good meeting place—at least for the man who had chosen it. In the very center of the *Innere Stadt*, near the Graben, with its statue to the victims of the great plague, there were no American installations anywhere in the vicinity. Worse, there was no vantage point from which to observe the area from a distance. At eight-thirty it would be dark, there would be little vehicular traffic and few pedestrians. At least Alex would not have any problem spotting his contact. Booth began to work out the details.

Five minutes before the meeting a case officer driving a shabby, Austrian-plated Volkswagen would make a final reconnaissance of the area to see if there was any sign of a stakeout or surveillance. As a man and a woman would be much less conspicuous than two men in a slow-moving vehicle, a station secretary would ride in the passenger seat to help with the observation and to handle the portable radio.

If Alex failed to identify the contact, he was to leave the area within three minutes. If he spotted his man—even in civilian clothes Russians were easy to identify—he would go directly up to him, announce himself in Russian, and walk his catch to the vehicle that would be parked on the Graben. They would drive along the Schottengasse to the Ringstrasse, then turn and head directly for the American sector and the safe house. The shotgun would follow them from the Graben, looking for any signs of surveillance. If the contact *was* a Russian, Alex would drive him back to the *Innere Stadt* after the meeting. Otherwise he could walk.

Booth knew the scheme was too elaborate, but there was no time to simplify it.

But Todd was an activist. He *knew* that a straight line was the shortest path to any objective and he resented the security trappings that appeared to interfere with a direct approach to any target—especially a Russian. The thought of committing *three* ops vehicles—all that the station had at the time—and *five* people to an operation that might be a hoax was too much for him.

"Couldn't we just have Alex meet the guy and take him to a safe house in a taxi?"

Todd had arrived in Austria after Otto's kidnapping, but he had a point. There was a taxi stand on the Graben and there was much to be said for simplicity. Radios had a way of not working when most needed, inexperienced case officers could hardly be counted on to improvise with ease if something went wrong, and Booth couldn't plan for every contingency.

There was also the first law of operations: if there is a way for things to go wrong they will. The station had postulated a second law: things will go wrong in direct ratio to the importance of the operation. But Alex would be blind-dating in an area that might have been picked by the KGB. Booth had to give him as much protection as possible, and if they *were* being set up it was important that the station know about it at the first possible moment. There was no choice but to do it by the book.

"If the guy agrees to go to the safe house," Booth said, "I don't want any shoptalk in the car." Todd nodded agreement. It would be important to get as much as possible of this first meeting on tape.

As Todd walked to the door to begin assembling the case officers who would be handling the surveillance cars and radio, Booth remembered Helms's advice and added one last caution. "Remember, only Alex is to know that it's a Russian we may be meeting. Tell the others it's a Czech refugee just come over the border."

Todd smiled. "A likely story," he said.

As soon as Todd left the office, Booth called for Ed Masters, the station technical officer. A former architect and ocean-racing yachtsman, Masters had served on a destroyer in the Pacific during the war. Ironically, his only command was a surrendered Japanese destroyer which he sailed to Pearl Harbor after the war. In 1951 when CIA was expanding rapidly Masters was recruited for maritime operations, a rather narrow field but one in which his background would be most useful. By the time he had completed a few weeks of operations training, whatever need had been perceived for him in maritime operations had disappeared. He was assigned to Austria.

No one, least of all Masters, knew for sure why he had been picked for that landlocked country. He could not speak a word of German and, as he was to discover, was one of those unfortunate individuals who, no matter how hard he struggled, would never be able to string a sentence together in anything but his mother tongue. By the time this had become apparent, Booth had learned that Masters had other skills—he was an expert ham radio operator and an enthusiastic amateur photographer. With the station desperate for someone who could make the fragile electronic gear work, and who could tell a lens from a light meter, the station had found the man to run the technical section. A bit more plumbing had been put in.

Masters had another great quality. He was an irrepressible optimist.

After Booth had briefed him, Masters read the requirements back from the notebook he always carried when he went into Booth's office.

"Radio contact between a moving vehicle in the *Innere Stadt* and a radio command post at Freddy's." For security reasons proper names were assigned to each safe house. If a telephone had to be used, and the station tried to avoid this, a case officer could say, "I'll meet you at Freddy's" rather than attempt to get the address across in double talk.

"Two room mikes in the living room at Freddy's to be monitored and recorded from the bedroom." There was a lot to be said for naval training. Masters might not be able to speak much German but he could trim his English conversation to the bone.

"Can you photograph the guy we're meeting?"

Masters studied the street map. He hated to admit that some things could not be done. "Not at that time of night. But we might be able to do something at Freddy's." He explained that by drilling a series of pinholes in the bedroom door and holding the camera against them he might be able to get a recognizable likeness.

"All we have to do is put in an extra floor lamp and make sure he is seated facing the camera."

"Okay, but the photographs are secondary. What we must have is the tape."

That, Masters said confidently, would be the easy part.

"If you think they will show in the picture, put a bottle of bourbon and some American cigarettes on the coffee table." It might be useful, Booth thought, to have a picture of the anonymous Russian sitting with someone who had access to things that obviously came from the American PX.

6
A NOISY LEICA

Because case officers were so vulnerable to surveillance, the station maintained several offices in Austria. When in Vienna, Booth and Roberts occasionally met in one of the buildings occupied by the high commissioner, a handsome stone edifice, rumored to have housed the Imperial Diplomatic and Consular Academy in the days of the Austro-Hungarian Empire. A generation of old-school diplomats had learned the fine points of protocol in the office Roberts borrowed. The room usually made available to Booth was less grand. He could not imagine what the aspiring diplomats might have learned in such a cubbyhole. But he used it only often enough to lend some verisimilitude to his cover. It was in another building more than a mile away that Booth did much of his work.

Formerly the headquarters of a large Austrian firm, the building had been requisitioned in 1945 to provide working space for some of the dozens of American units involved in the occupation. The offices usually allocated to Booth were on the top floor, and the constant flow of military and civilian personnel throughout the building provided excellent camouflage for the coming and going of the busy case officers.

Because of his senior position in the American occupation establishment, Roberts was tied down to offices where he could receive visitors, conduct the necessary liaison, and deal with the plague of administrative bothers that beset all secret intelligence field offices. As long as Roberts was at hand, Booth was free to spend his time with the operational sections of the station. This worked well enough for Booth, but was a constant frustration to Roberts who, like most station chiefs, had begun his intelligence career as a case officer and preferred the rough and tumble of operations work to the paper pushing that went with his job as station chief.

Roberts and Booth met every morning to read the incoming cable traffic and review any upcoming activity of particular interest. As a rule, Booth would return late in the afternoon to wind up whatever had unraveled during the day.

That morning Roberts's first question was about Todd. Although Booth had told Todd not to call him after the meeting—late at night "innocent" phone calls sometimes became so ostentatiously bland they could alert the Soviet telephone monitors—Roberts knew Todd well enough to know that if a Russian had made the meeting, Todd might not have been able to keep his discipline. Had he called?

"No," Booth said. "But that's all to the good. If it was a *Blind-gaenger*, a dud, he might have called just to take us off the hook. Maybe it's a good sign that he's kept his pucker."

They had begun to leaf through the morning cable traffic when the door to the office swung open and Martha, Roberts's secretary, brought in a porcelain coffee pot and two soggy doughnuts from the snack bar in the basement. The snack bar food was an affront, a grotesque attempt by an otherwise competent Austrian chef to imitate American short-order cooking; but few Austrians were capable of producing anything but superb coffee.

As she set the tray on Roberts's desk, Martha said in her soft Southern accent, "When you have a minute, Peter Todd is anxious to see you both."

Roberts groaned in frustration, but before he could say anything, Todd slipped through the door. Unsuccessfully masking her pique at this breach of office etiquette, Martha asked stiffly if Mr. Todd would like coffee. "Not this morning, dear," he answered and remained standing to close the door behind her.

After a moment's nervous groping, Todd fished a sheaf of scrawled notes from his breast pocket and began to talk.

"Like clockwork. Just like goddamned clockwork. The guy was there, right on schedule. Alex took him straight to the safe house. He didn't bat a goddamned eye."

Roberts turned and snapped on the radio he kept behind his desk. The station offices were regularly swept by counter-audio men, but the radio was used as an extra precaution. It wasn't much of a help: if it was on loud enough to bother any possible interceptor, Roberts and Booth had to shout to make themselves heard; if it was low enough to permit easy conversation, it merely provided background music for the monitors.

"So far, so good. Who is he?" Roberts was as impatient as Booth.

"He wouldn't identify himself. But he's a Russian, big as life. There's no doubt about that."

"How do you know?" Roberts asked.

"He said he was." Todd saw Roberts wince.

"He doesn't speak much German, his Russian is native and he had the bloody T/O with him," Todd said quickly.

"Did you get it?"

Todd reached into his pocket and tossed a wad of photostats onto the desk. "Look at the date—there's no doubt about it, it's the real thing."

And so it was. Two hours later, and after several redrafts of the paragraph covering the Russian's refusal to identify himself, Roberts signed the long, outgoing cable. A few minutes after that the station began to transmit its first Blue-Bottle message.

Whatever his motives may be, the role of a spy is to betray trust. A man who has volunteered, or been tapped, to commit treason cannot logically ever be trusted again. Every aspect of a spy's relationship with his case officer, or intelligence service, stems from this basic premise.

There is a corollary. Whatever reservations an agent may have when he signs on, the fact is that when an intelligence service buys a spy, it buys him *in toto*. No espionage service can tolerate the merest whiff of independence or reserve on the part of an agent. For the spy, espionage is a one-way street.

With a new agent, the case officer's first task is to maneuver him into a position where there is nothing that he can hold back—not the slightest scrap of information nor the most intimate detail of his personal life. Until this level of control has been achieved, the spy cannot be said to have been fully recruited. Only when the recruitment is completed can a "contact" or "source" (as they are sometimes called) be considered a spy, the creature of his case officer and the intelligence service he represents.

The idea of paying an anonymous source for information contradicts the most basic principles of agent control. It is anathema to all intelligence services and none will tolerate it for long.

The fact that the station did not know the Russian's name and as yet had no plausible means of identifying him meant that Roberts had some deft explaining to do in the first Blue-Bottle cable.

As an outside man and a newcomer to operations, Alex had done a good job. But as Todd pointed out, he had gone into the operation with one great advantage—he was not burdened with the knowledge of just how rare any operational contact with a Russian was and how potentially important it might be. Nor had Todd given him any indication that this was not a routine operation—business as usual at the station. Whatever anxiety Alex may have felt about the meeting, he was determined to prove that he could handle it as easily as if it were one of the training exercises he had sweated through in Washington. His matter-of-fact approach to it was something none of the old hands could have carried off.

Todd had begun briefing Alex by reminding him that the first thing any young reporter on a high school newspaper learns is that most news stories are based on a simple formula, the answers to six questions—who, what, when, where, why, and how. The formula for dealing with a walk-in was even simpler—who, what, how, and why. Who is he, what does he have, how did he get it, and why is he offering it? "If you can get the answers to these questions," Todd told Alex, "we'll be off and running."

Todd also briefed Alex on what he called a "one-shot." One-shotting has a particular appeal for imaginative amateurs who think they can make an anonymous, one-time transaction with an intelligence service—a packet of hot information for a wad of cash and no one the wiser. Grasping greenhorns have about as much chance of swinging a deal like this as the average football fan would have of surviving more than a few minutes in a Super Bowl game.

To guard against the possibility that the walk-in had such a proposition in mind, Todd coached Alex carefully. If Alex was satisfied that his contact was a bona fide Russian, in no circumstance was he to be allowed to leave the safe house without positive assurance that he would return. Most spies are mercenaries. No matter how much political gloss they daub on their motives, if money enters the picture at all, chances are overwhelming that money *is* the motive. Because the man had mentioned his price, it seemed likely he was primarily interested in cash and possibly intent on a single deal. It was Alex's difficult task to offer enough money to entice, sufficient to ease but not cancel whatever pressure had made him turn to American intelligence.

If this didn't work and the Russians refused to have a second meeting, Alex was to turn tough. He would tell the stranger their interview had been recorded and photographed. He was to say that if the Russian refused to continue the negotiation he had invited, Alex's boss could only assume that he had been sent by Soviet intelligence to bring back identification of American personnel and facilities. To discourage any further such fishing expeditions, he would have no alternative but to publish the pictures and the tape transcripts.

However unlikely it was that the station would ever have taken any such irreversible steps—or even that the pictures would be recognizable—was not important. In the tense safe-house atmosphere even empty threats have the impact of a knee in the groin.

Alex was well primed for his rendezvous.

It was dark at eight-thirty and, as Booth expected, the rain-washed streets were deserted. Alex was within a hundred feet of the corner before he spotted a man, half hidden in a doorway at the corner of Dorotheergasse and Stallburggasse. Without breaking stride he strained to see if there was anyone else, anywhere along the street. It was too dark to see who might be concealed in the deep doorways, but at least there were no cars parked along the Stallburggasse. Alex could not know what might be around the corner on the Spiegelgasse and for the moment at least preferred not to speculate on it.

As he drew closer Alex could see that the man was in civilian clothes; short, thickset, almost fat, but perhaps it was the broad-brimmed hat and bulky overcoat that gave this impression.

"I'm here about the letter," Alex announced in Russian. Later he admitted that he could not remember the Russian's response. But when the stranger answered in Russian, Alex took him by the arm.

"Come on—I haven't got much time. Let's go where we can talk."

Without waiting for any possible demurrer, or suggestion that they follow Viennese custom and do their business in a coffee house, Alex bustled the man along the gloomy street to the parked car. With the stranger slouched in the front seat, they sped across the Ringstrasse and on to the safe house—a grungy flat on the first floor of an apartment building.

It was not one of the station's high-security meeting places. Rather than risk compromising a better safe house on a walk-in, Booth had decided that he should be taken to one of the simple flats the station kept in buildings requisitioned by the army's Vienna command. The station used these places to interview walk-ins whose bona fides were suspect. If the walk-in proved bogus, all the station had to do was telephone the army housing office in the morning and the flat would probably be occupied by a grateful second lieutenant the next day. There would be no way a hostile intelligence service could trace the apartment to Alex or the station. If the contact looked promising after the first two or three meetings, a better safe house would be made available.

This was the sort of nip-cheesing that warmed the hearts of agency auditors—who invariably found the station to be spending too much money on safe houses that were leased for six months but might only be used once. It was also the sort of knee-jerk economy that had no place in operations. Booth was lucky that the first meetings were unnoticed by curious neighbors or the surveillance agents the Russians attempted to keep in circulation in the vicinity of the American quarters and offices.

As they peeled off their overcoats, Alex's first question exhausted his small talk. "Vodka or whiskey?"

The Russian eyed the two bottles on the coffee table. "Vodka," he said and began to talk even before the drinks had been poured.

He was, he declared, a field grade officer in the Soviet army, assigned to the Central Group of Forces headquarters at Baden bei Wien. It was embarrassing for him to admit it, but the fact was that after a night of hard drinking, he had been rolled by a bar-girl in the *Innere Stadt*, who had lifted all his cash. It was bad enough to lose his own money, but he was also carrying some official funds. If he could not replace this money within a few days, it would be missed and he would face a court-martial.

"How much money?" Alex asked.

"Not so much—three thousand schillings."

"That's not so little either," said Alex.

The Russian shrugged. "That's why I've come to you. It's little enough for what I have with me."

"That's something my boss will decide," Alex said. "But let's see what it is."

"This is the new table of organization for a Soviet armored division. We just got it, direct from Moscow. It's the first reorganization since the war and it shows how we're preparing to cope with tactical atomic weapons."

Aside from a few months of forced labor, building a *Wehrmacht* hospital in Germany during the last months of the war, Alex had no military background at all.

The Russian dropped a sheaf of photostats on the coffee table. As Alex bent to study the papers, they both stopped talking. Suddenly Alex's attention was distracted from the document. To his dismay he could hear the unmistakable click of the camera behind the bedroom door. He cleared his throat and in a questioning voice began to read aloud from the document. But not before the Russian had begun looking anxiously around the room.

"This may be all you say it is, but it doesn't look so unusual to me. How is it different from the old T/O?"

The Russian began to explain but Alex was not listening. At least their voices covered the clicking camera.

"Okay, maybe this is a new organization. And you may be a Soviet officer. But how do I know this? How come you are in civilian clothes? Who are you?"

"I'm just who I said I am—you don't expect me to come to a place like this in uniform, do you?"

"And you don't expect me to tell my boss that I've just given a total stranger three thousand schillings for some damned document he copied out of a newspaper, do you?"

"He'll know what it is."

"That's right, he will. But I don't. Until he says okay, I'm not going to pay for it."

"This is impossible. Just coming here, I put my life on the line. I need the money now—if you can't afford it, I'll go to someone who can."

"If you are who you say you are, you'll be better off dealing with me—how many letters do you think you can toss into automobiles anyway?'

The Russian wiped the sweat from his forehead and reached for the vodka.

"Look," Alex said. "I'll give you five hundred schillings tonight if you identify yourself. If the document is authentic, I'll pay you the rest in a few days—and give you a bonus to boot."

They argued for a few minutes until, to change the subject, Alex began to ask questions. Who is the commanding general in Austria? Who is chief of staff? How many divisions do the Soviets have in

Austria? In Hungary? Who is town commander in St. Poelten? In Baden? Where is the communications center for the Central Group of Forces? What offices are on the fifth floor of the Hotel Imperial?

Smiling, the Russian answered each question, casually adding information and volunteering data that could only be known to a serving officer. Alex poured another two drinks.

"This is all very well, but we'll get nowhere until I know who you are. Show me your ID card."

"I will not identify myself. Take the document to your chief. He'll know. But you won't get my name."

In a few more minutes they had agreed—the Russian would take seven hundred schillings on account. He would return the following week and pick up the rest—if the document was authentic.

"Don't worry, it is. And I am who I say I am."

They agreed to meet at the same corner in a week. If the Russian was not there, Alex would return the following night. If the Russian wanted to meet earlier he would telephone Alex.

"All you have to do is identify yourself as 'Max'—speak Russian or German. Just give the time you want to meet. I'll be there at any time you say."

The Russian nodded and copied the telephone number into his pocket notebook. As they rose to leave, he stared apprehensively around the room. There was no more noise from the camera and his gaze seemed to focus on an ugly oil painting on a wall across from the coffee table.

Once in a while, just often enough to give intelligence officers a false sense of confidence, a secret operation goes almost according to plan.

7
THE MEN FROM WASHINGTON

In the first cable to headquarters the station had sketched the operational developments—the letter tossed into the car, Alex's street corner meeting, the Russian's explanation of why he needed the cash, the substance of Alex's pitch—giving a tentatively favorable evaluation of the document the Russian had provided.

The cable had also speculated on who the man might be. There was little doubt that he was a Russian—native fluency in the language, effortless response to Alex's questions, and the palpably Russian aspect of his clothing. That he wore civilian clothes could only mean that he was a diplomat or an intelligence officer—all other Russians in Vienna were in uniform. The fact that the table of organization had been photocopied also seemed to support this speculation—not many Russians would have the facilities for making copies of documents. Although his rough physical appearance and blunt conversation suggested a military background, the station knew that all the Soviet intelligence officers in Austria carried military rank and most of them had been on active military service during the war.

Roberts's conclusion was that the Russian was an intelligence officer, that he did need the cash he was asking for and, most interesting of all, he did not seem interested in defecting. Whether he was in the GRU, Soviet military intelligence, or in the KGB—the more formidable intelligence and security service—Roberts refused even to guess. In either case, as far as the station was concerned, it had a very big fish on the line.

As exciting as this prospect was, Roberts did his best to convince headquarters that he knew the walk-in could be a Trojan horse. Still,

29

he assured Washington, he had not as yet seen any evidence of provocation, or any indication that he was trying to draw them out in any manner. Roberts promised that the station would keep its guard up and, insofar as possible, not expose anyone to the risk of kidnapping.

Roberts also made one urgent request of headquarters. He needed an experienced, Russian-speaking case officer and he had to be in Austria in time for the next meeting. It was twenty-four hours before Washington replied.

Alex had played his part perfectly, but he had one drawback, and this was reason enough to remove him from the operation as quickly as possible. Alex was born in the Soviet Union and had grown up there. His three years in Germany and four in the United States had neither erased his mannerisms nor altered the unmistakably Soviet flavor of his spoken Russian. CIA had not had much experience with Soviet defectors—and as far as Roberts or Booth knew, none at all with Soviet agents in place—but the agency had approached a few Russians and made strenuous attempts to recruit them.

One of the first things learned was that the cumulative impress of the Soviet Union's thirty-five years include a virulent strain of paranoia. In Stalin's Russia even the most sanguine Soviet citizens were leery of strangers. Abroad, at the height of the cold war, any Soviet officials who could, avoided foreigners. Russian-speaking strangers were even more likely to be shunned. If a foreigner spoke fluent pre-1918 Russian, he was almost certainly an émigré, and Soviet officials had been warned that all émigrés were enemies of the state and fascists and spies in the bargain. If a stranger spoke "Bolshevik" Russian—the language that had evolved since the revolution, with changes apparent to any native speaker—he could only be a defector, refugee, or KGB man engaged in a provocation. The prudent reaction for a good Soviet citizen was immediate flight.

The only Soviets with any latitude in dealing with émigrés were KGB officers detailed to émigré operations. Western intelligence had learned from bitter experience that most Russian officials were so impressed with the KGB's record of penetration and manipulation of the Russian emigration that they would as soon look death in the face as to confide in any émigré, let alone to use him as a conduit for an illicit relationship with a foreign intelligence service.

Therefore, although Alex had been nimble enough to hold his own during the first meeting, if the station was going to win the quarry's confidence it would be essential for an American case officer to take over the operation at once. And he would have to do so in Russian. Russian is not a language that lends itself to a simplified, pidgin form. Unlike German, Spanish, or even French, there is no such thing as "speaking a little Russian." One knows the language or not.

Some graduates of the intensified Russian study programs in the United States had already signed on with CIA. But as recent recruits they lacked operational experience and, as a rule, were far too young in appearance to hope to achieve the level of rapport and dominance called for in a case of this potential importance. A good man would be hard to find.

Headquarters' answer to the Blue-Bottle cable was succinct. The case was a potentially more important matter than anything else the station had at hand. Until proved otherwise, it was to take precedence over all other activity. A maximum hold-down on knowledge of the operation had been ordered at headquarters, and no one in the station not directly involved was to be given any knowledge of it.

Not only was the request for a case officer to handle the operation approved, but a backup man, a specialist on Soviet intelligence, would also be sent. Traveling separately, they would leave Washington on the next available commercial flights. The station was to fetch both from the airport and billet them separately. To preserve his anonymity, the case officer who would be meeting the agent was to be quartered in a safe house. His colleague, the backup man, would stay in one of the hotels requisitioned by the occupational forces.

Roberts was delighted. Headquarters had obviously accepted his evaluation of the operation and was giving the station even more support than he had asked for. As Roberts and Booth pored over the short cable, Booth suggested it could only have been drafted by Helms: there was not a headquarters desk officer who could have resisted adding the advice that the station should "proceed with caution," a bit of wisdom that invariably illuminated any traffic on new or risky ventures.

As Booth got up to leave, Martha came in with a second cable. Brooks Newby would arrive at 1300, Gregory Domnin at 1600.

* * *

Roberts and Booth recognized Newby's name at once. Neither knew Domnin or could recall his name. Brooks Newby was one of CIA's experts on the Soviet intelligence services. He also had a reputation for smoking the foulest cigars in Washington—worse, Booth had been told, than any of his many pipes. Before Booth left for Vienna, Newby had spent an entire day briefing him on the RIS. "RIS" was the agency's acronym for the Russian Intelligence Services. It was not an accurate term—SIS for Soviet Intelligence Services would have been better. But when the British intelligence service, which had long been known as MI–6, opted for a more stately label, it became the Secret Intelligence Service. CIA had no choice but to reserve SIS for the British. Not that it mattered much—old timers and the press continued for years to refer to it as MI–6.

Like many other World War II intelligence officers, Newby was teaching German when the war broke out. It had taken the assistant professor almost a year to convince the army that no matter how thick his glasses were, he was at least qualified for limited service. Assigned to the Washington area, Newby spent the war sweating strategic intelligence out of a select group of German prisoners shipped to this country.

In April 1945, with the market for strategic intelligence on the Third Reich collapsing faster than the demand for membership in the Nazi party, G–2 scheduled one of its last VIP prisoner flights from an airfield in Belgium. At a military airfield near Washington, a handful of German prisoners had filed off the plane when the reception team was startled to see a general and six other high-ranking officials striding down the gangway. Their field-gray uniforms were familiar, but the large epaulets and the distinctive shield-shaped insignia on the left sleeve identified the prisoners as members of the ill-fated Vlasov army.

Lieutenant General Andrey Vlasov was a Russian who had been captured by the *Wehrmacht* in July 1942. He had an outstanding combat record but, unlike most Red Army generals, could scarcely conceal his hatred of Stalin. After a few weeks' negotiation with German intelligence officers, Vlasov agreed to head a Russian National Committee and to form a corps of captured Soviet troops to fight on the German side. It is difficult to say whether Vlasov or his captors were the more naïve.

Regardless of its potentialities—and in the hands of a rational government the Vlasov movement could have had a significant impact on the USSR—the idea of Hitler fostering a political movement bent on establishing noncommunist, nationalist governments in Russia and the Ukraine was doomed from the start. Despite the pleas of his advisers, Hitler could not be budged from his lunatic plan to turn the USSR into a giant slave state. And, as hard-pressed as the commanders on the east front were for troops, the German General Staff could not, at least until the closing weeks of the war, be persuaded to employ large combat units of Russians under the command of Russian officers. The prospect of the renegade Russians defecting en masse to their countrymen at the first opportunity was more than the headquarters generals chose to risk. By May 1945, when the General Staff was desperate enough to take the chance, a Vlasov division did change sides—it routed a German SS unit and turned Prague over to the Czech resistance and Soviet troops.

Under terms of the Yalta agreement, Allied military commanders were under strict orders to return to Stalin all Russians captured fighting in *Wehrmacht* formations, recovered Soviet prisoners of war, and even displaced persons. With few exceptions, this was done.

Whether the seven officers were put on the plane by mistake, or because some anonymous intelligence officer deliberately took advantage of the confusion of the final days of the war to slip these valuable sources into the United States is not known. In any event, the Vlasov officers gave American intelligence one of its first inside looks at the USSR.

Although he planned to make his academic career in Germanics, Newby began to study Russian while still at Heidelberg prepping for his doctorate. There, in 1929 he spotted an Intourist advertisement for low-cost travel in the USSR and postponed his return to the United States long enough to spend a few weeks in the Soviet Union. Because it was one of the first such Intourist tours, Newby had little trouble drifting away from the group and exploring Moscow, Leningrad, and Kiev on his own.

Thus for Newby, the arrival of the Vlasov prisoners was a windfall. Not only could he exercise his rusty Russian, he could also get an insight into what he suspected would become an even more difficult intelligence target than Nazi Germany had been. His study, based on what he had learned from the Vlasov prisoners, was completed in 1946. It was the first paper by a U.S. intelligence officer on the organization and methods of the NKVD. A few weeks later Newby applied to the Strategic Services Unit (SSU) of the Central Intelligence Group.

This was the temporary organization President Truman had established to keep a cadre of former OSS personnel and files together until Congress could pass the legislation necessary to establish a central intelligence agency.

The officer in charge of Soviet operations in SSU had read Newby's study and thought enough of it to have circulated it within the unit. When Newby telephoned, the response was immediate—it was a unique job applicant who spoke German and Russian, had traveled in the USSR, and had written a study of the NKVD. Newby was assigned to Special Project Division/S. With two junior case officers, a secretary, and a scant drawerful of files, Newby's office was scarcely a threat to either the NKVD or the GRU. Dubbed—however inaccurately—"Speedy Suzy," the SPD/S began its work on three fronts.

It collected all the published literature on Russian intelligence: in the twenty-nine years since the revolution, the Cheka, OGPU, NKVD, and GRU had inspired a fair number of books and memoirs. Researchers also rummaged through university libraries and the Library of Congress. However fanciful some of the material turned out to be, it provided a framework for research. The FBI and military organizations were solicited for contributions and the remaining OSS files ransacked.

Captured German and Japanese documents yielded some information on Soviet espionage during the war. In Japan the net established by Richard Sorge was brought under study, and in Europe, German files were mined for data on the wide-ranging networks partially exposed by the Gestapo, the *Sicherheitsdienst* (SD) and the *Abwehr*. Research into the most extensive of these *réseaux*—called the *Rote Kapelle* (Red Orchestra) by the Germans—kept a handful of analysts busy for almost a decade after the war.

While surviving members of the communist espionage nets in Europe and the Far East were being questioned, foreign intelligence agencies in liaison with SSU field stations were canvassed for contributions. In England Kim Philby personally selected background material for SSU. As a Soviet agent so well covered that he had recently been named chief of the British intelligence Soviet operations branch, Philby made sure that the material he forwarded—a list of one hundred "known Russian agents" and a few hoary scraps of data on the organization of the Soviet espionage services—was worthless. Philby, whose sense of irony had been well polished during his years as a penetration agent, must have laughed aloud when he recounted this incident to his Russian case officer.

Fortunately, one researcher uncovered a press clipping on Ismael Akhmedov, a GRU major who had defected from Soviet military intelligence in Turkey in 1944. Although he had been questioned at length on local matters and later by the British on a broader scale, Akhmedov agreed to another debriefing. He flew to Frankfurt, Germany, and spent four weeks in a safe house with Newby.

It was during this interrogation that Newby was struck by the fact that each time he opened a new topic, Akhmedov would say, "But you must know this, I went over it in detail with the British." Philby, who had handled Akhmedov's interrogation for the British, had given SSU but a few scant pages of data from him. He had also taken the trouble to add a comment deriding Akhmedov as a source. This struck Newby as odd. Dated as some of the information was, Akhmedov was a trove of background data and leads. How could so bright a chap as Philby was known to be have misjudged an important defector so badly?

Newby was not the only SSU officer struck by Philby's curious appreciation of Akhmedov. James Angleton, who had started his intelligence career in X–2, the counterespionage section of OSS, had recently returned from his post in Italy. He had known Philby in London during the war. Not only had Philby muffed the opportunity to secure the defection of Konstantin Volkov, an NKVD man posing as a Soviet vice-consul in Turkey, it now appeared he had been equally obtuse about Akhmedov. Philby *was* smarter than that. Inexplicable lapses of performance on anything as important as Soviet operations are almost calculated to attract the attention of suspicious counterintelligence officers. In time, the Volkov and Akhmedov incidents became links in the chain of analysis that led to Philby's exposure as a Soviet agent.

As familiar as Roberts and Booth were with Newby's work, they drew a blank on Gregory Domnin. The name sounded Russian, but if he really was a "senior case officer" and a "fluent Russian speaker," how could it be that neither had heard of him? They would not have long to wait—Domnin's plane was due in six hours.

8
THE CASE OFFICER

Newby and Roberts were still closeted in Roberts's office when Todd brought Domnin into Booth's office a few blocks away. After forty-eight hours of waiting in crowded airports and bucketing about in propeller-driven aircraft, he was exhausted and looked it. But if the Russian showed up on schedule, there was still much to be done: Booth had no choice but to put Domnin to work. Braced with a cup of coffee, Domnin began to leaf through Alex's report. Between grunts which neither Todd nor Booth could interpret, he asked questions, mostly to clarify Alex's English syntax. English was not Alex's best language. Finished with the report, Domnin turned to the tape recorder and pulled on the earphones. He began to take notes, switching the tape back and forth on the machine.

Pretending to shuffle through the mound of paper in his in-box, Booth tried to size up the man who would play such an important role in the case. He looked as if he had been dragged into town on a rope. His dark suit was corrugated with wrinkles. The collar of his white shirt, gone gray on the trip, was unbuttoned. His tightly knotted necktie was pulled down from the collar and lay across his massive chest like a lariat. Powerful, sloping shoulders, chunky arms and thick thighs bulged against the suit. His paunch eased over the low-slung pants, straining against a thin leather belt. Cowlicks of dark hair rose from his large head, like a chop in a riptide. Strangely small feet belied the bulk of his upper body. His broad face was puffed with fatigue.

Peter Todd intercepted Booth's stare: "He'd just got back from four weeks in the Far East when Helms grabbed him," he said. Maybe that did account for it, Booth thought. No one could have gotten that rumpled in the time it had taken Domnin to get to Vienna. It was almost an hour before he switched off the tape deck.

"How much time have we got?" he asked.

"If the guy shows, Alex will take him directly to the safe house tomorrow night, probably about eight-thirty."

"That's plenty. In the meantime, if it's all the same, I want some soup, a little vodka, a bathtub, and a bed."

Booth sketched the schedule—an early-morning meeting with Alex to get his impressions of the Russian, a conference in Booth's office to review the meeting plan, and then a quick trip to check out the safe house. Domnin agreed.

"Good enough," Booth said. "After that we'll meet here late in the afternoon for a windup with Joel Roberts."

"Okay. Can someone get some *zakuski*?"

"Some what?" Booth asked.

"*Zakuski*—little things to eat. The poor son-of-a-bitch will need something with the vodka."

Todd spoke up: "Hors d'oeuvres, herring, sour-cream, red caviar, some cold meat—I'll take care of it."

Domnin had gotten up to leave but Booth could not let him go without one last question: "Greg, just one thing before you flake out."

"Sure."

"Can you tell anything about who he is from the tape?"

Domnin rubbed his red-rimmed eyes. "He's a Russian, a Great Russian. Maybe from around Moscow somewhere, but he's definitely a country boy. I don't think he's faking. If I'm right, this could be a pretty good thing."

Todd went to the supply room for a bottle of vodka. There was plenty of good vodka in Vienna. Most of it came onto the black market from the Soviet commissary.

If Alex was disappointed at being pulled out of the operation he was a good enough soldier not to show it. As he helped the Russian out of his bulky overcoat in the dark hallway, he spoke. "I've brought a friend to see you. I'm going to leave you with him. Don't worry, you'll be in good hands."

In the living room, Domnin rose to greet the Russian. After a lingering glance around the apartment, Alex pulled on his trench coat, turned back into the hallway and slipped out the door.

"*Privet*," Domnin said. "I'm glad you could come—I've had a long trip." Domnin's Russian was fluent and educated. There was no trace of a Bolshevik accent.

For a moment the Russian stared at him. "I've not come so far," he said, "but it's not such an easy trip for me either." They shook hands and sat down facing one another across the coffee table. Half hidden by the vodka and bourbon bottles were a yellow pad and a collection of ball-point pens. Although Newby, Todd, and Ed Masters were locked in the bedroom to monitor and record the meeting, Domnin would take notes. At that time tape recorders were even less reliable than they are now. Even when the recording was good, notes were always useful in making a transcript of an agent meeting. There was another disadvantage. The more notes a case officer takes, the less likely the agent is to worry about the possibility the meeting place is wired.

Domnin reached for the glasses. "Vodka or whiskey?"

"Vodka."

As Domnin poured the drinks, the Russian looked anxiously around the room, his glance tarrying once more on the ugly oil painting, a still life with flowers.

"Have you checked the document?"

"It seems to be okay, but only Washington can really tell."

"What about the money?"

"Money's no problem, I've got what you asked for and a bit—"

The Russian interrupted. "Then let's have it."

"... and a little more." Domnin did not like to be interrupted. "Look, you're supposed to be a Russian. Stop acting like a bloody businessman—let's have a drink."

The Russian raised his glass. "*Na zdorov'e.*"

"Your health," said Domnin in English.

"How much time do you have?" Domnin asked.

"I haven't got any time if you don't come through with the cash. I can't spend the night drinking commissary vodka and arguing with you about a few hundred schillings."

"Don't you want to know who you're doing business with?" Domnin asked.

"We're not going to do any business until you pay me for the document."

Domnin took a wallet from his hip-pocket. "My name is Grossman, Lieutenant Colonel Harry Grossman. I've come all the way from Washington to see you." He tossed a laminated identity card onto the coffee table.

According to the ID card, "Lieutenant Colonel Harry Grossman" was born in the United States in 1917. In fact, Domnin had been born in St. Petersburg in 1912, three years before his father, a Russian diplomat, was posted to the Imperial Russian embassy in Washington.

The Russian picked up the card. "Very nice." He paused and looked up at Domnin. "I suppose this means you want to look at mine?"

Domnin nodded: "That *is* the next step."

The Russian reached into his breast pocket and pulled out a thick, black wallet. He riffled through the papers wedged into the wallet pockets. After fumbling for a moment, he selected a laminated card and dropped it onto the table. A little bigger than Domnin's, it identified—in Russian and German—the bearer as Major Pyotr S. Panov, a civilian employee of the Soviet delegation to the Allied Control Commission for Austria. Domnin bent over the coffee table, studying the identity document.

"Take a good look—it's just as phony as yours."

Domnin grinned: "Okay, then who the hell *are* you?"

The Russian stared straight across the table. In a strained voice he said, "I am a graduate of the Military Diplomatic Academy, now assigned to the Strategic Intelligence *rezidentura* of the GRU in Vienna. My office is in the Imperial Hotel."

Domnin nodded. The Russian reached into the side pocket of his jacket and pulled out a dark, red leather card case. Holding it open, he handed it across the table. Domnin looked at the card. It was an official identification document issued by the *Glavnoe Razvedyvatel'noe Upravlenie*, the GRU or Chief Intelligence Directorate of the Soviet General Staff. It was complete with the name, photograph, and serial number of the bearer.

"*Khorosho*," said Domnin and raised his glass to Major Pyotr Semyonovich Popov of Soviet military intelligence.

With less scrimmaging than Domnin had thought possible, he had gained the first objective—when Popov disclosed his operational pseudonym and his true name, he had taken another step beyond the point of any possible return.

In the bedroom Newby stared incredulously at the tape recorder. Without removing his earphones, he tore a piece of paper from the clip-board on his lap and scribbled a question to Todd. "Why has he come around so easily?" Todd shrugged, shook his head, and wrote "don't knock it" at the bottom of Newby's note.

But Domnin had no time to ponder Popov's reasoning. To keep the initiative he lunged into the first of the questions Todd and Newby had prepared on the chance that the Russian would admit he was an intelligence officer.

"Tell me something about the GRU here. Is there more than one *rezidentura*?" A *"rezidentura"* or *"rezidency"* is similar to a field station in Western intelligence parlance.

"There's only one Strategic Intelligence *rezidentura*."

"No Tactical Intelligence *rezidentura*?"

In Soviet military intelligence at that time, Strategic Intelligence *rezidencies* worked against sensitive, strategic targets and were authorized to run operations almost anywhere in the world. Personnel were carefully selected and better trained and usually more competent than case officers working on tactical intelligence. Tactical Intelligence *rezidenturas* worked at a lower level, and their activity was usually restricted to the country in which they were based.

"Sure, their headquarters is in Baden."

"How is your *rezidentura* set up?"

"We've got four Strategic Intelligence points, each under a different cover. But they all come under the *rezident*."

In the GRU and in the KGB, the *rezident* is the equivalent of a CIA station chief and has command responsibility for all operational activity in the country. In Austria an "intelligence point" was the rough equivalent of a branch in a Western intelligence station.

"Who's the *rezident* here?"

"Colonel Aleksey Vasiliyevich Romanovsky."

Romanovsky was well known to Western intelligence and occasionally appeared at diplomatic receptions in his cover role as an official of the Soviet delegation to the Allied Control Commission for Austria.

"His deputy?"

"Colonel Vitali Aleksandrovich Nikolsky. He's a tough bastard, but a real professional. One of the best in our service."

"Is there a chief of operations?"

"Not really. Nikolsky has both jobs. He's more a chief of operations than the deputy. I think they gave him that title so he could get the *papakha*." A *"papakha,"* or big hat, is the distinctive cap worn only by full colonels and general officers in the Red Army. When an officer is promoted to full colonel, or to general, he is said to have been given a *papakha*.

"Who's your boss?"

"Colonel Ivan Ivanovich Yegerov, a real *zhopa*." In the most polite terms *zhopa* might be translated as ass. It is also the trade name of a popular Austrian ice-cream, the advertisements for which were an unending source of jokes among the Russians in Austria.

"What's your assignment?"

"I'm a case officer on the Yugoslav line."

In the bedroom Newby felt a flash of disappointment. Yuglosavia was an important target, as much so for CIA as for the Russians. But given a choice, Newby would have opted to have Popov assigned to something nearer the knuckle. On the American line, he could have tipped Domnin to GRU operations against the United States.

For a moment Domnin stopped writing. He would risk one more sensitive question before Popov lost his momentum.

"How many agents do you control?"

Popov flinched. "Eight," he mumbled.

Later Domnin was to learn that he was bragging. Popov never had more than six agents in his stable. And recruiting new spies was a nightmare for him.

It was time for a pause. Domnin spilled another half tumbler of vodka into Popov's glass. "Let's try the *zakuski*."

Domnin had chosen a good point to relax. Popov had been forthcoming enough on the anatomy of the GRU in Vienna, but it was much too early in the game to probe for the identities of his own agents. Even defectors had proved reluctant when it came to uncovering agents they had recruited in good faith. There would be no point in pushing Popov on something that might be this sensitive until Domnin had a more precise reading of his motives.

As they spooned red caviar onto crackers and heaped smoked sturgeon and herring on the plates, Domnin turned to another topic.

"How'd you get along with my friend?"

"He's all right. But he's a Russian. It's a good thing you came along. I won't work with a Russian."

"He's an American."

"The hell he is. He's some goddamned deserter, maybe a refugee. Those guys are all *nashi*."

"Nashi," which means "ours," is Soviet intelligence slang to indicate an agent or collaborator. As Booth had suspected, Popov had been well briefed on the KGB's exploitation of émigrés and refugees. The KGB had not been nearly as successful as they made out, but they knew the value of advertising. It had a useful cauterizing effect to imply that all native Russian speakers were *nashi.*

"Who do you think I am?"

"You're an American. You act a little like a Russian, but you don't look Russian. What I can't figure out is how you learned the language."

"That's a long story, I'll tell you about it some day." Domnin never did tell Popov that, after the revolution, when his father had decided to remain in the United States, he had insisted the children be tutored in Russian—the revolution could not last for long and the family would soon return to Russia. Domnin had also spent several months during World War II working as a liaison officer, living with the Soviet naval and air force personnel who were supervising the shipment of lend-lease material to the USSR. This put the final edge on his language and had given him an almost unique chance to study the "new" Russians, the men his father had so despised.

Domnin had bought a little time and this slight give and take had relaxed the atmosphere.

"Don't worry about Alex. I'm the only person you'll be dealing with from now on."

As they tucked into the *zakuski,* Domnin continued to ask questions. Before the session ended, he had identified twenty-four GRU officers, learned their cover names, and pinpointed their operational assignments. It was almost eleven before he pushed the yellow pad aside. The vodka bottle was empty.

"It's late, but we've got one more bit of business to take care of."

"It's about time." For the first time Popov smiled.

"Let me give you some schillings now. We can work out a permanent arrangement next time—when can you come back?"

"Let's have the cash."

Roberts had agreed that if the meeting went well, Domnin would pay the Russian between three and five thousand schillings. It would be important to erase any bad taste the earlier bickering might have left with him, but Roberts did not want to risk giving him more than was absolutely necessary. Nothing would be more dangerous for a Russian than a sudden show of affluence. To avoid flashing any more cash than was necessary, Domnin had put three thousand schillings in one pocket and five thousand in another. It would be up to him to decide how much he should offer. Roberts hoped he would remember which pocket he had put the five thousand in.

"Here's three thousand schillings," said Domnin as he handed over a sheaf of bank notes—a little more than a hundred dollars. "You see—money is no problem."

"Maybe not for you—but I'm the one with the problem."

"Tell me about it."

"It's too late—we can talk about it next time."

"When can you come?"

"In a week. I'll come right here, at the same time."

Domnin helped Popov into his overcoat.

"Do you want a ride?"

"Sure, just drop me in front of the Imperial—one of my KGB neighbors can open the door for me." Popov grinned as he pulled on his hat. They shook hands and Domnin watched as the stocky Russian hurried down the short flight of stairs.

Domnin walked back into the room. Pushing aside the remains of the *zakuski*, he took another bottle of vodka out of the sideboard. As he twisted the cap he remembered that Newby, Todd, and Masters were still locked in the bedroom.

"It's over. Why don't you guys come out and mingle?"

The door of the bedroom swung slowly open—Newby, his thick glasses reflecting the light of the floor lamps, peered cautiously around the room. Satisfied that all was clear, he motioned to Todd and Masters. Still in stocking feet—to avoid any unnecessary sound, everyone in the back room had removed his shoes—the trio came tumbling out. There was another rule. Never under any circumstances was there any drinking in the room with the tape recorders. It was almost eleven-thirty, they had been locked in for four hours. As Newby rushed for the hall toilet, Todd and Masters made for the sideboard. Todd poured three double shots of bourbon.

"Not bad, Greg," he said. "And you've been in Austria for only forty-eight hours."

9
DIGGING IN

Roberts's first question took the words away from Booth. "Before we get started," Roberts said, "tell me something more about our friend. Who is he and what's his background?"

Roberts, Domnin, Newby, and Todd were meeting in Booth's office. The room was a light, institutional green, a color presumably selected by a committee of military psychologists and chemists as being dirt resistant and inoffensive. It was neither, but at least it did not clash with the scruffy furniture and threadbare carpet. The only wall decorations were maps—a large Vienna street plan covered the wall behind Booth's desk and small-scale maps of Austria and its eastern neighbors were mounted on the other walls. Shabby as the office was, it did offer a splendid view of the back of a military motor pool.

Domnin took a swig of coffee. "He's about thirty, maybe a year or two older. He was assigned here in August 1952, about a year after he got out of the Military Diplomatic Academy. In CIA terms he's a case officer in the Jug section of Branch 4 of the Strategic Intelligence of the GRU in Vienna."

Newby nodded his concurrence. "That's the usual career pattern for someone they brought in after the war. He must have been picked for the Military Academy in 1945—they were in a bind then to replace the officers they lost during the fighting." It was only nine o'clock but Newby had already reduced his first stogie to a soggy three inches.

"Is the Military Academy a regular officers' school, like West Point?" Booth asked.

"It's more like an infantry school," Domnin answered. "It's got nothing at all to do with intelligence."

"My guess is that the GRU recruited him while he was still there," Newby added. "They must have sponsored him for the Military Diplomatic Academy. That's a much more advanced school. Most of the career intelligence officers—GRU and KGB—go there."

"It's like a university, with separate schools sponsored by each of the services—the military has schools for each branch of service, ground forces, air force, navy. The GRU school cover name is VASA," Domnin added.

"That means he was graduated in 1951, probably in June," Newby said. "That would give him a year or so on an area desk at GRU headquarters before getting the Vienna assignment. That squares exactly with what we know about the way they train case officers."

Roberts glanced at Booth. At the time, CIA case officers were supposed to have four months' operations training before going to the field: not everyone in the station had had that much.

As Newby and Domnin began to sketch the results of the meeting, Booth tried to fit the data into what he knew about the RIS in Austria.

The core of any intelligence service operating abroad is its official cover offices and personnel, usually discreetly tucked away in an embassy, consulate, trade, or military mission. To the casual observer, intelligence personnel under diplomatic cover are identical with their bona fide diplomatic compatriots. They have diplomatic titles and appear to have legitimate diplomatic functions. They enjoy all diplomatic privileges; and most important of all, when official cover case officers are on the street, they are as immune from arrest and search as their licit diplomatic colleagues. In the *rezidentura* offices, case officers can study their case files, draft reports, and rummage through dossiers as nonchalantly as if they were in Moscow.

The ability to stuff embassies with operations officers, more or less convincingly togged out as diplomats, is a measure of an intelligence service's clout with its own government. In some Soviet embassies the intelligence staff occupies sixty percent of the diplomatic slots. In the days following Senator Church's attack on the agency, CIA was lucky to keep its nose under the official tent in some areas.

But in Austria in 1952 cover was the least problem. The occupation had spawned such an abundance of military and civilian agencies, organizations, and offices, that the intelligence services could create cover units at random and cull choice office space from a dozen or more requisitioned buildings. The only real problem was the choice of a likely but bland name to daub on the door. However plausibly a "Regional Typewriter Repair Section" might explain the small office and workshop occupied by the station's technical section, it was not satisfactory cover. As soon as the name went on the door, and the phone was listed in the military directory, the busy techs would have to stave off an avalanche of broken typewriters.

Best was a title with "plans" in it. During the occupation, plans and planners were as common as *Wienerschnitzel*. But as far as could be told, no one ever actually needed a plan, or thought to talk with anyone who advertised himself as a planner. The "Plans and Review Section" rubric which covered the station's Soviet branch was an invention of genius. It exuded such an authentic bureaucratic stench that no one with a legitimate query ever came near it.

In Vienna, Russian intelligence didn't need to be even this imaginative. The *rezidentura* offices were like redoubts built deep within Soviet-requisitioned buildings. For cover purposes Russian case officers were accredited at random to the various components of the Soviet occupation establishment. Unless some operational need was perceived, few of these case officers ever appeared in their cover offices or made the slightest pretext of doing their cover jobs. All of their office work was done in the redoubt areas. A few, usually those prospecting for British or American recruits, were assigned to the Soviet diplomatic staff and did their digging at embassy receptions and the endless negotiating sessions between the occupation powers.

This proliferation of cover was a boon to the operatives on both sides but it added an unwelcome dimension to what was already a complex counterintelligence problem.

The first job of the counterintelligence section of a field station is to keep book on the opposition—the espionage staffs of the various communist embassies. Since the terms of the occupation forbade Austria to have a counterintelligence service, the foreign intelligence agencies had only one another to worry about. It was problem enough to sift a few dozen intelligence officers from hundreds of their straight colleagues.

Except for the one representative the Office of Naval Intelligence kept in Austria, CIA was the smallest unit in the American intelligence community—the military intelligence staffs outnumbered the station by a factor of five or more. In any field post, Western intelligence commits a sizable chunk of its manpower to studying and building up background data on the Soviet diplomatic, military, and intelligence establishments. This research is essential if human targets—Russians who might conceivably be susceptible to recruitment—are to be identified. Soviet intelligence and the Eastern European services work against Western targets in exactly the same way. The data accumulating from this research also provides the base needed to question agents or defectors and to check on the fanciful yarns peddled by fabricators. Elaborate rosters and organizational charts are kept, listing every member of a target embassy whose name can be learned and whose assignment can be uncovered.

Biographic files are the heart of any intelligence service and personal data on any possible target is eagerly collected by every intelligence agency. Diplomats are easy pickings and in time their dossiers are swollen with notes on their enthusiasms, indiscretions, and eccentricities. Officials who rarely appear in public are most difficult, but through the years enough bits and pieces of data can be accumulated to make a rounded picture. Because intelligence officers tend to keep casual acquaintances at arm's length and are experienced at role-playing and dissembling, they are among the toughest targets. But in Austria a number of Soviet intelligence officers had been identified.

A few RIS case officers were identified by double agents operating under station control. Many of these DAs, as they are called, were Austrians or stateless refugees employed by the occupation agencies. Hundreds of these locally hired employees handled administrative, clerical, and housekeeping work. This was a hefty saving in American manpower and a boon to the Austrian labor market, but it played hob with security. Austrians with relatives living in the Soviet-occupied zone of Austria and refugees with families trapped in Eastern Europe were paradigmatically prone to Soviet blackmail.

Although the local employees rarely had direct access to classified information, they could report in detail on their offices, occasionally snitch a document, and, even more to the point, give detailed reports on the possible vulnerability of their American associates. The recruitment of American—or British—agents was the root objective of most RIS operations of this sort.

Some of the local employees resisted the blackmail and reported to their American supervisors or the Austrian authorities. Others went to a security officer in desperation after having been browbeaten into recruitment. There were others that the station had to winkle out.

A few of the volunteers welcomed the chance to strike back at their tormentors and to work as double agents under the station's control. Those who lacked the temperament to chance this risky double game were usually resettled out of harm's way in western Austria. Some of those the station uncovered welcomed discovery and volunteered to cooperate. Others, usually those with more mercenary motives, resisted questioning or gave only partial confessions. They were sacked and blackballed with the Allied employment offices. This was in marked contrast to the treatment given Western agents detected by the Russians. After brutal interrogation they were usually transported to a Hungarian prison or sent to labor camps in the Soviet Gulag. Few returned.

To establish credibility, most of the information reported by double agents has to be accurate—deception comes late in the game. Because of this, the station usually ran these agents only long enough to get a line on the case officer and the information the RIS was after. By studying the questions Soviet case officers put to "their" agents, a good analyst could determine which sectors of the American community the Russians had well covered and those on which they were most ignorant. Perceptive, detailed queries about a certain office were usually positive proof that another agent was, or had been, active in that area and that the Russians were merely verifying his reports or testing the newly recruited agent by having him report on data that was easily checked. With this sort of lead a case officer could, by a complicated process of elimination, surveillance, and records checking, usually spot the other RIS source.

As useful as these DAs were, they could only identify one Russian, their own case officer. Not all the DAs could even do that. Soviet case officers invariably use simple aliases when running spies—every field station's RIS *modus operandi* files are strewn with observations on "Boris," "Anton," and "Michael." In Vienna there was even an amiable chap who called himself "Charley" when sidling up to GIs in a *Bierstube*. But unless a case officer had a photograph to show the DA, he was usually told that the Russian operative was of "average height," spoke "accented German," and looked "exactly like a Russian."

What the station needed was a mug book. But as Booth learned, RIS case officers were skittish, almost as hard to photograph as a bishop in a brothel.

One of the first buildings seized by the Russians when the Red Army smashed into Vienna in April 1945 was the city's largest and best hotel, the Imperial. It became the headquarters of the Soviet

Control Commission and provided posh office space for the highest-ranking Soviet military and civilian officials in Austria. Although no one could be certain, it seemed likely that both the GRU and KGB headquarters were on the top floors of the Imperial. Fragmentary agent reports suggested this and several of the Soviet case officers who had been identified appeared to be frequent visitors. The RIS was known to have several other offices in Vienna, but the Imperial looked like the honey pot.

The initial reconnaissance of the area uncovered one interesting possibility. A few hundred feet away and across the Ringstrasse—a broad, four-lane boulevard with streetcar tracks on each side and rimmed with spacious sidewalks—was another Soviet-requisitioned hotel. Despite its impressive name, the years of occupation—first by the *Wehrmacht* and then by the Russians—had not been kind to the Grand Hotel. But tacky as it was, the Grand was handy enough to the Imperial to make a convenient officers' billet, and the kitchen and dining rooms were big enough to feed the Imperial's Soviet staff. To get to lunch, the Russians crossed the Ringstrasse at a traffic light on the Dumbastrasse. If the right hidey-hole for a cameraman could be found it might be possible to turn this crosswalk into a photographic shooting gallery.

Nothing is more likely to put the wind up in an intelligence officer than a decrepit, windowless panel truck parked in an unlikely spot—since the advent of the wheel, spies have been peeking out of shabby vans. Nor is a man sitting patiently in a parked car likely to escape notice. Prisons are cluttered with optimists who thought they could stake out a bank from the front seat of a Ford. If the station was going to operate on Russian turf—both hotels were in the *Innere Stadt*, but so heavily guarded that most passersby gave them wide berth—it would have to be a bit craftier.

This was an assignment that saw Ed Masters at his best. Along with a keen interest in photography, he was an amateur radio operator, a skill he had honed while ocean racing. At various times Masters also toyed with model sailing boats and had built one sloop he could control by radio from the shore. As an avid reader of photographic magazines, he knew that wildlife photographers frequently rigged cameras near water holes and triggered them from a distance. Sports photographers had also found remote-control cameras a boon when required to work close to dangerous sports like motor racing. But as far as Masters could learn, these cameras were only good for one shot, after which the film had to be advanced manually.

At the time, Leica offered a mechanical device that supposedly advanced the film and cocked the camera, but the only examples Masters could find in Austria were balky and notably unreliable. Rummaging around in a Vienna camera shop, he uncovered the Robot, a small 35mm camera which he later learned had been developed by the Luftwaffe. It had a spring enclosed in a small housing on the top of the camera which, when wound, would automatically advance the film and cock the camera after each exposure. Allegedly the Luftwaffe had mounted these cameras in the wings of fighter planes so that potential aces had positive proof of their kills.

After hours of experimentation, Masters constructed a miniaturized Rube Goldberg device which, when attached to the camera, could be activated by the same signal he used to change course in his model sloop. With a reliable camera—and before he was through Masters had cornered the Austrian market for the cameras to cannibalize parts—he could promise Booth a series of as many as twenty exposures triggered by a miniature radio from a hundred yards or more away.

Today highly efficient remote-control cameras are available in neighborhood camera stores and more sophisticated versions are in daily use by professional photographers, private detectives, and, one may safely assume, intelligence and police services.

The only remaining problem was concealment.

No one could remember how the fad started, but it was a boon for Masters. At the time, no Austrian-owned automobile was complete unless it had a mascot—usually a stuffed animal stretched out across the rear window. The favorite talisman was a toy tiger; the smaller the car, the fancier the tiger. They were almost as common as license plates.

It took weeks of experimentation before Ed Masters perfected it, but when he did it worked as smoothly as the vault door on the *Credit-Anstalt*, Vienna's biggest bank. All the agent had to do was to park an artfully dilapidated, Austrian-plated sedan in the right spot on the Ringstrasse—previously marked with an inconspicuous splash of paint to show exactly where the front wheels should be—and the eye of the toy tiger (and the lens of the radio-operated camera concealed in the beast) had a perfect line of sight on the crosswalk most favored by the Russians hustling from the Imperial to the Grand for lunch.

Loitering some distance away—and within easy running distance of the American-requisitioned Bristol Hotel—a case officer with a concealed radio could trigger the camera whenever a likely target stepped onto the crosswalk. When the luncheon rush was over, an agent would pick up the car and drive a circuitous route to a safe-house garage in the American sector.

Occasionally it was possible to supplement these shots with others taken by a bold agent with a small, automatic camera concealed precariously in his hat, or a briefcase. But this was not habit-forming work—few agents were willing to get this close to Russian intelligence officers in Vienna.

To avoid attracting attention, the concealed camera was rarely worked more than one day a week; it was not always possible to get the required parking place, and hunting was poor on rainy days when the quarry wore hats. But dozens of pictures were collected, many of them excellent mug shots.

These photographs and the data case officers were slowly developing from agents working in the vicinity of the Soviet installations were funneled into the Soviet branch. There an analyst put the data into operational notebooks on each of the separate Soviet organizations, or targets, as they were called. It was slow work and much of it was speculative; without an inside source the station could not be sure how dependable the analysis was. Todd's section needed an accurate picture of the Soviet targets before it could hope to penetrate them—with agents, audio operations, and telephone taps.

As Domnin and Newby poured out Popov's information, Booth realized that at last he had a litmus against which he could test the hours of analysis Todd's section had made.

As it turned out, Todd had not done so badly. A third of the case officers cited by Popov were in the files, correctly identified as GRU operatives. Now, with the inside knowledge Popov had given, the station had the cover names, true names, and specific operational assignments of the ranking GRU staff in Vienna. As Domnin continued the briefing, it became apparent that the information was solid, not sensational. It was about what might have been expected from the first few hours with a defector. Once again Roberts preempted Booth's question.

"Greg, why is he doing this? He must have known he didn't have to give us his name—he could have strung us along for weeks with an alias."

Todd spoke up. "He said he was in a jam. Maybe he did get rolled, maybe he's got a girl. One thing's sure, none of them has enough money to horse around very much."

"What about the black market?" Newby asked. "Could he have stubbed his toe in some deal?"

This made no sense to Booth. There were Russians in the black market—certainly vodka and occasionally bits of Soviet equipment turned up in Vienna—but as far as he could tell most of it came from garrison towns some distance from Vienna. If any officers were involved, they almost certainly used enlisted men as cutouts for what was a very dangerous activity. RIS personnel were better paid than their military colleagues and Booth assumed they were under much tighter control, even surveillance. It was inconceivable that a major in military intelligence would be desperate enough to take such risks.

"What about his family?" Roberts asked. "Is his wife here with him?"

Domnin shook his head. "I didn't have time to ask. Anyway, it wouldn't have been such a hot idea. This isn't the time to remind him that he could be getting his family into a jam."

Soviet justice had not changed since the purges of the thirties. CIA knew what happened to the families of the innocent victims of Stalin's show trials in Eastern Europe. Stripped of their apartments and personal property, they became "nonpersons," lucky to find even the most menial labor.

"There's one thing I'm sure of," Domnin said. "He's an honest-to-God peasant. I don't know where he comes from—east of Moscow somewhere, along the Volga probably. But surer than hell he's a peasant. And damned few of them have ever set foot in the Military Diplomatic Academy."

"But Greg, half the General Staff are peasants." Booth also remembered that Michail Ivanovich Kalinin, the first president of the USSR, had bragged about his peasant origins and had been puffed in the Soviet press as a friend of the peasants.

"That might have been true twenty-five years ago," Domnin said. "Some of the old guard were peasants. But the guys who are talking so much about it today are the sons of peasants—they didn't grow up in one of those damned villages."

Nobody agreed with Domnin about peasants, but no one was sure enough of his ground to take him on.

Domnin picked up his sheaf of notes. "If I'm right about that, then money hasn't got a damned thing to do with it. He's got a grudge."

As it turned out, Domnin was right. Popov was a peasant and money didn't have much to do with it. But it was months before the station found this out.

The weeks that followed set the pattern for the station's handling of the Popov case. The morning after a meeting, Roberts, Domnin, Newby, and Todd would gather in Booth's office. With the radio blaring, Domnin would brief Roberts and Booth on the highlights of the session and Newby and Todd would flesh out Domnin's account with their impressions from the back room. Free from the pressure of face-to-face contact with the agent, they could often spot things that Domnin had missed.

These initial briefings were kept as short as possible so that the probing would not inadvertently color Domnin's firsthand impressions of the meeting. As soon as the briefing was over, Todd and Booth would draft a short cable summarizing the highlights of the session. This reassured headquarters that Popov had showed up and tipped them to any new areas of intelligence he might have disclosed. It also gave the Washington reports staff a leg up in preparing questions for the next meeting.

While this was being done, Domnin would begin the onerous job of peeling the most salient intelligence off the tapes. Like most agents, Popov rarely covered any one topic in detail, in a logical sequence or without prompting for details. As scrupulous as Domnin was in trying to cover every facet of each topic, omissions were inevitable. When this happened, headquarters would come back with urgent demands for clarification. Sometimes the information could be pulled from the tapes. More often, it was necessary to follow up at the next meeting.

As soon as Domnin had completed the intelligence cables—sometimes more than twenty pages of tightly worded reports were sent on one meeting—he would begin to make a transcript of the meeting. This was nerve-racking work. No matter how hard Masters tried to produce clean, easily audible tapes, the recordings were bedeviled with extraneous sounds. If Popov did not begin to drum on the table at a critical moment, one of the noisy Vienna trams would rattle past the safe house. If not this, a neighbor could be counted on to try to start a balky motorcycle beneath the window. Only when there was a gap of three weeks or more between meetings could all of the paper work be finished.

The station followed this pattern for each of the meetings with Popov in Vienna.

The information Domnin had received from Popov at their first session was more than enough to convince Roberts and Booth that Popov knew what he was talking about. It was so detailed that it seemed unlikely the GRU would release it merely to build up Popov's reputation with CIA. If Popov had been sent to the station in some arcane counterespionage caper, someone had been guilty of overkill. A fraction of the data would have been enough to keep the station running after him.

Headquarters was less convinced. Their cabled response to the station's enthusiastic appraisal of Domnin's take was guarded. It agreed that much of the data squared with what was known and that it was valuable enough. But, the cable asked, why was Popov risking his life to provide it? What were his motives? If money was the root cause, why did he not demand more? Why hadn't he mentioned defection?

Until more data was at hand, headquarters would reserve its evaluation of the operation. Meanwhile, the station was to keep its head and to press hard for more intelligence.

10
THE GIRL FRIEND

As uneasy as headquarters professed to be about Popov's bona fides, a torrent of questions were unleashed for him. So many pages of requirements rocketed through the code room that Booth knew he would have to make arbitrary deletions if time were to be reserved for finding out more about the agent.

For his second session with Popov, Domnin had three tasks: to answer the highest priority intelligence questions, to learn more about Popov's background, and to probe more deeply into his motives. Having covered so much ground at the first meeting, Booth wanted Domnin to maintain his momentum, to keep Popov talking freely. It would be best, he reasoned, to open with a topic important to the station, but not so close to the nerve that Popov might hedge. Certain that all Russians loathed the secret police, he decided to have Domnin begin with a round of questions on the "neighbors," as GRU officers habitually referred to their KGB compatriots.

Here it is necessary to sketch the bloody chronicle of the Soviet secret police, the seed from which Soviet intelligence sprang. Too often these pages have been left to specialists and intelligence historians. But neither the USSR nor the Soviet intelligence services can be understood without a grasp of this history. From its inception in 1917 to the present, the secret police has provided the barbed wire that holds the Soviet world together.

The histories of the GRU and the KGB have unfolded in markedly different patterns, but both were minted from the same source. The KGB's parent organization was first on the field and to this day the KGB is recognized as the "senior service."

A scant two weeks after the Bolsheviks seized power in 1917, Lenin ordered the suppression of the non-Bolshevik press and the arrest of the liberal party leaders. When it became apparent to Lenin that the existing police forces were better equipped to cope with civil crime than political offenses, he bade the Council of People's Commissars, in effect the revolutionary cabinet, to take action. On 20 December 1917 the council established the All-Russian Extraordinary Commission for Combatting Counterrevolution and Sabotage—an organization that was to become better known by its acronym, Cheka.

Today, more than sixty years later, KGB officers still refer to themselves as Chekists and, at home and abroad, celebrate each anniversary of their service.

Under the leadership of Felix Dzerzhinsky, an ascetic, well-born Pole, who had spent twenty years in the underground fighting the Okhrana, the czarist secret police, the Cheka was not long in earning its reputation as the "sword and shield of the party." Facing violent unrest throughout Russia, Dzerzhinsky with Lenin's enthusiastic support adopted a policy of outright terror. Speaking to the press in June 1918, "Iron Felix," as Dzerzhinsky came to be known, minced no words. "We stand for organized terror. . . . Terror is an absolute necessity during times of revolution. . . . The Cheka is obliged to defend the revolution and conquer the enemy even if its sword does by chance sometimes fall upon the heads of the innocent."*

Lenin was equally outspoken. "The energy and mass nature of terror must be encouraged," he said and sent a cable ordering a regional Cheka office to employ "merciless mass terror." While cutting down all non-Bolshevik political activity, Chekists began the random extermination of landowners, businessmen, ex-czarist officers, aristocrats, intellectuals, and prosperous farmers. The Cheka also found time to make a few clumsy attempts to collect foreign intelligence. On the correct assumption that the foreign embassies were hotbeds of espionage and counterrevolution, Chekists began the surveillance of the diplomatic colony.

In September 1918 the Cheka was given formal authority to sentence and even execute the unfortunates it had arrested. Not that this official license was necessary—the Chekist police had long usurped

---

*Ronald Hingley, *The Russian Secret Police: Muscovite, Imperial Russian and Soviet Political Security Operations. 1565–1970* (London: Hutchinson of London, 1970), p 122.

the authority of judge and executioner. By 1921, when the revolutionary government realized that organized terror had served its purpose, a conservative estimate is that more than fifty thousand persons had been put to death by the Cheka.* Another one hundred and fifty thousand victims had perished of "natural causes"—starvation and neglect—in the Cheka concentration camps. These figures dim when compared with those that were killed in the years to come, but from the Chekist point of view it was a start, and the impact of the terror had had the effect Lenin intended. Political opposition was throttled, the population cowed, and the authority of the Cheka graven on the Russian mind.

When the Cheka was formally abolished in 1922, it had grown to an organization of over thirty thousand members and had cemented the foundation that would last until the present. The responsibilities seized by the Cheka were immense—the surveillance of the entire population, press censorship, security protection of the party leadership, counterespionage (at home and abroad), supervision of the transportation and communications systems, care of the hundreds of thousands of orphans cast up by the revolution and civil war, the suppression of religion, supervision of the prison camps, command of special troops and border guards.

However heavy this load, the Cheka had also shouldered responsibility for foreign intelligence operations. Here it stumbled—a resounding intelligence failure which resulted in the birth of the GRU.

In 1920, when a Polish military expedition was fighting its way into the Ukraine, Lenin ordered the Red Army to make a retaliatory invasion of Poland. The Cheka's failure to provide adequate intelligence and to gauge the Polish spunk and capacity to resist was a major factor in the Red Army's defeat. Dzerzhinsky and Lenin moved quickly. Jan Karlovich Berzin, a Latvian, was seconded to the Cheka's "Registry Section"—an innocuous cover for the foreign intelligence branch.

Lenin's judgment of his associates was often eccentric. It is perhaps fortunate for the noncommunist world that few of the men he favored proved to be as talented as the wily Latvian. Berzin was a brilliant choice. A born leader, a man of subtle intelligence and an acute perception of human nature, he also had a formidable flair for conspiracy. He was an authentic espionage genius.

*Ibid., p. 126.

As a veteran of the underground—with two death sentences lodged against him to prove it—Berzin had commanded the Latvian regiment that served as Lenin's praetorian guard during the civil war. In 1918, with the civil war raging, Berzin found time to entice the notorious Sidney Reilly, a colleague of Bruce Lockhart, a British diplomatic agent more self-confident than prudent, into financing a national counterrevolutionary plot. The bona fide counterrevolutionaries attracted to the false flag were easily rounded up and Lockhart, despite his diplomatic immunity, was arrested. Lockhart survived and was eventually bartered for Maxim Litvinov—the British having had the foresight to detain the future foreign minister in England.

Berzin's "Registry" soon shed its cover name and in 1920 was moved to the Red Army. There it became the Chief Directorate of Intelligence (GRU), a component of the General Staff.

Although the GRU was ostensibly a military intelligence service, Berzin's seasoned operatives—veterans whose operational skills had been honed in the communist underground—ranged across the entire spectrum of secret operations and espionage. Political, industrial, and scientific data flowed into Moscow from GRU agents scattered through the capitals and laboratories of Europe, the Far East, and the Western Hemisphere. From its inception until the late 1930s, the GRU scored a string of espionage coups, collected a wealth of information, and made dazzling agent recruitments. Under Berzin, the GRU concentrated on espionage operations—it had no police function and such security and counterespionage work as it undertook was usually connected with its own operations.

The transfer of Berzin's espionage apparat from the Cheka to the General Staff did not mean that the Cheka had surrendered its own foreign intelligence mandate. But saddled as it was with immense police and security responsibilities in the USSR, the Cheka concentrated its foreign activity on counterespionage and the penetration and political manipulation of the Russian emigration. The collection of intelligence was relegated to second place. Later, under Stalin, who tolerated and even encouraged overlapping responsibilities within his government, the secret police increased its emphasis on foreign espionage. When World War II broke out, the NKVD, one of the Cheka's successor organizations, was challenging the GRU's espionage primacy. But by that time Berzin had been liquidated and the GRU gutted in Stalin's blood purges.

In 1922, with the civil war burned out and the communists settling into power, the sinister reputation of the secret police had become a burden to the Soviet government. The Cheka was formally abolished and replaced by the State Political Directorate—the GPU. Aside from its new name, no other change was apparent. As a subordinate component of the NKVD, the People's Commissariat of Internal Affairs, the GPU retained the Cheka's functions, personnel, and leadership. In 1923, with the formal federation of Soviet republics, the GPU became the OGPU—the United State Political Directorate. Again, the change in nomenclature was meaningless—it was still the Cheka.

"Iron Felix" died in his bed in 1926—an achievement that was to be denied to at least four of his successors. Under the leadership of Vyacheslav Menzhinsky, the OGPU consolidated its position in the USSR, extended its internal agent networks, and began to expand its espionage activity abroad.

When Stalin decreed the collectivization of agriculture in 1929, it was the OGPU that enforced the law and carried out the dispossession of the *kulaks* and other landowning peasants. Some four million perished in the process, and another cosmetic name change was deemed appropriate. In 1934 the OGPU became the GUGB, the Main Administration of State Security, and was made a part of the NKVD, the People's Commissariat for Internal Affairs. This time the acronym did not stick—it was easier to refer to the NKVD than to its subordinate element, the GUGB. Not that it mattered, GUGB or NKVD, it was still the Cheka.

In 1934 Menzhinsky died, possibly of poison administered by his deputy and successor, Genrikh Yagoda. Like Dzerzhinsky and Menzhinsky, the malevolent Yagoda was a Pole and a veteran Chekist. After having cut down thousands of Russians during the early days of Stalin's first purge, and working up the stagehands necessary to produce the sophisticated show trials, Yagoda was dumped. According to Stalin, Yagoda had been dilatory in unmasking Trotskyites. Transferred from the NKVD, he survived until 1937. Then, at his own show trial, Yagoda admitted having slipped a potion to his predecessor. Yagoda had another distinction—he was the first Soviet secret police chief to be forced to admit in court that he was a foreign agent. This was manifest nonsense, but it served Stalin's purposes by discrediting the chief of security he wished to be rid of and helped increase the "spy consciousness" of the Soviet public. If the capitalists could recruit the secret police chief, who could be trusted?

Nikolai Yezhov, Yagoda's successor, was only five feet tall, but what he lacked in stature he made up for in attention to business. The "Bloody Dwarf" ran the NKVD for some two years, long enough for Stalin to do in every possible enemy and to disembowel the Soviet establishment. The slaughter of the officer corps was typical—in 1937–38, thirty-five thousand Red Army officers were executed. About one half of the officer corps fell—the higher the rank, the greater the casualty rate. Eighty percent of the colonels were murdered; ninety percent of the general officers were liquidated.* The Soviet High Command was all but destroyed.

The intelligence and secret police services fared little better. In 1937 three thousand NKVD officers were liquidated; others committed suicide; some merely disappeared into the Gulag. The GRU suffered similar losses. Of the many intelligence officers stationed abroad, some were lured back to the USSR for execution, a few were murdered *en poste* abroad. Berzin who (using the cover name General Grishin) had gone to Spain during the civil war, was ordered home for execution in 1937. Anyone known to have been close to him—and this included the most brilliant operations officers and agents in Soviet intelligence—was suspect. Many were executed, a few defected or went to ground. The GRU was never to recover from this bloodletting.

An afternote to Stalin's singleness of purpose came during World War II. Richard Sorge, a long-time German communist and Comintern agent, was sent by Berzin to Tokyo in 1933. There, under a flimsy journalistic cover and using his true name, Sorge ingratiated himself with the German embassy and the Japanese government. Not the least of his many achievements were his reports on Hitler's plan to invade the USSR and Japan's determination to remain at peace with the Soviet Union. After they arrested him in 1941, the Japanese authorities made secret overtures to exchange Sorge for Japanese known to have been imprisoned in the USSR. In lofty terms, Stalin denied ever having heard of Sorge. It was not until 1964, twenty years after Sorge was hanged in Tokyo, that this great agent was rehabilitated. He was awarded the USSR's highest decoration, Hero of the Soviet Union, a street was named for him, and a flood of articles surfaced in the Soviet press. In 1965 a four-kopek stamp appeared with Sorge, shown full face against a scarlet background, the first time a Russian agent—and German citizen—had been so honored.

Yezhov, the "bloody dwarf," remained chief of the secret police for two years, long enough to lend his name to the peak years of the purges. The "Yezhovshchina" as it was dubbed, echoed the Oprich-

*Ronald Hingley, *The Russian Secret Police* (London: Hutchinson, 1970), pp. 170–171.

nina—the secret police who from 1565 to 1572 had slaughtered tens of thousands of the subjects of Ivan the Terrible. Not surprisingly, Stalin is known to have spoken favorably of the "progressive role" of these early murders.

Lavrenti Beria, a Georgian and a man after Stalin's heart, replaced Yezhov in December 1938. Yezhov was named Commissar for Inland Water Transport, an ironic last post for the first Russian—his three predecessors were Polish—to have been secret police chief. Yagoda is known to have been executed in the cellar of the Lubyanka, a few floors beneath the offices from which he had directed the secret police. Yezhov simply dropped out of Soviet history—almost certainly executed by his erstwhile subordinates.

Under Beria the NKVD, like many huge capitalist corporations, expanded and diversified its interests. By 1941 the secret police were managing a sizable part of Soviet industry and, as one writer put it, "virtually all of Siberia."* Many of these responsibilities were so completely at odds with the primary functions of a secret police and intelligence agency that the GUGB was eventually separated from the parent organization and became the NKGB, the People's Commissariat for State Security. Beria retained his post as head of the NKVD but ensured his hegemony over the NKGB by naming one of his toadies, Vsevolod Merkulov, as secret police chief.

In 1946, the war over at last, another reorganization was decreed. The NKVD became the Ministry of Internal Affairs (MVD) and the NKGB, the Ministry for State Security (MGB). The MGB was the operational arm, responsible for counterintelligence and security within the USSR and for intelligence and counterintelligence abroad.

For a while the Soviet Union attempted to create its own central intelligence agency, the Committee of Information, or KI, incorporating all the foreign intelligence sections of the MGB and the GRU—much to the fury of the General Staff. Beria, who saw the various chiefs of the KI as potential threats to his own status, succeeded in separating the GRU from the KI in 1948. Three years later he persuaded Stalin that Lieutenant General Victor Abakumov, who was head of the KI, had suppressed evidence of a plot against Stalin. Abakumov was arrested and Semen Ignatiev took over the MGB. From then on it was business as usual, and the MGB and the GRU resumed their independent operations abroad.

---

*John Barron, KGB. *The Secret Work of Soviet Secret Agents* (New York: Reader's Digest Press, 1974).

The death of Stalin in March 1953 produced another, fundamental change in the secret police. With his eyes on bigger things, Beria arranged for the merger of the MGB and MVD under his personal command. With direct control of the secret police at home and abroad, the internal militia, special troops, some two hundred thousand border guards, the prison system, a significant part of Soviet industry, and the Soviet nuclear and guided missiles programs, Beria was a man to be reckoned with. And it did not take long for his colleagues to do so. Having survived Stalin, they had no intention of letting Beria assume the throne. On 26 June Beria was lured to a meeting in the Kremlin. As he strode through the conference room door, his colleagues jumped him—literally. (A probably apochryphal story attributed to Khrushchev has it that he was strangled on the spot—one can only wonder if it was in the room in which Brezhnev receives distinguished visitors.) Whatever actually did happen, it was not until Christmas Eve 1953 that *Pravda* reported Beria's execution. Along with his other shortcomings, or so the government of the Soviet Union would have us believe, Beria had long been a "foreign agent."

In March 1954 yet another reorganization of the secret police was announced and the Committee for State Security, or KGB, was formed. Shorn of the peripheral responsibilities Beria had grasped, the KGB retained authority for all secret police and security activity within the USSR and would continue to command the border guards. It would, of course, continue its secret operations abroad. In 1973 Yuri Andropov, then the KGB chief, was made a full member of the Politburo. It had taken twenty years, but the secret police chief had once again made his way into the USSR's highest council.

Even though the Western world has to some degree been conditioned by the documented depravity of the Nazi movement, it is still difficult to comprehend the extent of the barbarities inflicted by the Soviet secret police. In his study of the terror,* Robert Conquest accepts the probability that from 1936 to 1950 there was an average of eight million Soviet citizens confined in prison camps in any given year. In all, some twelve million of these prisoners were worked to death, executed, or permitted to die of starvation or neglect.

---

*Robert Conquest, *The Great Terror, Stalin's Purge of the Thirties* (New York: Macmillan, 1968), p. 533.

Taking the pre-Yezhov period into account and adding the very conservative figure of three and a half million who died as a result of the collectivization, Conquest reckons that twenty million persons died at Stalin's hand—in effect were put to death as a result of secret police operations. Conquest suggests that this figure, based on very conservative estimates, may be too low. The actual total for Stalin's twenty-three years in power might be thirty million.

It was the secret police—the Cheka, GPU, OGPU, NKVD, NKGB, MGB, and the KGB—that carried out this terror. From the merest peasant to the mightiest marshal, no Soviet citizen will ever forget it.

Except for the hiatus during the brief life of the KI, the GRU had since its inception in 1920 retained authority to conduct independent clandestine operations abroad. In the course of this long history the GRU had faced many security problems—senior officers had defected, Nazi and Japanese police had arrested high-ranking agents and smashed their networks. At the height of the purges two of the GRU's best officers, Ignaz Reiss and Walter Krivitsky, deserted their posts in Europe. Between them they might have exposed enough secrets to maim Stalin's European networks.

Reiss was gunned down by the NKVD before any Western intelligence service even knew he had broken with Stalin. Krivitsky fared a little better, but only a fraction of his information had gotten to Western sources before he was found dead in a Washington hotel room, an ostensible suicide.

But in November 1952, the GRU was oblivious to a new threat unique in its long history. One of its trusted officers had been recruited by CIA.

As Booth had hoped, it did not take long to get Popov rolling. Before he stopped he had supplied a comprehensive picture of the organization and key officers directing KGB operations in Vienna. Under the command of Evgeny Kovalov, more than seventy officers were deployed in fourteen different sections. Kovalov was well known. He appeared on the Soviet diplomatic list as counselor of the Soviet High Commission for Austria and was one of the few senior espionage officers in the Soviet apparat who even went through the motions of keeping his cover.

Most interesting to Roberts and Booth was Colonel Vasily Romanovich Sitnikov, a beefy, hard-drinking Russian whom station officers had frequently encountered at diplomatic receptions. As Booth had suspected, Sitnikov was head of the Anglo-American section of the KGB *rezidency*. He spoke German, but as far as Todd had been able to discover had not bothered to learn English.

One officer who rarely circulated outside the Soviet community was Lieutenant Colonel Vladimir Prybitkov, acting chief of the SK, or *Sovetskaya Kolonia,* the section responsible for the security of every Soviet citizen in Austria. It was the SK's job to spy on the Russians, to make sure that none had been recruited or were planning to defect or were violating any of the strict regulations governing Soviet behavior abroad. The station did not know it at the time, but it would not be long before it would get an inside look at the SK.

The KGB *rezidentura* in Vienna was a large one, but it was much like those in every other capital. Officers were assigned to every possible intelligence target, the best officers to the most important tasks. There was a highly qualified technical support staff to train agents in secret ink, ciphers, and radio transmission and a warehouse bulging with the impedimenta of espionage—concealment devices, miniature radio transmitters, surveillance gear, and disguises. Recondite chemical potions, knockout drops, alcohol "extenders" and "interrogation aids"—the truth serums Soviet intelligence had been experimenting with since Yagoda's time—were also on the shelves.

As Popov's voice rose, Domnin's pen sped across the yellow pad. When he interrupted with a question of detail it seemed only to spur Popov to talk faster, to try to cover more ground. For the first time Popov's shield had slipped and Domnin had an intimate glimpse of at least part of what bedeviled him. Popov loathed the secret police and all the trappings of state security. He made no distinction between the Okhrana—the czarist secret police that had disappeared five years before his birth—and the Cheka and its long chain of offspring. He hated them all with an undiscriminating fury.

By the time Popov had finished his second tumbler of vodka Domnin knew he must change the subject. There was other ground to be covered. As they walked to the sideboard for *zakuski,* he said, "Tell me something about the jam you're in."

Popov shrugged and began to pile smoked salmon on the plate. "I guess it's not the first time you've heard this kind of a story. But I didn't think it could happen to me."

Domnin's question had dampened the emotion ignited by the discussion of the KGB. Domnin watched as Popov walked quietly back to the coffee table. He was shorter than Alex had thought, no more than five feet ten at the most. Powerfully built, stocky, almost thick, he seemed close to the ground. His restless brown eyes were set deep beneath his forehead. An odd, old-fashioned conceit contrasted sharply with the rough, unfinished aspect of his face and made him look older than his thirty years. As Popov told Domnin later, five years of interaction between his helmet and scalp had left the top of his head as smooth and shiny as a Siberian apple. To mask the bald spot, Popov combed his remaining hair across his pate and plastered it in place with a scented hair oil. It was a curious vanity for a peasant.

For as Domnin had suspected, Popov was a peasant. Born in a village near Khady in the Ivanov Oblast on the Volga, Popov had grown up on the dirt floor of a peasant hut. He had not worn leather shoes until he was thirteen.

Domnin brought his plate to the coffee table and eased into the overstuffed chair opposite Popov. Popov speared a piece of salmon and stared warily around the room. "It was a dumb thing, but I got involved with a woman."

Domnin was relieved. Easing Popov out of a bind with a girl would be less of a problem than helping him out of trouble with the GRU. "How'd it happen?" he asked.

"She's someone I recruited, a Serb. My wife hadn't gotten here yet. Things just took their course."

"She's blackmailing you?"

"No, nothing like that. She's all right. She just doesn't have any money and I've been helping her out. When my wife and daughter got here I was broke. They needed things, Lyuba needed things. I just didn't have money enough to go around."

"Did you take anything from your operational funds?"

"Not much. It's already covered—no thanks to that damned banker, your friend Alex." Popov took another long pull of vodka. "She's not a bad agent, but I wanted to give her more money and my boss caught it. He's a bastard and he hates me. This was all I needed with him."

"Is she a communist?"

"Sure, but not a party member. She's a Serb, she hates Croats almost as much as the Nazis. That's why she's willing to work for us."

"Are you in love with her?"

Popov shifted uneasily in his chair. He had never discussed his personal life with anyone. "Look, I love my wife. I love my daughter. They're what's important. I don't know what I feel about Lyuba. She's completely alone, she lost everything in the war. She's had a rotten time and she needs someone to help her."

"What's her last name?"

Popov bristled, his eyes flashed. Domnin had gotten too close to a nerve.

"Don't you want me to make a check?" he snapped. "For all you know she may be a CIC agent, reporting on you." CIC was the U.S. Army Counterintelligence Corps. The Vienna detachment was well staffed and very active, but their operations were more aggressive than subtle. When the controlled press in the Soviet zone wanted a whipping boy, it was CIC they singled out.

Popov managed a slight smile. "Bielic," he said. "Lyuba Bielic,* she lives in the Second *Bezirk*." He took another sip of vodka. "If she's not working for CIA, maybe you can sign her up to spy on me."

Domnin laughed. "You know better than that. All I'm going to do is have a look in the files."

The Second *Bezirk*, or district, was in the Soviet-occupied sector of Vienna. It bordered the *Innere Stadt* and stretched out across the Danube canal.

"Are you still seeing her?"

"Of course, she's my best agent. She knows every Yugoslav in Vienna. I meet her every week." Popov had stopped eating and was staring around the room as if he expected to see the hidden microphones that were recording his admissions.

"That's not what I mean," Domnin said. "Are you seeing her on the side?"

"Sure. Every chance I get."

Domnin shook his head and poured another round of vodka. Popov was already a little drunk.

"You know what kind of risks you're taking? One whiff of this and your ass will be back in Moscow. And a week later you'll be counting the trees."

Counting the trees is a peasant expression dating to czarist times. Anyone counting the trees has been deported to Siberia. If Popov's

---

*A pseudonym.

relationship with his agent was detected he might not be sent to a labor camp, but he would certainly be busted out of the GRU and possibly out of the army as well.

"What are you going to do about it?"

"I don't know. But it's all right for now. I could have handled it without your money. I'll make out if I can get my boss off my back."

It was almost ten-thirty. If he was going to get to the military and political questions Washington had sent, Domnin knew Popov's problems with Lyuba and his boss would have to be postponed until the next meeting.

An hour later, Domnin had covered most of headquarters' priority questions. It was clear that despite the hours he spent in the weekly Communist party meetings, Popov had little insight into Kremlin politics or foreign policy. But as an army officer he was required to attend military training and briefing sessions held for the military personnel of the GRU and KGB. Here he was more at home. Four years of active service, three years in the Frunze Military Academy and four at the Military Diplomatic Academy had given him a liberal military education. Although Domnin eventually managed to increase Popov's interest in Soviet political developments and foreign policy, the data he was to take from his military briefings became the most important part of the intelligence reports the station funneled back to Washington. These reports also sparked the most urgent queries from Washington.

As he watched Popov walk unsteadily out of the safe house, Domnin wondered whether he was going back to his quarters at the Grand Hotel or would continue on to a shabby side street in the Second District.

11
A SMALL, TIGHTLY KNIT
RESISTANCE GROUP

When Domnin reminded Popov that his mistress might be an agent reporting on him to a Western intelligence service, he was not merely trying to talk his way out of a tight corner. The use of spies—called "access agents"—to size up a recruitment candidate is an espionage commonplace. In Austria, where Soviet ground rules forbade social contact outside the Russian community, any Russian involved with a local woman was courting catastrophe.

Soviet experience from the earliest days after the revolution had convinced the security forces that many defections of Russians stationed abroad had been triggered by social entanglements outside the Soviet community and that the most dangerous liaisons were romantic. On the other side of the fence, the fact that Soviet security regarded even the slightest flirtation as a harbinger of treason or defection, was enough to convince Western intelligence that any Russian it found in such dalliance was indeed a potential defector or agent. Certainly illicit romance has contributed to some defections. The case of George Agabekov, the OGPU operative in Turkey, who became so besotted with the prim English girl he had hired as a language teacher that in order to marry her he defected in 1931, may have influenced Soviet security doctrine. But the fact remains that in recent years none of the most important Soviet defectors appears to have been influenced by romance. Some defectors were saddled with unhappy marriages—and usually left their wives behind—but in no case does a love affair appear to have been at the root of defection.

But just as an illicit affair with a foreigner may indicate that a Russian is at odds with the system, anyone, on either side of the ideological fence, who is out of step is worth close attention by adversary intelligence operatives.

Much of Todd's operational activity was directed at ferreting out contacts—social, professional, or sexual—between Russians and outsiders. Other allied intelligence agencies were working the same vein. As, of course, were the Russians—hence their keen interest in recruiting Austrians working alongside Americans in the various American establishments.

The morning after Domnin had learned the story of Popov's girl friend, and minutes before Roberts was due to arrive for a briefing, Todd burst into Booth's office. He had completed his check of the station files for any possible trace of Lyuba Bielic. There had been only one piece of paper in the file, but there could be little doubt that the station had a record of Popov's mistress.

Late one night in August a district police station in the Soviet sector of Vienna had received an excited telephone call. A drunken Russian officer was shouting and kicking at the door of an apartment on Am Werd Strasse. Fraulein Bielic, a stateless Yugoslav refugee, did not have a telephone. It was her alarmed neighbors who made the call.

By the time two *Schupos*—uniformed Austrian patrolmen—arrived, the Russian had calmed down enough to explain that it was all a mistake. After giving his name as "Major Petrov," he apologized and left the scene. Unless a serious crime was involved, the early-morning misadventures of Russian officers in the Soviet-occupied sector of Vienna were something the Austrian police were content to leave to Russian authorities. Since Fraulein Bielic had no interest in making a complaint, a brief report was filed in the precinct station and the episode forgotten. Or at least it would have been if one of the station agents had not heard a policeman gossiping about it.

A week later a case officer dropped the agent's report onto Todd's in-box.

It was a slim lead, but as Todd's scribbled instructions on the report indicated, the refugee's possible relationship with the Russian was worth checking out. If "Major Petrov" was interested enough in a Yugoslav refugee to attempt to kick her door down, he had strayed a long way from the collective. Todd's note instructed a case officer to add Bielic to the target list. As a first step in exploring the lead, the case officer was to obtain the woman's full name and address and to trace Austrian police and alien registration files for further information on her. Under the provisions of the occupation statutes, all four occupying powers were given access to all Austrian police records.

To avoid swamping Todd's section with more preliminary investigative work than it could handle, Booth restricted the "leads roster" to the most likely looking prospects. Only when a lead had been resolved—found worth a recruitment attempt or too ephemeral to warrant further effort (as was most often the case)—was another lead added to the roster. Lyuba Bielic was number eight on the list. As soon as the Austrian file data were at hand, the next move would be to look at her "on the ground"—to place her under light surveillance. Depending on what was found, the final step would be for an agent or case officer to approach her, attempt to win her confidence, and to ask about her friend Petrov. Fortunately, Todd had not yet requested any of the Austrian files on her.

Todd's reaction to this unwelcome news—any police report involving a Soviet citizen might come to the attention of Soviet security at any time—was mixed. He was satisfied that an agent had been alert enough to pick up the story, but anguished at having nearly launched an investigation which, if blown to the Russians, would surely have landed Popov in a jam. But whatever glimpse of Popov the report may have afforded, there was the chance that, because the incident had occurred in the Soviet sector and had involved a Soviet officer, the Russians might have tumbled to it. This was a distinct and unhappy possibility.

Prudently, Todd and Domnin had begun Roberts's briefing with an account of the meeting and what Popov had reported on his mistress. Preoccupied with the police report, Booth's attention wandered until he heard Roberts raise his voice.

"This is something we can damned well do without."

For a moment Booth thought he was talking about the blaring radio. But as he looked up, Roberts's glare was directed at Todd and Domnin, the messengers who had brought the bad tidings—and they had not yet got to the police report.

"It's also something we're not going to be able to do anything about," Todd shot back. "He's been sleeping with her for months.

We've had three meetings with him—it's not likely that Greg can just tell him to knock it off."

"That's right. I can't do it," Domnin said. "Even if he agreed to drop her, she might not let him—and one peep from her and our friend goes down the spout."

"Easy does it," Booth interposed. "There's more to come." Gingerly, he handed Roberts the police report.

The argument went on for an hour. But there were cables to be written and finally the meeting broke up. Todd went back to his office to put the case officer assigned to the Bielic lead on some other, "higher priority" assignment and to make sure the section's interest in the Yugoslav was erased from the station files.

Alone, Roberts and Booth reviewed the options. They were in no position to give Popov orders. He obviously knew more about protecting himself in the Soviet community than Domnin could tell him and would probably, and justly, resent any second guessing. However dangerous Bielic might be, it was more important to bolster Domnin's ties with Popov than to issue orders that would be disregarded. Later, Booth reasoned, when Domnin had cemented his relationship with Popov, perhaps he could be persuaded to drop her. Meanwhile a contingency plan would have to be devised to deal with the possibility that the Russians would uncover his risky liaison, tear off his epaulets, and ship him home. Domnin would now have to discuss the possibility of defection with him. He also had to push deeper into Popov's reasons for coming to the station.

When Roberts left his office, Booth began to rough out a comment for headquarters. As dicey as the situation was for Popov, Roberts and Booth had concluded that masterly inactivity was the only specific for the dilemma. This was the station's sole recommendation to Washington, and Roberts signed the cable with some apprehension.

No matter how thoroughly a field station reports, nor how well its case is made, only rarely can headquarters perceive more than a fraction of what is actually going on in the field. Issues that might be settled in a few minutes of conversation often result in weeks of testy correspondence.

To Roberts's surprise, headquarters accepted the station's reasoning and agreed to wait and watch. They also consented to Domnin's preparing Popov for the possibility that he might have to escape. Pages of additional intelligence requirements choked the code room.

Popov was punctual, a common obsession of operations officers. As they settled down in their accustomed places, facing each other across the low coffee table, Domnin began to plow through the detailed military questionnaires. After an hour, Popov flagged.

"Let's eat something," Domnin suggested.

At the sideboard Domnin said, "There's one thing I don't understand." Popov scooped *Kartoffelsalat* onto his plate.

"You know, Pyotr Semyonovich, you still haven't told me why you came to us in the first place. It doesn't seem to me that you really needed the money at all." It was the first time Domnin had used Popov's first name and patronymic.

"That's right, I could have gotten by without it."

"Then why all the haggling about money?"

Popov looked up from his plate and reached for his glass.

"Meeting Alex put me off. I thought I'd be dealing with an American. I didn't expect anyone like Alex."

"Then why did you come back?"

Popov looked up from his plate. "I wasn't going to, it was too damned risky with Alex. But I heard the camera. I knew you had compromised me."

"What camera?" Domnin was honestly surprised.

"The camera behind the picture, right there on the wall. You guys are clumsy. I should have busted out right then."

Domnin was baffled. He hadn't seen any photographs.

Masters had done his best with the negatives, but there wasn't enough light and the film was almost blank. In the pressure of briefing Domnin for the first meeting Booth had forgotten to tell him that Popov had apparently heard the camera. As it was, Masters had shot from behind the door, there was nothing behind the ugly still life. Popov had not been compromised, and if he had chosen not to come back, the chance the station could have found him again would have been slight.

"But you were fussing about money with me?"

"I thought that being an American you would understand it better if I put it all on a business basis."

Domnin sighed, loudly enough to be heard on the tapes.

"But you didn't have to give me your real name—you could have stuck with the alias document."

"You'll never understand." Popov shrugged and put down his empty glass. "I'm fed up with all that lying. I wanted to start on the level with you. That's important to me. I've already talked more to you than I would with my brother. I'd never tell anyone about Lyuba."

"You know how dangerous it is—seeing her, I mean?"

"Sure."

"You damned well don't know how dangerous it is," Domnin said as he leaned across the coffee table and began to tell Popov about the police report.

For a moment after Domnin had finished, Popov remained silent. Then, wiping the sweat from his forehead, he began to speak. "I hadn't been so drunk since the war. It was the dumbest thing I ever did," he said.

"No, it's not. The dumbest thing you ever did was not telling me about it right off the bat. We were within days of calling on your girl friend. If the Russians had gotten hold of that, you'd have been in Moscow in twenty-four hours."

Flustered, Popov toyed with the food on his plate.

"I can't make you get rid of that girl, but for your own good you'll have to do it, and the sooner the better."

"You're right, I'll do it. But not right now, she's too important to me as an agent."

"I guess that will have to be up to you," Domnin said. "Meantime, just in case, we'd better make some plans."

For half an hour they went over the escape plan. It was as simple as Booth could make it. If Popov felt threatened, if there was any chance he might be arrested or rushed back to Moscow, he was to telephone and give a code message—the shortest Booth could devise.

No matter how weak his German might be, he would have no trouble with *"Max ist krank."* Nor would the duty officer be likely to confuse "Max is sick"with any more innocuous message. Soonest, within fifteen minutes Booth hoped, Popov would be picked up at the corner of the Waehringerstrasse and Berggasse in the U.S. sector. If he couldn't call, he was to take a taxi, or walk, to the *Stiftskaserne*, an American military police station in a former Austrian military building on the Mariahilferstrasse, near the *Innere Stadt*. There he was to request asylum and ask to see "Colonel Grossman"—

Domnin. The station had easy access to the building and would be able to pick him up within minutes.

When Popov was given the telephone number, he reached for his pocket notebook. Domnin interjected: "I don't want you to write this down—the phone's right in our office, there's no way you could explain it in your notebook."

"I'll add two digits to each number," Popov explained quickly.

Domnin shook his head. "How long do you think it would take your 'friends' to figure that out? Talk about our being clumsy, you couldn't fool the Okhrana with an old trick like that. It wouldn't even look like an Austrian telephone number."

Popov nodded. "I'd better get rid of the number Alex gave me." Domnin winced. He had forgotten that Alex had allowed Popov to make a note of the first telephone number.

After thumbing through his pocket notebook, Popov tore the corner from a page. "I'll take that," said Domnin, and added the scrap to his pile of notes.

It had not been one of Popov's best days. As he began to memorize the number, he held out his glass for another drink.

"You're drinking too much," Domnin said as he poured a small drink into the glass.

"It gets on my nerves, talking like this."

"Being drunk won't help. You need a clear head, now more than ever."

Popov took a sip of the vodka. "There's one more thing," he said.

"What?" Domnin pushed his notes aside.

"I won't come without my family."

"For Christ's sake, Pyotr, do you think we'd expect you to? Of course you're going to bring your family."

However reassuring Domnin sounded, he knew that if Popov fell under suspicion there would be little chance he could get his wife and daughter away with him.

"*Khorosho*," said Popov, "that's good." For a moment he relaxed. "I can't see you for a few days—I'm duty officer and I'll be busy all next week."

"That's okay. Do you want to set a date now?"

"I can't be sure, I'll have to call you."

"Just use the new phone number, say 'Max' is calling, and tell whoever answers when you can make the meeting."

"Will he be able to speak Russian?"

"No, but that doesn't matter. The last thing we want is someone speaking Russian on that line. You'll have to speak German. Just tell whoever answers when 'Max' will arrive. I'll be here. But no Russian on the phone—your KGB neighbors may be listening."

Popov squirmed in the overstuffed chair. "My German's not so good."

Domnin had suspected as much. For this reason Booth had made the emergency signal as short as possible—"*Max ist krank.*"

"You speak enough to give the days of the week and the time, don't you?"

"Sure, but I like to work it out in advance. What I can't do is carry on a long conversation on the telephone. Whoever answers better not ask a lot of questions."

"Don't worry, no one is going to ask any questions."

Domnin, a natural linguist, was puzzled. "What the hell do you do when you go to a *Bierstube* for a drink?"

"I just say *ein Bier bitte.*"

"How do you expect the waiter to know if you want *Flaschenbier, ein Seidel, ein Krugerl, helles oder dunkles?*"

Popov's expression showed that there was more to ordering beer in Austria than he had realized.

As Domnin drilled the agent on the basic German to be used on the telephone, he wondered how Popov could possibly hope to succeed in a GRU Strategic Intelligence *rezidentura*, even as a Serb specialist. It was no problem for a Russian to make himself understood to a Serb, nor to understand someone speaking Serbian—both were Slavic languages—but whatever his specific assignment was, any Soviet intelligence officer working abroad was expected to know the language of the country he was working in. Popov scarcely knew enough German to take a taxi. He could barely read the newspapers and could not hope to handle an agent in anything but Russian or Serbian. No wonder he was in trouble with Colonel Yegerov.

Because of the pervasive threat of hidden microphones, miniaturized radio transmitters, and even old-fashioned eavesdropping, intelligence officers customarily mask operational discussions with professional jargon—a kind of oral shorthand—and an abundance of pseudonyms and cryptonyms. If the true name of an agent must be used, it is scrawled on a bit of paper. Not once in the hours spent discussing the Popov case in Austria was his name mentioned. If a simple pronoun was not sufficient, Popov's cryptonym—"Attic" would be used. As the operation progressed, even the cryptonym was changed every few months.

Case officers and other field personnel are also assigned pseudonyms which, like the cryptonyms for agents, are used in all cables, dispatches, and records kept in the field. Experienced operations personnel have a working vocabulary of hundreds of these cryptonyms and pseudonyms.

It was thirteen days before Popov telephoned, long enough for Domnin and Newby to bring most of the paper work up to date—and for Booth and Roberts to begin to worry. Even headquarters was fretting: "Advise soonest date next Attic meeting" was the cable that rocketed into the signal center an hour before Popov made his first call to the new telephone number.

To add a measure of security to Popov's communication with the station, Booth had reserved a separate telephone line in the duty officer's room for his exclusive use. If this telephone rang while Domnin was in the office, he would rush to pick it up. After hours, or in Domnin's absence, the duty officer handled the call. Unless the duty officer was one of the handful involved in the Popov case, all he knew was that "Max" was an agent of the greatest importance and that the call was to be handled exactly as prescribed in the duty officer's handbook. The "Max" phone, as it became known in the office, was equipped with a recording device. No matter how difficult it might be for the duty officer to understand Max's German, there would be a recording for Domnin to work on.

Alongside the telephone was a top-secret folder, called after airline procedures the "Mayday book." It outlined exactly what the duty officer was to do, and whom he was to call in the event Max gave the danger signal—*Max ist krank*. Never during the three years Popov was active in Vienna were there fewer than two case officers who could be alerted within minutes to pick him up at the appointed place or to retrieve him from wherever he might have fled. To make sure it was functioning, a case officer made a daily call to the Max phone. The scramble procedure was tested less frequently, but often enough to satisfy Booth that the Mayday team could respond within very few minutes.

Popov's first telephone message was loud and clear. *"Hier Max. Ich komme heute Abend. Selber Zeit."* Obviously he had rehearsed his German.

The flustered duty officer burst into Booth's office within seconds of putting down the phone. The Popov team prepared for a busy night. Todd dashed off to buy the *zakuski*; Domnin, with Brooks Newby in tow, picked up the notebook bulging with requirements and bustled into Booth's office for a quick briefing session. Masters rushed to the safe house to test the audio equipment and to settle down for a long night in the back room. Unfortunately, Popov had other plans.

"I've brought a little something to make up for missing the last time," Popov said. He reached into his pocket and pulled out three carefully folded sheets of onionskin paper. "When I was in Baden bei Wien to get my duty officer briefing, Orlov, the Baden finance officer—a tight little bastard—asked me to bring the payroll sheets to Vienna for the boss. Orlov's too lazy to seal it up and give it to the regular courier. All I had to do was wait until our administrative officer had left and then, as duty officer, I could keep it in my workbox until morning. I thought I might as well make a copy for you."

The payroll listed every GRU officer, technician, clerical worker, and driver working in the Vienna *rezidentura* and in the Baden offices and gave their rank, date of grade, pay, and allowances. It even showed how many rubles they had converted into schillings in the GRU finance office. Popov wrote a clear, carefully disciplined hand. Like many who have fought for an education, he was proud of his handwriting. It had taken him most of the night to copy the paper. It was a windfall for the station.

As Domnin began to study the document, Popov stood up. "I'm sorry, but I can't stay tonight. I've got to see someone I may be able to recruit. I'm in real trouble with Yegerov, my boss. He wants three more recruitments from me. I don't see how I'm going to do it. There just aren't that many Yugoslavs around here."

"What does he do, give you a quota?" Domnin asked.

"You're damned right, only it's assigned by Moscow, not from here. We have to make five recruitments a year—and replace any agents we may have dropped. One of my agents has left Vienna. That means I'm on the hook for six this year. I've got three, but I don't see how I'll ever make the next three."

Popov got up and moved toward the hallway where his coat was hanging.

Domnin was nonplussed—he had pages of priority questions for Popov.

The next morning Booth changed the format of Domnin's workbook. The questions were carefully sorted out and a notebook was prepared with sections tabbed for a meeting limited to fifteen minutes, half an hour, an hour, or a normal meeting—usually at least three hours. From then on, Domnin's first question to Popov would be "How long do we have?" He would then flip the notebook open to the appropriate tab and find questions arranged in priority according to the length of time he had to pursue them.

Although headquarters continued to swamp the station with requirements—in espionage jargon, questions for agents are known as "intelligence requirements," a pompous military phrase usually shortened to "requirements" or "RQMs"—it was up to the station to balance headquarters' enthusiasm for the intelligence product with the reality of agent handling. As important as Popov's reports were, Roberts and Booth had to ensure that he was not treated like an automaton. Like lovers, spies cannot be taken for granted.

Those involved with the Popov operation were constantly aware that they were dealing with a man who, from the moment of his first appearance, was risking his life to their advantage. Operational discipline and headquarters' thirst for intelligence notwithstanding, Domnin had to be prepared to respond to Popov's moods and emotional needs. In this, he was at his absolute best.

By nature warm and enthusiastic, Domnin was also perceptive. His ability to sense and respond to the feelings Popov only rarely expressed was a key factor in the operation. Only gradually did it become apparent to Booth that Domnin was at least as "Russian" as his agent—complicated, emotional, and given to unpredictable, at least to Booth, changes of mood. Aside from Newby, who was soon to return to Washington, none of the rest of those involved with Popov could speak fluent Russian, certainly not enough to second-guess Domnin's appreciation of his agent's personality. As the only person in contact with Popov, he bore the brunt of the strain involved.

Domnin's wartime intelligence experience had been in liaison. This had given him an understanding—possibly unique in the agency at that time—of the Soviet psyche, but it had little to do with operations work. Even after he joined CIA and was named chief of a branch in the Soviet division, Domnin had not been directly involved in agent operations. But he was one of the rare individuals who had a natural flair for working with spies. This, plus his empathy for Russians, and perhaps some of the advice showered on him, was enough. In the end, he was a fine case officer.

It was not an easy role. No matter how often Booth or Roberts attempted to reassure him, Domnin felt that the success of the case rested entirely on him and his ability to guide Popov safely between the demands of the agency and the menacing Soviet security system. Only once during the early stages of the operation did headquarters insist on overriding the collective wisdom of the station.

As weeks passed, a routine for meetings developed. Popov would meet Domnin as many as three times a month, the frequency being set by Popov and balanced against the time he might have available and the ease with which he could disappear from the Soviet community for even a few hours. As a GRU case officer, his time was more nearly his own than it would have been had he been in the army or on a diplomatic assignment. But every time he went to the safe house, he had to have a cover reason to explain his absence to Colonel Yegerov, his section chief. Notional agent meetings, reconnaissance of meeting places, and time spent prowling through the restaurants and barrooms favored by his Yugoslav targets were his most common alibis.

Brooks Newby's assignment to Austria was supposed to have lasted only a few weeks, but it was mid-February before he left. By then the Popov operation was four months old and, as Roberts and Booth thought, had outgrown its birth pangs. It was only a few days after Newby's return to Washington that headquarters waded into the operation.

Newby left Austria determined to convince the headquarters staff—still puzzled by Popov's motives—that Popov was the man the station had described, a witting collaborator, motivated by a deep personal fury against the Soviet system, and prepared to take the risks of fighting back rather than to adopt the safer course of defecting. As Roberts and Booth studied headquarters' cable, it was clear that Newby had carried the day—and had even been too successful in doing so.

Headquarters' brief message instructed the station to have Domnin raise with Popov the possibility of forming a "small, tightly knit resistance group of like-thinking comrades." Roberts was appalled at the prospect of involving an agent as important as Popov in anything as risky as "covert action."

For more than a year after its inception in 1947, CIA's sole operational component, the Office of Special Operations (OSO) was responsible for espionage and counterintelligence. But in 1948 the White House, State Department, and National Security Council realized that as menacing as the Soviet military forces were, there was still another threat, less tangible but equally dangerous. The communist takeover in Czechoslovakia and the political crisis in Italy had alerted Washington policymakers to the extent of Soviet subversive operations. Clandestine political operations, conducted through well-funded international front organizations and the various national communist parties—all heavily underwritten by Moscow—were expanding rapidly. Democratic countries struggling to recover from the effects of World War II offered little or no organized resistance to this subversion. Italy, Greece, France, Iran, China, and Vietnam seemed more likely to become victims of political subversion than to succumb to military attack.

To fight this activity on its own level, the United States embarked on a broad campaign of covert action (CA). In 1948 one of the first directives of the newly formed National Security Council ordered CIA to establish the Office of Policy Coordination (OPC). Under CIA's command but with close policy ties to the Department of State and the White House, OPC was to be CIA's covert action arm. It was to engage in a three-pronged operational program covering the spectrum of covert action: political, propaganda, economic, and paramilitary operations were to be undertaken at once.

First, OPC was to attack the communist enemy on its own terrain by supporting resistance movements in the USSR (primarily in the Ukraine and Baltic areas) and in the Eastern European countries; to support anti-Soviet émigré operations in the West; and to destroy Soviet morale by radio propaganda and written material smuggled across the borders by agents or air-lifted by balloons.

The second element of the OPC program was to contain, and even to roll back, communism in the West by subverting communist or left-wing governments; to support noncommunist governments threatened by communist overthrow; and to provide forums for noncommunist intellectuals.

OPC's third covert action mission was to counteract Soviet propaganda and political fronts by developing noncommunist political organizations, supporting noncommunist editors and writers, and subsidizing American student and labor organizations in fighting communist fronts abroad.

These ambitious undertakings were to be done so skillfully that each operation could be "plausibly denied" by the U.S. government. Considering that the operations involved such diverse enterprises as the overthrow of the governments in Iran and Guatemala—in years to come similar attempts would be made in Cuba and Chile—the underwritings of paramilitary activities in Albania (later in Vietnam and Laos) and the establishment of such large, overt activities as Radio Free Europe and Radio Liberty to beam radio programs to Eastern Europe and the USSR, the concept of "plausible denial" had an undeniable flavor of wishful thinking about it. Secret operations at this level are a contradiction in terms.

In 1949 the OPC staff was a modest 302 employees; in 1952 it numbered 2,812 and was active in some forty-seven foreign stations. (The idea that some 2,500 persons could be selected, subjected to security investigations, trained, provided with cover, and given some notion of their responsibilities in thirty months would have been hooted by almost anyone with experience in clandestine operations. Not every recruit was up to the job, but on the whole the OPC staff was a remarkably talented group and achieved considerable operational success.) Until 1952, OSO and OPC existed at home and abroad as separate commands. In Austria, as in most other foreign countries, there were in effect two separate CIA stations. The OSO station, of which Roberts was chief and Booth the deputy, was concerned only with espionage and counterintelligence. The OPC station, with its own chief and staff, wrestled with the covert action program. In Austria OSO and OPC maintained easy liaison, a situation that did not exist in many field posts, particularly when OSO and OPC were interested in the same agent prospect.

For OSO personnel one of the irritating differences between OSO and OPC was the matter of temporary duty trips to headquarters for consultation. As valuable as these trips were for ironing out plans and the differences that inevitably occurred between field stations and headquarters desks, they were rarely authorized by OSO. But OPC station chiefs were called home two or three times a year.

A few months after Booth arrived in Austria, the OPC station chief returned from a few days in Washington. As usual after such a trip, he stopped by Roberts's office to brief Roberts and Booth on his visit and the latest headquarters gossip. After listening to him sketch the ambitious covert action plans of other stations, Roberts, who was more understanding of the OPC mission than Booth could be, asked wryly if OPC Austria had been assigned any new tasks.

Yes indeed—along with everything else on its plate, OPC Austria was now "to shake the Hungarian government to its knees." This, he explained, would be accomplished by a propaganda effort within Hungary. Roberts rolled his eyes but forbore comment.

For years the OSO station had tried to infiltrate agents—called border-crossers—into Hungary. After weeks of preparation, a score or more of these operations aborted, usually before the agents even got to the border area. Other bolder agents were rounded up by Hungarian border guards within a few hundred feet of the barbed wire and mine fields. The few agents who actually succeeded in making their way into Hungary rarely produced even a whiff of intelligence. Roberts and Booth considered the OPC scheme of infiltrating political activists into Hungary so enterprising as to be lunatic.

In August 1952 General Bedell Smith, then CIA director, ordered the merger of OPC and OSO on a worldwide basis. Roberts assumed command of the combined Austria station and the OPC chief became deputy. Booth retained his function as chief of operations but continued primarily to concern himself with the OSO mission of espionage and counterintelligence.

In the political climate of the time—the most frigid days of the cold war—covert action was heady stuff. Because CA agents and contacts usually played public roles—labor leaders, politicians, prominent émigrés, journalists, and publishers—and were often well-known, not to say prominent, individuals, covert action was scarcely a back-alley activity. It was impossible to pump money into political parties, underwrite press campaigns, and overthrow governments without attracting a level of public attention rarely if ever visited upon spying.

In Austria, thanks largely to the good judgment of the OPC station chief, covert action was conducted clandestinely and with adequate attention to the principle of plausible denial. The most unrealistically ambitious headquarters schemes—ranging from revolution to smuggling propaganda across the Czech and Hungarian borders—were quietly relegated to the back burner. Propaganda campaigns against the USSR and international communism were pushed and usually flourished—there being nothing like the presence of the Red Army and a cohort of political commissars to stimulate anticommunist enthusiasms. Communist fronts were penetrated, and activities such as the World Youth Conferences were turned into forums in which young democrats would, with OPC's guidance and some funding, challenge the Stalinists on their own ground. These political operations were so successful that the Soviet Union was forced to abandon its international youth assemblies.

Even when considered against the background of John Foster Dulles's and President Eisenhower's campaign pledge to "liberate Eastern Europe," the notion of having an agent as valuable as Popov set about organizing a "tightly knit resistance group" of Soviet intelligence officers seemed the height of folly. Popov was fully occupied in reporting the highest level of military intelligence and a stream of inside counterintelligence data. Politely, or so he thought, Roberts urged headquarters to reconsider.

A few hours later a stinging reply crackled into the code room. The station's objections had been noted at a "high level"—jargon which might refer to the director of CIA or some even loftier personage not excluding the president. Headquarters was adamant. Domnin *would* broach this topic at the next meeting.

If possible, Popov was even less responsive to headquarters' proposal than Roberts had anticipated. In rejecting the idea out of hand, he read Domnin a grim lecture on what he called "Soviet reality." There were, he said, plenty of Russians who shared his opinions of Stalin, the secret police, and the Soviet system. But, said Popov, this was something he sensed. Never had he encountered any Soviet citizen at home or in Austria so foolhardy as to hint at dissatisfaction. Those who had, he presumed, were in the Gulag.

There was no one, Popov continued, not even his wife, to whom he could conceive of disclosing his thoughts on the matter. To do so was to invite denunciation. In controlling political activity in the USSR, the KGB had recruited agents in every cranny of Soviet society, in each office and agency of the government, and in the military services. So thorough was the KGB penetration of the Soviet establishment that Popov was convinced there were KGB agents within the

GRU *rezidency* in Austria. Even those friends whom he suspected of being closet dissidents could be KGB provocateurs. So pervasive was the KGB's clandestine presence that even Popov's subtle probing of a friend's attitude could be considered provocative. The only way a possibly disaffected friend could protect himself would be by denouncing Popov.

Not only would Popov not consider the proposition, but in no circumstance would he even give Domnin the names of anyone who *might* be dissident. The chance that a failed CIA recruitment attempt might somehow blow back on him was too great a risk. As far as Popov was concerned, espionage was a one-on-one proposition. He was prepared to continue on that basis. He would not put his safety and the future of his family in the hands of another Russian.

Washington's reply to Roberts's cable outlining Popov's reaction to forming a resistance group was brief. For the moment headquarters would table the proposal. It was not, however, a closed issue.

As far as anyone in the station knew, Popov was never again urged to form a resistance group. But headquarters' expression "a small, tightly knit resistance group" was etched on the memory of everyone concerned with the Popov operation. For years it was used as a pejorative, to describe any headquarters proposition that seemed to slight the operational facts of life as perceived by field personnel.

Roberts and Booth were preoccupied with the Popov operation but there was also a station to run. Plans had to be made for operations against other targets, going cases had to be supervised, sterile operations had to be weeded out, and new recruitments ventured. There was also the paper blizzard, relentless as the arctic williwaw. Audit reports, monthly progress reports, quarterly operations reports, special reports, cables and dispatches piled up on Booth's desk like snow drifting against a barn.

For all the planning the station did, there was much to be said for luck—if young Freddy Baer had not wanted to sit in the front seat that day, it might have been weeks before Popov's letter was found. Luck usually struck in unexpected places.

It was a sullen sort of day when Harriet Jones's call was put through to Booth's office. Paul and Harriet Jones had only been in Austria for a few weeks. He was a case officer, working for Peter Todd on his first field assignment. Neither he nor Harriet had been overseas before.

From the moment they moved into a small, rather isolated house on the edge of the Wienerwald, Harriet had developed the habit of telephoning Paul in the office several times a day. This violated the station's security canon—Booth assumed the Soviets were glued to most American phone lines and tried to keep the monitors on a starvation diet. But as much as the calls chafed Todd, he reasoned that Harriet would outgrow the habit before any real damage was done. He was more tolerant than Booth.

Because Paul Jones was out of the office and Todd was closeted with Domnin, a secretary, miffed by Harriet's telephone habit, deviously transferred the call to Booth. It had been a busy morning and Booth's cross-grained attempt to affect an avuncular tone could scarcely have encouraged Harriet. Was there, he asked loftily, a problem? There might be, she answered, but it was not anything she could discuss on the telephone.

Balancing the prospect of a long drive to the Joneses' house against the possibility of a bit of homely insecurity on the telephone, Booth asked if she could give him just a hint as to what the trouble was. Harriet paused, drew a deep breath, and whispered that it had to do with the office. Since she seemed to be going through the motions of discretion, Booth asked for a little more information.

"There are some strange men in the woods behind the house," she said.

"How many men?"

"Three."

Housebreaking was a fact of life in Vienna, but the thieves, usually displaced persons or refugees, were careful to make sure no one was at home before they entered.

"What are they doing?"

"They're burying something."

"Could they be workmen, fixing a sewer or a water pipe?"

"No. They're Russians, burying something right in the backyard."

"*Russians?*" he said. "In uniform?"

"No, they're civilians—floppy pants and big hats. Regular Russian civilians."

By this time Booth's paternal pose had faded. "Let's get this straight, Harriet. In broad daylight, three Russians are burying something in your backyard?" This was hyperbole. There never was any *broad* daylight in Vienna.

"Yes, damn it. There are three Russians burying a box behind the house. I can see them now, right from here."

"What does it look like—a bomb? Have they got shovels?"

"Of course they have shovels, little shovels," she answered. "It's too big for a bomb. It looks like a square box, about three feet around—anyway, why would anyone want to bury a bomb in our backyard? If you ask me it's a radio."

"Okay, Harriet. Paul won't be back for a while, but I'll ask Mr. Todd to come over and take a look. He'll be along as soon as he can."

"You'd better tell him to hurry—they're getting ready to leave."

Always the activist, Todd was glad to get away from the office, however skeptical of the reason for his outing. It was more than an hour before he called back.

"This is pretty damned odd, but the fact is someone *has* buried something about three hundred feet behind Paul's house. It's just inside the woods."

"Okay, Pete, I'll take your word for it. If you can spare the time, you'd better dig it up. If it's not a dead dog, bring it into the office."

He agreed.

"Pete—one more thing."

"Yeah?"

"I understand the Russians always booby-trap their dead."

"The same to you, chief." Todd hung up.

It was a beautifully constructed, heavy plastic container, two by three feet and about twelve inches deep. The seams were sealed with melted plastic. It was an expensive, professional job and should have kept the contents dry for years.

Masters pried the case apart with a chisel. Inside were three separate packages. Even before the inside wrappings were peeled off, Booth guessed—ruefully—that Harriet had somehow been right: she had uncovered an agent radio set. Like most Russian radio gear, the markings were in English and German. Aside from this, it was like no transmitter the station had ever seen.

Two days later an expert came to examine it. It was indeed a Soviet set and the most advanced model he had ever seen. Weeks later Booth learned this was the first Soviet "squirt" radio transmitter to fall into CIA hands in Europe. Squirt or "burst" transmitters are equipped with a device that permits an agent to punch his enciphered messages on a tape. When the message is ready to transmit, a special keying device is activated and the tape fed through the transmitter at two hundred and fifty or more words a minute. With this equipment, the clumsiest spy can transmit a long message and be off the air before the set can be pinpointed by radio direction-finding equipment.

The station never did learn why the Russians had chosen such an unlikely spot to bury the set, but Booth's guess was that they had entered the Vienna woods from the Soviet sector, misread their map, and assumed they were farther from the American sector than they were. Nor could anyone fathom why they had failed to realize they could be seen from the Joneses' house. Possibly they had been drinking on the job.

Todd kept the site under surveillance for a few days but, perhaps because of all Booth's chatter on the telephone, no one was spotted in the vicinity. If Todd had nabbed an agent, he might have explained why the Russians insisted that he excavate a bulky box when the radio could have been handed to him in complete secrecy in a Russian safe house.

Later, when Booth apologized to Harriet, she was too polite to admit that she had detected his shirty assumption that no amateur, least of all a housewife, could ever hope to make a contribution to such a "macho" endeavor as spying. At the time most of CIA's women officers were restricted to office work, usually as analysts.

It was more than a year before the first CIA squirt transmitters—better, the station was assured, than the Russian version—arrived in Austria. Booth always suspected that the agency communications staff had profited considerably from Harriet's set, but no one would admit it. Nor was Booth's suggestion that the set be given the code name *Harriet* ever acknowledged by headquarters.

12
HOME LEAVE

At 8 A.M on 4 March 1953 a Moscow radio commentator, his voice choked with reverence, announced that a "misfortune had overtaken the party and the people." Not everyone in the Soviet Union agreed with him. For some, the "serious illness of Comrade J. V. Stalin" was a portent of better things to come. Pyotr Semyonovich Popov, major, GRU, was not of this opinion. Weeks before Stalin's death, he had told Domnin that as long as the KGB was in existence there would be no real change in the USSR. "No matter who's in charge, no matter what they say, it will be the same damned prison it's always been."

As Khrushchev related the story in his memoirs,* Matryona Petrovna, Stalin's housekeeper, found the dictator stretched out on the floor of his *dacha* at Kuntsevo early in the morning of 1 March. Assuming that the "little father" was sleeping off a night's drinking, she summoned the guards to lift him onto the sofa bed in his study. After tucking him in, the old woman went on about her business.

Although 1 March was a Sunday, Khrushchev expected a call from Stalin—at this stage of his life the dictator hated to be alone. But when Stalin had failed to call by midnight, Khrushchev went to bed. Minutes later, Malenkov telephoned. The *dacha* guards, worried by the lack of movement in Stalin's quarters, but unwilling to risk disturbing him if he was at work, had asked Malenkov to come to *Blizhny*, as the *dacha* was called. Prudently, Malenkov asked Khrushchev to meet him at the *dacha*. He had already called Beria and Bulganin.

Khrushchev Remembers with Introduction, commentary, and notes by Edward Crankshaw, trans. and ed. Strobe Talbott (Boston: Little Brown and Company, 1970), pp. 316–320.

After questioning Matryona Petrovna and talking to Vasily Khrustalyov, the chief of the *dacha* security force, the nervous foursome decided not to risk disturbing the dictator. They returned home.

Within an hour Khrushchev's phone rang again. Petrovna had taken another look at Stalin. This time she had told Khrustalyov there *was* something strange about the way Comrade Stalin was sleeping. Malenkov summoned Beria, Voroshilov, and Kaganovich and alerted the Kremlin medical staff. Khrushchev sped back to the country house.

In the absence of Vasily Vinogradov, Stalin's personal physician— he had been arrested in November 1952 on the antic charge of conspiring with American and British intelligence to murder the Soviet leadership—Professor P. E. Lukomsky began gingerly to examine the unconscious Stalin. It was soon clear that Stalin had suffered a massive stroke, his right arm and leg were paralyzed.

Malenkov and Beria took charge and ordered that, along with the medical team, Khrushchev and Bulganin or Malenkov and Beria would remain with Stalin at all times. Stalin's daughter Svetlana and his son Vasily, an air force general, were summoned.

After a few minutes at his father's bedside, Vasily Stalin, who had begun World War II as a captain and ended it as a lieutenant general and an alcoholic, began to berate the doctors and to accuse them of murdering his father. Escorted out of the room by the security guards, Vasily made his way to the servants' quarters where he could continue drinking.

Early on the morning of 4 March, when it had become unmistakably clear there was no hope for Stalin, a confidential report was made to high Soviet officials. At 8 A.M. the first public communiqué was broadcast. After the initial announcement, three bulletins were issued by the doctors. Stalin was pronounced dead at 9:50 P.M. on 5 March, but it was not until early on 6 March that the Soviet radio audience was told that "the heart of the wise leader . . . of the Communist party of the Soviet Union has ceased to beat." It was almost two weeks later before Domnin could meet with Popov.

The station knew Popov was not an expert political observer and probably had less intimate knowledge of Kremlin politics than many Western political pundits. But he was an "inside source" and headquarters had prepared a battery of questions for him.

In Austria, Popov said, the Russians were watching and waiting. Except for the Soviet press reports and photographs, the Russians, like the political analysts, had little data to study. The most revealing signal of the new status was the group photograph taken at Stalin's bier. Malenkov, with Beria close beside him, stood slightly apart from Voroshilov, Bulganin, Kaganovich, and Molotov. In a second row, after Vasilevsky, Konev, Sokolovsky, Zhukov, and Mikoyan, came Khrushchev. Khrushchev's picture seemed slightly different from the others—perhaps it had been superimposed over that of Nikolai Shvernik, president of the USSR and chief of state. The fact that Shvernik was missing from the group was a clear, and not unexpected, signal that he would not hold office much longer.

"There's one thing you can be sure of," Popov said. "Those bastards are sweating. They couldn't even announce that the old man was dead without starting to talk about preventing panics."

With an amused expression he unfolded a copy of the official announcement that had been circulated to the Soviet personnel in Austria.

"Listen to this," he said, as he began to quote the document, mimicking the diction of a radio announcer. "They want us to be sure 'to guard the monolithic unity of the party as the apple of our eye.' They even tell us that the most important job of the government 'is to insure uninterrupted and correct leadership' and to 'prevent disorder and panic.'

"As long as Beria is number two, and that won't be long—he'll take over or land on his ass trying—they don't have to worry about any panic," Popov said. "Nobody is going to do anything, except maybe in the Kremlin."

He handed the announcement to Domnin.

"What happened in the United States when Roosevelt died?" he asked. "Did Truman make a speech telling everyone not to panic? When Churchill was deposed, did the king say anything about the unity of leadership? Even when there's a war on your governments don't worry about panics."

Domnin smiled, "Churchill wasn't deposed, he just lost an election. But I see what you mean."

By 28 June, when Popov's prediction about Beria had come true and the secret police chief had been apprehended by his erstwhile Kremlin colleagues, Popov had left Vienna for home leave in the USSR.

*   *   *

As a rule Soviet diplomats and intelligence officers on duty abroad are allowed home leave every two years. But in Austria at that time most intelligence officers, diplomats, and high-ranking military men took leave every year. However long the train ride from Vienna to Moscow, security officials considered it worth the time and expense to bring the foreign staff home every twelve months. Prolonged exposure to the capitalist world might otherwise dim their appreciation of the Soviet state.

Popov had six weeks' leave. While he spent a few days in Moscow at the Arbatskaya Square headquarters of the GRU, Gallina and their daughter would visit her mother in Tula. As soon as Popov finished his duty in Moscow, he would spend a few days in Solnechnaya, where his younger brother and sister still lived in the hut Popov had grown up in. Popov had not been home since 1949. After this, if it could be arranged, Popov, Gallina, and their daughter would spend a few days at one of the vacation resorts, Sochi or Kaliningrad, where special accommodations were available to GRU and KGB personnel. The family would return to Moscow to catch the train back to Vienna.

Booth had planned to have Domnin spend one of the last two scheduled meetings briefing Popov on the military questions he hoped the agent would be able to find answers for in Moscow. The position of the military in the new government, the reorganization of the security and intelligence services under Beria, and any changes that might be planned for the GRU were topics Popov could be counted on to cover. Headquarters also wanted insights into the political plans of the new regime, but the station doubted Popov—who was not one for political nuances—could add anything to the reports coming from the Moscow embassy and the press.

Anxiety is the occupational disease of espionage. Spies are the most heavily afflicted, but few case officers are immune. In his double role as a GRU case officer and CIA spy, Popov was under awesome contradictory pressures. When he began to work with Domnin, Popov's hard-won status in Soviet intelligence became the vital cover for his work as a penetration agent. But to protect his cover and to keep pace with his GRU colleagues, Popov had to work as convincingly as ever to produce intelligence for the GRU. He also had to maintain easy social relations with his fellow GRU officers, most of whom he liked.

As a CIA agent, Popov labored to provide information on the USSR for the station.

In his work for Soviet intelligence, Popov risked detection by the various Western counterintelligence agencies deployed in Austria. As a CIA agent, Popov faced both the KGB and GRU security systems.

Nor was his personal life less tangled. Despite Domnin's coaching, Popov had continued his relationship with Lyuba Bielic. The recently discovered pregnancy of Gallina and the turmoil of the post-Stalin period accented the stress. Lyuba, a communist and GRU agent, could share little of her lover's life. Their occasional meals and furtive embraces only underlined the illicit and temporary compass of the relationship. Gallina, doing her best to make a home in the shabby hotel room, was completely cordoned from her husband's life. At no time in their marriage did Popov as much as hint at his political disaffection. Nor could he discuss his GRU work with her. Soviet intelligence officers are strictly enjoined from mentioning any aspect of their operational work to their families.

There was no one to whom Popov could speak freely but Domnin, the case officer he met clandestinely. In the six years they worked together, Popov never learned Domnin's name, nor could he ever indulge in what for Russians was the customary and somehow reassuring practice of using his friend's first name and patronymic.

Aside from his work, his family, and Lyuba, Popov had few interests. Like many Russians, he was a passionate fisherman and whenever possible went out into the Soviet occupation zone in Austria to the streams reserved for Soviet personnel. With his friends, he regularly poached on privately owned fishing streams. He was also an expert marksman—in Solnechnaya ammunition was expensive and like his older brother Aleksandr, he had learned to make every shot count—but in Austria there was little time for hunting. His deepest interest was in farming.

To offer Popov a slight respite from the constant shoptalk in the safe house, Domnin kept the living room stocked with a selection of illustrated American magazines—*Life, Look, Holiday*, and even *Better Homes and Gardens* were on a side table. Occasionally, Popov would pick up a magazine and flip through the glossy pages, but rarely was his curiosity sufficiently piqued to ask Domnin for an explanation of a photograph or some aspect of American life. Once in an inspired moment, Todd filched a copy of the *American Farm Journal* from the

Special Service's library. Popov was fascinated. Questions tumbled from him as he studied each photograph and advertisement. Always he returned to the same point. Is this propaganda? Do farms really look like this, do farmers really live like this in America? From then on, copies of the magazine were regularly mailed to the station from Washington.

Despite his interest in American farming, Popov gave little thought to life anywhere but in Russia. The safety and well-being that defection and resettlement in the United States would offer him and his family was of no interest. He might have to defect, but he would only do so if he had to flee and then *only* with his family. Defection was not an alternative, only a means of escape.

The strain showed. Popov was tired and the half-empty bottle that marked every meeting with Domnin was token enough that his inclination to ease his anxiety with vodka had become more pronounced. Neither Roberts nor Booth had any idea how much he was putting away on his own, but it was clear that Popov was drinking too much.

To give Popov a chance to unwind before he left, Booth had planned to have Domnin keep the final meeting on a social level. There would be no agenda, but special *zakuski* and a bottle of wine. Perhaps in the relaxed atmosphere and the absence of the customary shoptalk, Domnin could steer Popov into a discussion of his background and glean a little more insight into his motives.

For all the station's good intentions, headquarters had cabled a page of urgent questions which Domnin would have no alternative but to cover at this last meeting. As the case officer worked his way through the briefing, the agent began to fidget—it was time for Popov to tell Domnin that he had business of his own to transact in the Soviet Union. Reluctantly, Domnin finally closed the notebooks, still stuffed with requirements for the forthcoming trip. Popov hesitated for a moment and then began to explain that along with putting the best possible face on his operations in Vienna, he also planned to remind a friend in the GRU personnel department that his promotion to lieutenant colonel was overdue.

"There's something else," Popov added, almost shyly.

Domnin poured a glass of port, the only red wine Popov would drink, and looked up. "Yes?"

"You know we can't have too many rubles here. The finance people keep a close watch on how much money we draw and how much we spend," Popov said.

Years of experience had taught Soviet security officers that the best device for keeping Russians away from capitalist fleshpots was a short financial leash. Forty percent of the monthly salary due Russians abroad is arbitrarily deducted from their wages and held in escrow in the Soviet Union. Even with this financial hobble, Russians on foreign assignment can, by scraping, acquire consumer goods denied to everyone but the Soviet elite at home. With what seems to be congenital generosity, Russians returning to the USSR lavish gifts on their less fortunate kinfolk.

Relatives are not the only beneficiaries of this largess. Sensible diplomats and intelligence officers are also careful to distribute consumer items among their colleagues working on area desks at headquarters. For an intelligence officer, the next best thing to a foreign assignment is a posting to a headquarters desk supporting operations in the United States or Western Europe. They expect, and get, a tithe from each returning acquaintance. Called *blat*—the swapping of favor for favor—the custom is built into the Soviet bureaucracy and society. (Sometime before General Ivan Serov was relieved as chief of the GRU, a newspaper photograph showed him wearing a sweater purchased by CIA and given Serov—as *blat*—by a CIA penetration agent.)

"I've got schillings enough to take care of things for friends at headquarters and Gallina's mother, but I want to do something for my family in Solnechnaya. I haven't been home since 1949."

Domnin nodded.

Popov hesitated. "Can you give me fifteen hundred rubles?"

This was the first time Popov had mentioned money in weeks. Fifteen hundred rubles, then about four hundred dollars, was a sizable sum, more than a GRU major might have been expected to save from the portion of his salary he collected abroad.

"I've got the rubles all right, but how are you going to cover it?" Domnin asked.

"Don't worry. The only place they check is at Chop. The guards don't worry too much about Russians coming in. They expect a little chocolate and tobacco, but they're not going to search me. It's the foreigners they go after."

Chop is the border point where the Russians crossing from Hungary went through Soviet border controls and changed to the broadgauge Russian trains to complete the trip to Moscow.

"That's a lot of money," Domnin said. "You can't throw that kind of cash around Moscow without someone noticing it."

"Don't worry, I'm not going to spend it in Moscow. I'll tell you about it when I get back—there's something I have to do."

After Domnin's first meeting with Popov, headquarters had decided to budget four hundred dollars a month for Popov's salary. These modest wages, less than some station agents were being paid, had nothing to do with the value of the information Popov was producing, the risks he ran, or headquarters' regard for him. It was based on an exaggerated estimate of the amount Popov could securely handle. One of the biggest threats to a spy—certainly to a Russian working in place—is sudden and unexplained affluence.

As Domnin had first explained it to Popov, the bulk of his money would be kept in escrow, available for him to draw on if he needed it—and then only if Domnin agreed that he had a plausible cover for having it. The money Popov didn't use would be banked for him, against the day he might be forced to flee.

Rarely, if ever, did Popov draw more than fifty dollars a month. Aside from a raincoat, a pair of trousers, and a bargain-basement suit, Popov gained no material benefits from his wages. Most of the money Domnin gave him was spent on gifts for his family, Lyuba, and, oddly enough on one occasion, to support a GRU agent.

Booth tumbled to this when Popov asked Domnin for a thousand schillings, about forty dollars. Since a request for this much money was completely out of pattern, Domnin was curious. Sheepishly, Popov explained that one of his agents, code name *Matros*, or Sailor, had lost his job on a Danube barge. When Colonel Yegerov, Popov's section chief, refused to advance Matros enough money to tide him over, Popov had begun to slip him money out of his own funds. A few weeks later Matros was still unemployed and Popov was fifteen hundred schillings out of pocket.

Domnin was not impressed. "What the hell are you thinking of?" he exploded. Crestfallen, Popov explained that Matros was broke and needed the money for food.

"Didn't they teach you anything at that damned academy?" Domnin roared. "An Austrian family could eat for a month on fifteen hundred schillings."

"What could I do? The poor guy had no work—I might have lost him if I hadn't helped out."

"That's great, maybe for the Red Cross. But what the hell are you going to do when another case officer takes over and finds you've been giving that creep more money than the record shows? Yegerov will have your ass."

Chagrined, Popov agreed.

This was the last time he asked CIA to underwrite GRU operations. But Booth was not sure he had learned the lesson. The more Domnin reported on him, the more Roberts and Booth began to sympathize with Colonel Yegerov: maybe Popov was too nice a guy to deal with spies.

However little Popov was paid, there was no way to put a price on the information he delivered. For years one of the Pentagon's highest priority requirements was to obtain a copy of the 1947 Soviet army field regulations, the first basic manual of Red Army organization and tactics issued after World War II. At a meeting of an interagency intelligence requirements committee in Washington, a Pentagon representative had become so keen on getting the document that he put a price of five hundred thousand dollars on it. He might as well have gone for a million—the bulky manual was classified secret and as far as could be learned at the time, copies rarely circulated below division level. It was not the sort of document an absent-minded Soviet general might leave in a taxi.

A few months after Popov was recruited, Domnin asked if he could possibly get his hands on the 1947 document. Popov looked puzzled.

"I may be able to bring out one of the 1951 manuals, but I don't know where I could find the old one. Copies of the '47 issue were withdrawn when the new one came out." This was the first the Pentagon had heard of the new manual.

Domnin and Popov spent an entire meeting photocopying the document Popov had slipped out of the GRU offices in the Imperial Hotel. As pleased as the Defense Department was when CIA disseminated it, nothing was ever said about the five hundred thousand dollars.

The day after Popov left, Domnin returned to headquarters. He would be back in Austria a week before Popov's scheduled return. Domnin, who had come to Austria expecting to stay for a few weeks, had been living out of a suitcase for eight months. Although not as tired as Popov, he also needed a breather. Besides, Allen Dulles, who had joined CIA in 1951 and replaced Bedell Smith as director in 1953, wanted a firsthand briefing on the Popov operation.

That summer Joel Roberts left Austria for a headquarters assignment. His replacement arrived a few days before Popov was scheduled to return to Vienna. By that time, Domnin, still glowing faintly from the two-hour interview he had had with Dulles, was busy indoctrinating a new assistant into the Popov case.

Mike Andenko, an amiable giant of a man, had been assigned to the station to fill the gap left when Brooks Newby had returned to headquarters. He spoke fluent Russian and had worked on the Popov case at headquarters. He would monitor the meetings from the back room and help Domnin with the exhausting task of preparing précis of the tapes. Calm and rather strait-laced, he was to become a perfect alter ego for the emotional Domnin.

No matter how often Booth tried to persuade Domnin that everyone concerned with the case shared responsibility for the Popov operation, he remained convinced that if a slip occurred, the fault would be his alone. If anything, his long session with Dulles had reinforced this conviction.

In the months he had worked with Popov, Domnin had deftly juggled the double role of tough case officer and understanding friend. In fact, Domnin had become so devoted to Popov that it took all of his willpower to exert even the slightest discipline.

Hours were spent in Booth's office as Domnin manfully attempted to rationalize Popov's drinking, his continuing relationship with Lyuba Bielic, and to explain away the difficulty Popov was having meeting Colonel Yegerov's demands for new recruits. Repeatedly Domnin tried to convince Booth that the station should provide Popov with a brace of agents he could ostensibly recruit for the GRU *rezidency*. He spent hours digging through station files in the hope of discovering a lead to an agent he might possibly turn over to Popov.

As enticing as this proposal—which originated with Popov—was, Booth could not agree with it. It would not be possible to hand an agent to Popov without the agent knowing that he had been offered to Soviet intelligence by an American case officer. There might be no problem as long as Popov retained control of the operation and the agent remained loyal. But if something went wrong, if Popov's superiors came to suspect him or decided to insert a different case officer into the operation, there would be no way to prevent a sudden interrogation by the Russians or even a kidnapping. The security of the Popov operation would be no better than that of the agents the station had supplied to him—and there is no way of ensuring the continued good faith of any spy. Reluctantly, Booth decided that Popov would have to line up his own recruitments.

It was five tense days after his scheduled return before Popov called to arrange a meeting.

Despite the pressure from headquarters for the latest information from Moscow, Booth was reluctant to let Domnin put this first meeting on a business-as-usual basis. After the six weeks Popov had spent in the USSR, Booth was not sure that Domnin could simply take up where he had left off. In working out the meeting plan, it was decided to set aside a large chunk of time to allow Domnin to reinforce his personal relationship with Popov. As it turned out, this was a wise decision.

13
IVANUSHKA DURACHOK

From the safe-house window, Domnin watched anxiously for Popov to turn the corner. Even in the late summer shadows he was easy to identify. No matter what the weather he always wore a hat. Short and stocky, he was light on his feet and walked with quick, impatient steps. Now he seemed more hurried than usual as he strode brisky past the safe-house entrance for a hundred yards before abruptly whirling and retracing his steps—a routine maneuver to see if anyone was behind him. Satisfied there was no one there, Popov stepped into the entrance.

Domnin stayed at the window for a moment. Then, certain that the street was still empty, he turned and hurried across the living room to open the door.

He was surprised to notice Popov's face creased in a broad smile as he stepped into the apartment. Closing the door and snapping the extra lock Masters had installed, Domnin hesitated for a moment and then enveloped the smaller man in a bear hug. "*S vozvrashcheniem,* Pyotr Semyonovich," he said. "Welcome back."

Flustered, Popov took off his hat. With a furtive glance at the hallway mirror to see that his hair was still plastered in place, he walked into the living room.

"It's good to be back," said the Russian as he looked around the living room. "It seems like a long while, but I'm glad to be here again."

It was the third safe house Booth had assigned to Popov, but each was much the same—a three- or four-room apartment on the second floor of an apartment house in the U.S. sector and close by a tram or bus line. Three doors opened from the hallway leading into the living room and dining room. The doors to the kitchen and toilet remained slightly ajar. The bedroom door was locked from the inside.

At one corner of the living room, heavy overstuffed chairs were ranged around a low coffee table. To muffle street sounds that played hob with hidden microphones, heavy draperies were drawn across the windows. At one end of the dining area a massive sideboard doubled as a bar and table for the *zakuski*.

In the bedroom, Ed Masters had installed the elaborate electronic and taping gear behind a false partition built into a deep closet. Todd and Mike Andenko, each with a clipboard, sat facing each other across a card table littered with yellow pads. Each carried a loaded pistol. Masters had little use for handguns—his semiautomatic shotgun, loaded with buckshot, stood beside the bedroom door. No one really expected trouble, but if the KGB should uncover Popov, it would be best to be prepared to resist any violent intervention they might make.

Domnin splashed vodka over ice in the two glasses on the coffee table. Booth had decided that ice would help take the edge of the vodka.

"How was it, how was the trip?"

"Good, mostly pretty good. But. . . ." As he picked the ice out of his glass, Popov paused.

"Problems?" Domnin asked.

"No, not with the work. That bastard Yegerov gave me a bad report, but I think I got that straightened out. That's not it," he said.

"Gallina is all right? There's no problem with the baby?"

"No, no, the kid will be along in a few weeks. A real little Austrian, born in Vienna."

"You saw your people in Solnechnaya—they're all right?"

Popov hunched forward in his chair and unbuttoned his suit coat. "You know, when someone asks a peasant how he is, he always answers 'better than tomorrow.' There's only one thing wrong at home—my people are peasants."

Popov took a swig of his drink.

"Maybe I shouldn't have gone home. That damned village, it's just the way it was when I grew up, maybe even worse. But I had to let them see my uniform. One summer, when I was a kid, I remember walking with my father. A postman came by, peddling a bike along the road. My father doffed his cap. Imagine, a man, half crippled from thirty years' labor, pulling off his cap to some little turd on a bicycle. And now I'm a lieutenant colonel, a big shot."

Surprised by Popov's offhand reference to his promotion, Domnin leaned across the table and shook hands.

"That's great, Pyotr—you've made it. *Za tvoe povyshenie.* I toast you. I drink to your promotion."

Popov raised his glass. "I guess I'm the only officer ever to come from Solnechnaya. A couple of guys were sergeants, but they didn't make it through the war." With a grin he added: "It's the peasants that die first."

Domnin thought uneasily about the briefing books on the corner of the coffee table. It did not look as if Washington would be getting any answers tonight.

"It's quite a system," Popov said. "A peasant goes through two academies, makes lieutenant colonel and his brother and sister still live in the same old *izba*. There's not even a floor in our hut—just boards on the dirt. There's no one in Austria who lives the way we do in the village. No one here even knows what it's like."

Domnin nodded. The condition of the peasants, still more than fifty percent of the population, was a closely guarded secret. Since the war most peasant villages had been off-limits for touring correspondents and Moscow-based diplomats. The one or two showplaces near Moscow and in the Ukraine had too obvious a Potemkin aspect to be convincing to Western observers.

"All the propaganda Moscow puts out about helping the peasants—there's still no country that treats its own people the way Russians treat Russian peasants. When they need someone to beat, it's a peasant. When they need cannon fodder, it's the peasants. We work to live and we live to work. That song—even the Austrians sing it—*Burlatskaya*, "The Volga Boatmen." A nice song, but no one ever stops to think what it means—the boatmen were harnessed to the barges. They pulled them like oxen." Popov's eyes glistened.

"I'm a lieutenant colonel now," he said with a grimace. "But I was thirteen before I had a pair of leather shoes. It was Sasha—Aleksandr—my big brother who got them for me when he made me go to school in Khady. For two weeks he worked like an animal to buy one pair of shoes—too big so that I wouldn't outgrow them. If he hadn't done that I'd have gone to school barefooted. I was prouder of those shoes than I am of my promotion."

Slowly, Domnin eased back into his chair. The few days in Solnechnaya had stripped the veneer from Popov's feelings. This was not the time to interrupt him.

Popov hunched forward, his fingers drumming on the table. "What kind of a government is it that grinds down its own people? Peasants aren't some kind of foreigners, we're not even a minority. There are more of us than any other single group in the country. And we're Russians, just as much as those pasty-faced city boys in Moscow."

In the back room, Mike Andenko's pencil raced across the yellow, legal-sized pad as he watched the tapes spin slowly on the recording machines. Masters had installed two complete audio systems, microphones and recorders, as a hedge against the possible malfunction of the unreliable gear.

"No matter what Moscow says it's going to do for the peasants, nothing will change until there's a war and the whole thing is overthrown. Even the damned Germans could have done it, but they couldn't believe what they found. They could have had the peasants with them. Even after the first killings and burnings, they could have won us over. If they'd offered anything, just a little decency and some land, we would have gone over and fought with them against Stalin. I don't know how it would have come out, but at least Stalin and that gang would have been gone forever."

For Popov it was a long speech.

"You always want to know what made me come to you, what makes me keep coming back. It's so simple, I don't know why you can't understand it."

"It's not all that simple, Pyotr," Domnin said. "There are a hundred thousand Russians right here in Austria—how many think the way you do? How many are willing to put up a fight the way you are?"

"That's the trouble,"Popov snorted. "We're too tough, we can take too much. Peasants or serfs, we stand it for too long. But every so often we explode and there's blood to be paid. It happened in 1671, all over Russia the peasants rose. Again in 1775 we killed the landowners and burned the great houses. But every time we lost out. We didn't have any leaders. No one knew what to do."

With the back of his hand, Popov rubbed his eyes.

"In 1917 we did it again. If the damned dumb peasants being butchered in the army hadn't said to hell with the officers and started walking back home, where would Lenin and all his deep thinkers have been? Just a gang of intellectuals sitting around some cellar talking about a revolution."

Popov looked around the room. "Well, it happened to me here in Austria when I finally found out how the 'poor, oppressed workers' were living. That, and that damned Colonel Yegerov treating me like Ivanushka Durachok, Ivan the Little Fool. Well, I'll teach him something, that *svoloch*, that shit-dipped son-of-a-bitch."

Domnin remembered a children's book, one of the first he had read in Russian. It was the story of Ivanushka Durachok, a Russian folk figure, a country bumpkin who, apparently without any guile, always managed to outwit the smart alecks who tried to dupe him.

Staring into Domnin's eyes, Popov paused and hit the table with the flat of his hand.

"Whatever happens to me, just remember one thing. Everything I've done has been for my people, the peasants."

Popov got to his feet and began to pace around the small living room.

"I'm not so much," he said quietly, "and there's not a lot I can do. But you can do it. No matter what happens in the next war, just treat us decently and you'll see. You're the only chance we've got. Treat us like human beings, not serfs. All we need is a little hope and decent treatment. After such a long time, that's not so much."

For two hours Popov spoke. For once the smoked salmon and matjesherring seemed to be disappearing faster than the vodka. Before he finished he had described the village, his hut, and the string of events that had thrown him off the treadmill that had consumed generations of his family.

Popov's village, Solnechnaya, is a few kilometers south and east of Khady. In summer it is a half-hour's walk to the Volga. The area is one of the poorest in the Ivanovskaya district. Built on open ground, it is much like thousands of other peasant villages. More than a hundred log huts are ranged along an unpaved road. At one end of the village is the *kolkhoz* center, the *Narodni Dom*, or meetinghouse, and a consumer's cooperative store. A gasoline generator supplies power for the center, the only building with electricity. In front of the meetinghouse is an artesian well and pump, one of four that serve the village.

At the other end of the road is the village blacksmith shop and alongside, a wooden shed providing winter shelter for heavy farm equipment. Beyond the shed is the village granary, a low, sod-covered structure. In winter the road separating the huts is packed with snow, frozen hard as a billiard table. When spring comes the road is an impassable swamp of slush and mud. By early summer it has become a river of dust. Only a low dirt bank separates the road from the huts on either side.

There is little difference between one log hut and another, but the roofs of the older buildings are covered with moss. Spaced far enough apart—about four hut-widths—from its neighbors to prevent fire from spreading from one roof to another, each hut, or *izba*, has two small windows facing the street. Under the eaves of the low-slung, one-story buildings are remnants of scrollwork, still showing traces of the bright paint that provided the only decoration before the war made paint an expensive luxury. Beneath the windows outside, a wooden bench runs along the front of each hut. In summer old people sit there, watching the children play along the banks of the road. In late afternoon, when workers return from the fields, they relax there for a few moments before entering the *izba*.

The only entrance to the hut is from the back, through the *dvor*, a rubble-strewn courtyard banked by a dirt wall. Along the top of the wall, a crude wooden fence provides a rough windbreak for chickens or any livestock the family might be lucky enough to have. Against the back of the hut are a tool shed and a small stable. At the rear of the *dvor* stands a privy.

A low door leads to the *seny*, a narrow hallway crowded with winter clothes and boots, which opens to the large room where the family lives. A huge brick oven, a *pech*, dominates the room. This primitive space heater is whitewashed but streaked with soot. Two steps lead to the flat top. In winter, children play there and at night the old people and children sleep on the warm bricks. It is also the family hospital, anyone too sick to work can rest there during the day.

A worn wooden table, two benches, and a few straight-backed wooden chairs are the only furniture. In one corner of the dark and fetid room is an ikon. On a shelf in the opposite corner is a small mirror. Along the sides of the room are *polati*, deep shelves for storage and sleeping. In the larger huts a door opens from the left of the central room to the *klet*, a bedroom used by the parents until a son is old enough to bring his wife into the hut. Then the parents move to the big room.

With slight regional variations—in the south they are made of earth bricks—millions of peasants live and die in these huts.

* * *

It was 1930 before the convulsion that shook the Russian agricultural system to pieces struck Solnechnaya. It would have happened earlier, but the countryside was so barren that the Moscow-based agricultural commissars had given it a low priority for collectivization.

For the peasants, the trouble had begun in 1928 when Moscow, preoccupied with its industrialization program, awoke to a developing crisis in food supply. Unless something was done, there would be a two-million-ton shortfall in the grain supplies needed to feed the cities. Although the land seized from the large estates in 1917 had given the peasants more fields to cultivate, by 1927 the absence of consumer goods had begun to sap the farmers' initiative to produce the food necessary to feed the burgeoning urban population. In an effort to jack up food prices, peasants and *kulaks* began to withhold grain from the market.

A *kulak*—in Russian, "fist"—was a prosperous peasant who, through hard work, and in most cases considerable luck, had scratched together enough capital to hire farm labor, lease land, and even dangle shylock loans in front of the less fortunate farmers. As rapacious as most of the hereditary landowners, these self-made capitalists had acquired land which was farmed for them by hired laborers, often working off loans taken at one or two hundred percent interest. Even before the communists made *kulak* an all-purpose epithet, *kulaks* had few friends in Russia. But for all their faults, the *kulaks* were never quite the monsters Stalin's propaganda made of them.

Under Lenin the Bolsheviks had established a political base, smashed the economic power of businessmen and landowners, and destroyed all opposition political activity. But the peasants and small landowners—then more than sixty percent of the population—were largely untouched by communism. Left to work the land and to produce food, they ate more, but lived pretty much as they had in the past.

Stalin's solution to the food shortage was admirably simple. He would declare the *kulaks* and the more prosperous peasants enemies of the people and expropriate from them the food needed for the cities. The "poor peasants" would then take over the *kulaks'* land and the program of collectivized farming would be intensified. That the *kulak* class represented something less than four percent of the peasant population and that there were few peasants indeed who might be considered prosperous was immaterial. Also ignored was the fact that in a country as backward as Russia, not even the most visionary agricultural planner could have thought that a scheme as radical as collectivized farming could be achieved in less than a generation.

But if Stalin was to continue his drive for heavy industry, he needed workers and workers needed food. Moreover, if the Soviet Union was to be ready to fight off the attack from its capitalist enemies—which communist propaganda regularly predicted—the Red Army would need an assured food supply. A policy of coercion, Stalin thought, would supply food, and the liquidation of *kulak* holdings and the manpower saved by collective farming would add workers to the urban population.

In 1928 the Central Committee decreed emergency measures and a campaign against the *kulaks* was launched. Crops were confiscated, property requisitioned, and farms raided. Rather than surrender their crops and livestock on the vague promise of better things to come, peasants and *kulaks* alike resisted. Grain was hidden, cattle slaughtered and eaten. When the panicky peasants ran civilian administrators out of the villages or lynched them, Red Army and GPU military units were deployed to smash the offending villages and deport the survivors. As Hugh Seton-Watson has said, "It was a war of the Communist Party and its armed forces against the Russian . . . peasantry."*

When Stalin ordered the liquidation of "*kulaks* as a social class" in January 1930, five million alleged *kulaks* were uprooted and driven from the land, the lucky ones to work in factories, the others to be transported to underpopulated regions or labor camps. The rural population of the USSR was halved, those remaining on the land were again at the bottom of the heap. The peasants were totally subjugated.

When the result of forced collectivization—the complete dislocation of the Russian farm system and a catastrophic drop in livestock—was borne home to Stalin, he stepped deftly to one side. It seemed, he said in a *Pravda* article published in March 1930, that some agricultural administrators had been too zealous in carrying out collectivization. The program would be slowed down. It was too late. In the famines of 1931–33 an estimated nine million Russians died.

As nearly as Popov could remember, collectivization came to Solnechnaya in the late spring of 1930. After a village meeting at which

---

*Hugh Seton-Watson, *From Lenin to Malenkov* (New York: Praeger, 1953), p. 157.

young party functionaries from Moscow attempted to explain collectivization to the assembled peasants, officials visited each *izba*.

Patiently the pale-faced young commissar began to explain to the Popov family the details of the collective farming plan. The hundred or so families in Solnechnaya would form a *kolkhoz*, or collective farm, an independent economic unit encompassing all the land worked by the villagers. Peasants would work a minimum of a hundred and fifty days for the *kolkhoz*. All produce in excess of the peasant's individual needs would be given by the *kolkhoz* to the state—grain, potatoes, cucumbers, and other vegetables. In future, cattle would be slaughtered only by permission of the village chairman or an assistant.

Popov was eight. His brother Aleksandr was eighteen and already the tallest and strongest man in the village. He had worked alongside his father for five years, but his ambition was to become a hunter—stone marten and sable thrived in the wooded areas to the north. Aleksandr's strength and willingness to help other peasants in the fields had won him many friends.

The commissar repeated the words spoken at the village meeting—no longer would the family own the land it had worked for a century.

"We'll work for the government, just as we did for the *pomeshchiki*, the landlords. But the land is ours." Popov's father's statement echoed the centuries-old peasants' creed—"You may own us, but the land is ours."

Again, the commissar explained. Like industrial workers and city dwellers, each peasant would be given enough food for his family and seed would be allocated for next year's planting. Soon, tractors and other heavy farm machinery would be made available to the *kolkhoz*. Meanwhile, anyone hoarding grain or killing cattle without authority would be judged an enemy of the people.

Popov could remember the raised voices and harsh words. Suddenly Aleksandr lunged from the wooden bench. With a roar he grabbed the astonished commissar and dragged him across the rough boards covering the dirt floor and into the *seny*, the corridor leading to the only door. Stumbling, he threw the official against the door. There was a loud crack, the crude latch broke and the stunned commissar rolled out into the refuse in the courtyard behind the hut. Scrambling to his feet, he bolted through the wooden gate.

"You stupid *kulaks*, I'll see you all in hell," he shouted as he stumbled back to the road.

"To call us *kulaks* was a joke," Popov said. "Even in the best of times there were no *kulaks* in our area. The land was no good, we were all too poor to be bothered with."

Three days later two horse-drawn wagons rolled down the village street. Three armed soldiers, their blue collar-tabs identifying them as GPU troops, and two civilians stepped down from the cart and crowded into the Popovs' *izba*. Citizen Semyon Ivanovich Popov had been declared a *kulak*. Popov and his family would be deported. They had time to pack clothing and cooking utensils before being taken to Khady to await transportation to the east.

Popov could not remember where the family was held in Khady, but recalled that at least thirty other families—rounded up from other villages—were also crowded into the open courtyard. There they awaited their fate, probably transportation to Siberia.

"It was Sasha who saved us. He got the idea of writing to Kalinin. He was president then. It was a ceremonial job but Kalinin, an old revolutionary, was a peasant himself. He liked to be known as the 'friend of the peasant.' He never lost a chance to brag about his background.

"It's funny," Popov continued, "but a few years later our whole district was named for Kalinin. Sasha was ahead of time when he decided we should write him."

As they walked to the *zakuski* on the sideboard, Popov continued. "We hadn't done anything—God knows we weren't *kulaks*. Neither of our parents could write, but Sasha had been to school—part time—for five years. With the help of a clerk from another village, we managed to compose a letter to Kalinin."

Popov laughed. "I can't remember what we said, but we put in everything—'Beloved Comrade Kalinin, we beseech you to take a moment to read these lines from the poorest peasant family in Solnechnaya. We have nothing but our *izba* and a few strips of land. We are not *kulaks*, just poor peasants. We don't know what happened, but you can ask anyone in our village. We are good Russian peasants, not *kulaks*. We implore you to let us go home again. This is all we ask. We have done nothing."

Even in those days, Popov explained, strong elements of traditional Russian paternalism still existed in the USSR. Anyone could write to Stalin or the president and no minor official could stop the letter.

"By some crazy miracle, our letter actually got to Kalinin's desk. The railroads were still a shambles from the civil war and this was our best luck. We must have been held in Khady for a month at least waiting for a train. Suddenly a big shot, a regular city slicker, came into the holding area. Kalinin had given us a pardon. All at once the bastards couldn't do enough for us—the protégés of President Kalinin," Popov said.

"They carried us back to Solnechnaya—in all Russia we were probably the only peasant family that ever returned."

Traditionally peasants, trapped in the same abysmal poverty, stick together. A peasant would think nothing of stealing from a landlord or the government. But to steal from a fellow villager was unthinkable. The Popov hut was exactly as they had left it, their few possessions untouched.

Impressed by Aleksandr's initiative and the regard the villagers had for him, the commissar offered to make him an "official," an assistant to the brigadier who would supervise the Solnechnaya collective. Aleksandr was shrewd enough to know that he did not have the temperament to work with Moscow bureaucrats. He refused the job, but made a counter-offer. He would like to leave the village and become a hunter and work part time with the lumber trust in the forests. It was an odd request, but not one that could be refused to a protégé of Kalinin. Aleksandr had broken away.

When Popov's father died in 1935 Aleksandr returned to the village for a few days. Because Popov's mother and sister worked with Popov and his younger brother on the *kolkhoz* land, the family was as well off as any in the village. To Popov's chagrin, Aleksandr made a decision. At least one member of the family was to have an education and—no matter how much he might protest—it was to be Pyotr Semyonovich. Popov, barely literate, was enrolled in one of the special schools where accelerated classes were being established for peasants. Aleksandr stayed long enough in Solnechnaya to earn the money to buy his brother a pair of leather shoes and to escort him to Khady. Popov was thirteen.

In 1928 the Soviet school system had gone through a counter-revolutionary change. Gone were the progressive schools that had flourished after the revolution—where homework was barred, student governments were more powerful than teachers, and examinations and grades abolished. Sound basic education was needed if young peasants were to become workers, able to fulfill a role in industry.

After three years, Popov had progressed enough to transfer to a middle-school in Tula, some three hundred miles from Solnechnaya. A year later, in September 1939, German panzers cut swiftly across Poland. As Polish resistance collapsed, Soviet forces swept across the eastern frontier and occupied part of the ravaged country.

Popov got his first taste of military life in April 1940 when, a few weeks after the Soviet Union invaded Finland, the Tula school was abruptly transformed into a military training academy. Popov and his classmates were officially enrolled as officer cadets. When Hitler's forces rolled across the Soviet frontier in June 1941, the class had completed a scant twelve months of military training. It was enough, however, to earn its members commissions as junior lieutenants. With only six years of formal education behind him, Popov was assigned to the ammunition train of a quartermaster battalion servicing front-line artillery units.

"For four years I sweated. If every rocket I carried to the front killed even one Nazi, I must have won the war myself. But I've got no complaints—I was only hit twice, neither time bad enough to make any difference. Most of the time I was on the central front, in the Moscow area at first."

Like many officers with a clean security record and experience in the communist youth organization, Popov was accepted into the Communist party in 1943, when he was twenty-one. In wartime it was a simplified procedure, a natural progression from his Komsomol—Young Communist League—activity at the military school in Tula.

For all its kowtowing to communist doctrine, the Soviet army owes a significant debt to a czarist marshal, Aleksandr Vasilyevich Suvorov. Along with his tactical teachings, Suvorov, who died in 1820, preached a revolutionary system of military training. According to Suvorov it was only through intensive training that a soldier could acquire the self-confidence that would carry him to victory on the battlefield. He also insisted that military training be structured so that it could be understood by the lowliest peasant in the ranks. In the face of the then almost total reliance on mass armies trained on the parade ground, Suvorov wrote, "Wars are not fought with numbers, but with knowledge." For Suvorov, training, more than any other factor, was the father of victory on the battlefield.

After his death, Suvorov's doctrine was put aside and the Russian army went back to its traditionally harsh discipline and endless parade-ground drill. It was only after the Crimean War that a few Russian officers recalled Suvorov's concepts. They could not arouse the General Staff from its lethargy, however, and by the outbreak of World War I only a few young officers had been able to put Suvorov's theories into practice. But the scattered success of their efforts was impressive enough to convince some of the officers who would later form the Red Army that intensive training for all ranks would be as essential as bullets and boots.

Through the darkest days of the German invasion the Soviet military academies continued to function. To this day the Soviet officer corps spends more time in training than any of its potential antagonists.

The Red Army officer corps had barely begun to recover from the bloodbath of Stalin's purge when the Nazi armies attacked in 1941. By the time Stalin had finally called a halt to the slaughter in 1938, some 35,000 Soviet officers had been put to death and the "Red Army officer corps" had become a misnomer—it had been bled white. Among the victims were 3 of the 5 field marshals; 13 of the 15 army commanders; and 110 of the 195 division commanders. As the disorganized and ill-prepared army stumbled backwards in a fighting retreat, hundreds of thousands of casualties were suffered, and by the end of the year, an incredible 3,600,000 Soviet soldiers had been taken prisoner.*

Nowhere were the combat losses more visible than in the officer corps. Replacements were needed for the best troop commanders— as always the first to fall—as well as for the incompetent officers who were identified and culled from the combat units.

Officer cadets were hurried to the front and battle-proven NCOs were commissioned in the field, but these were short-lived emergency measures. Only when the battle lines stiffened and the full force of the German attacks was spent, did replacements begin to match combat losses. Throughout the war, the appalling attrition of combat officers made the replenishment of the officer cadre a critical problem. However great the pressure for officer replacements, the Soviet General Staff stuck to its training doctrine and officers were regularly pulled from the front for long periods of additional training.

*Trumbull Higgins, *Hitler and Russia: The Third Reich in a Two-Front War 1937–1943* (New York: The Macmillan Company, 1966).

In December 1944 Popov and a handful of officers from his regiment were summoned to corps headquarters for interviews with a mandate commission, scouring the front for candidates for the Frunze Military Academy, the Soviet command and staff college. With only six years of education on his record, Popov was astonished even to have been selected for interviews. However slight his chances, he welcomed the three days in the relative comfort of the corps headquarters. But for once his peasant pessimism was misplaced—the mandate commission had a quota to fill.

In peacetime, candidates for the highly prized appointments to the military academy are selected on the basis of competitive examinations. Even to take the tests, officers must have shown outstanding military potential as well as some academic promise. But in 1944, combat records, security background, and availability were the criteria. Training programs notwithstanding, wily combat commanders were often reluctant to release their best officers and sometimes recommended those they could most easily spare from combat duty.

Popov's military record was good, if not outstanding. In almost four years of combat service he had risen from an immature and half-trained junior lieutenant to a battle-smart captain. Twice wounded, he had won the respect of his brother officers and the trust of his superiors. His stubborn determination to follow orders more than made up for his peasant lack of initiative. Popov's peasant background reinforced his ability to weather the roughest combat conditions without complaint and contributed to his popularity with battalion officers. But in his ingenuous evaluation of his chances, Popov did not realize that he had an additional qualification, one that was all-important in the Soviet system.

Of pure peasant stock, neither Popov nor any of his family had ever been abroad or exposed to any political influence that might reflect negatively on his security record. With the exception of Aleksandr's fracas with the commissar—and this had presumably been erased by Kalinin's intervention—no one in the Popov family had ever attracted the attention of the secret police. Even better, he had become a party member at the first opportunity. Captain Popov had an impeccable security and political background.

In March 1945 Popov was ordered to Moscow and assigned to the Frunze Military Academy. If he could complete the three-year course, his future in the military would be secure.

* * *

General Mikhail Vasilievich Frunze had commanded the Red Army units that finally bested Admiral Kolchak and General Wrangl's White Russian troops. Later he replaced Trotsky as people's commissar for military and naval affairs. In 1925, at the peak of his career, Frunze died mysteriously on the operating table, a circumstance that probably saved Stalin the subsequent trouble of shooting him. The Frunze Military Academy is one of his monuments. Basically an infantry school, the academy is the first step in the advanced education of any Red Army officer, and the successful completion of the course qualifies outstanding officers, those headed for general rank, for the Voroshilov General Staff school.

Popov had barely begun the struggle to keep pace with his class at the Military Academy when, for the first time in his life, he fell in love. The cause of this unexpected distraction was a slim blonde schoolteacher who, with her mother, had fled when Tula was attacked by German invasion forces. In Moscow Gallina had begun teaching German at a combat intelligence school. They met at the Frunze officers' mess. Popov had little time for courtship, but in December 1945 he married Gallina.

Marriage brought Popov the first taste of the perquisites of his new status. As a fledgling member of the military elite, Popov was able to present his bride with an incredible wedding present—a private apartment. By Moscow standards at that time it was a luxury flat— two small rooms, a kitchen and toilet to be shared with only two other families.

In 1946 a daughter was born and named Gallina for his wife and Popov's mother. Later, when a son was born in Vienna, he was named Vladimir in honor of Popov's younger brother who had lost a lung to tuberculosis during the war. He survived, but was unable to continue working in the fields. Made the clerk and bookkeeper for the village collective, he lived at home with Lyuba, his sister. By the time Lyuba was of age, the eligible men had been called up for military service. Many of those who survived the war took jobs in industry or construction instead of returning to the mean life offered by the village. Lyuba never married. With his sister as housekeeper, Vladimir remained a bachelor.

In April 1948, a few weeks before he was to be graduated from the Military Academy, Popov was called before another mandate commission. Would Captain Popov, the major general chairing the committee asked, consider an assignment to the *Glavnoe Razvedovatel'noe Upravlenie,* or GRU, the chief intelligence directorate of the Soviet General Staff? If so, the general continued, he would be sent to VASA, the military intelligence school that was one of the many special departments of the Military Diplomatic Academy.

Popov blanched.

"The last thing I wanted was another three years of school. But when a major general asks a captain if he is interested in an assignment," Popov added, "that means the transfer has already been made."

Popov had seen a number of security and counterintelligence officers during the war, but he had rarely brushed against any GRU personnel, most of whom worked at division or corps headquarters.

"I didn't have the slightest idea what I was getting into, but it didn't take long for me to make up my mind. If there was going to be another war, I'd rather be at headquarters than carting ammunition around."

Popov had only one question for the selection committee. Like most peasants, he was not prepared to give up anything he already had in hand.

"When the general laughed—it was Konovalov, then chief of the European division of the Strategic Intelligence Directorate—and said I could keep my Moscow apartment, I accepted. I wasn't sure I could make it, but I knew Gallina could help. She was teaching at a middle school in Moscow by then and had already completed two years at the university."

Popov was graduated from VASA in June 1951. It had been an exhausting three years, but he had made it. His first assignment was to the Austrian desk of the European Directorate under General Konovalov. A year later he was assigned to Vienna.

"Little Ivanushka Durashok had stolen a pretty good education," Popov said with a grim smile.

Now CIA knew as much of Popov's biography as it was ever to learn. As Booth began to study the transcript of this meeting, and to fit it together with the bits and pieces of evidence Popov had already disclosed about himself, the picture of the agent came into focus.

Popov had had an extraordinary run of luck. By a fluke, he and his family avoided the deportation that had destroyed millions of other peasants. He had come through the war with minor wounds and a record strong enough to qualify him for the military academy. Relentless application, an unassailable security file, and the paucity of other candidates had carried him to another, even more senior school.

It had been a ten-year struggle but now, as a graduate of the Frunze Military Academy and the Military Diplomatic Academy, a field grade officer and a member of the GRU, Popov had battled his way into the privileged level of Soviet society. Even though he was only a marginally competent intelligence officer, his future was secure—if the intelligence assignment didn't work out, he could easily resume his military career.

Yet, of his own volition, Popov had sought out the Soviet Union's staunchest adversary and had volunteered to risk his life and his family in a lethal clandestine struggle to overthrow the system that had given him the best it had to offer.

Popov would forever see the world through a peasant's eyes. No success would ever erase the imprint of Popov's early years in Solnechnaya and the misery of his family. For Popov, Stalin had been a maniacal tyrant. His successors—henchmen in Popov's terms—who had inherited the empire with its repressive arm intact, could not be better. The solution, he was convinced, would come in the eventual conflict between the USSR and the West. Until the Soviet Union was smashed, he could see no hope for the Russian peasants.

Popov had little knowledge of democracy and only a pragmatic interest in it. He needed no more proof of a political system's worth than that at some time in its history it had permitted the peasants to evolve into farmers and landowners. This, and the absence of secret police, was as much as Popov wanted.

As the Popov operation eased back into its exacting routine of meetings, the station continued its operations in other areas. Some of the new operations came after weeks of planning. Others seemed simply to explode upon it. The pressures and tensions of the secret world can generate powerful spontaneous combustion.

14
THE MAN FROM SIBERIA

Most of what the station knew about Popov had come from Popov himself. It seemed beyond doubt that he had done his best to paint an accurate picture of himself, his work, and the Soviet microcosm in which he lived in Austria. But this was a self-portrait with background, no more perceptive than Popov's assessment of himself. He was scarcely introspective and his evaluation of events concerning himself was often superficial, invariably sanguine. If Domnin was to help Popov protect himself, he needed an accurate picture of Popov as he was seen by his colleagues and, if possible, even by Soviet counterintelligence.

There was another more important reason to search for an ancillary view of the agent. However convincing Popov's motives for dealing with CIA seemed to Domnin, operational prudence mandated that neither the case officer nor any of the others most directly concerned with the operation ever forget the possibility that he might actually be operating under Soviet control. The impression Popov gave and the vital nature of the secret data he was reporting argued strongly against this proposition, but Soviet intelligence had a formidable reputation for its deception operations and ability to manipulate double agents. It was possible—perhaps only barely so— that his whole story was just that, a melodrama concocted for American consumption. The notion that doubts had stirred in a Russian peasant as he struggled up the rungs of the Soviet system *could* be the sort of soft clay that a Soviet counterespionage officer might provide for CIA to thumb into whatever image best fitted its preconceptions of Soviet ideological dissidents. If Popov had been served up, the agency would be open to Soviet deception in particularly sensitive areas—Soviet military capability and weapons research and development programs.

Even if Popov was as straight as Domnin and the others were convinced he was, there was another concern: how accurately did Popov assess his personal situation? Because his personal life was so decidedly irregular and his deceptions of the other side so casually constructed as to seem almost half-hearted, could they be as effective as Popov seemed to think? Had he really been able to muffle his hatred of Stalin's system, to conceal the extent of his relationship with Bielic? How much of his day-to-day account could be taken at face value? Without a litmus to test Popov's view of himself, Domnin could have no idea of how safe the agent was at any time, or how best to protect him.

Sometimes case officers snatch a third-person glimpse of an agent by surveillance, from the reports of an informant in his vicinity, or even from a telephone tap. With Popov this was impossible. The chances of recruiting an independent source close to him were remote—indeed the energy spent in any such effort would have been better budgeted to piercing another of the shuttered compartments of Soviet intelligence, preferably the KGB. Popov could not even be tailed without the surveillance agents knowing that they were behind a man named Popov, a Russian of special interest to American intelligence. If the surveillance were detected or if one of the tails peached, Popov would be compromised. Soviet telephone security and the geography of Vienna made telephone taps impossible. The need for an independent view of Popov nagged at the station.

In the course of another investigation, the station got enough insight to help verify Popov's story, but not enough, as it turned out, to keep him safe.

Even for Vienna it had the makings of a foul February. Rain and sleet with an occasional bonus of snow had been falling since Christmas. The ponderous baroque buildings, shabby apartment houses, and wet streets blotted out what little light filtered through the dark skies. Maybe it was the grim weather that got to Anatoliy Skachkov, an official of the Soviet Petroleum Industry in Austria. In any case, after a boozy night at the Moulin Rouge—Vienna nightclubs were expensive anodynes and this place was no exception—Skachkov went home, picked up some clothing, and told his wife he was "leaving for the Americans."

With some one hundred thousand Russians encamped in Austria and several score Eastern European diplomats, intelligence officers, and trade officials assigned to the various embassies and missions in Vienna, there were bound to be a number of dropouts. In one twenty-four-month period, defectors from each of the major Eastern European intelligence services came to rest on the station stoop.

When possible, defectors were hustled out of Vienna as soon as plans could be made for their reception in West Germany. No matter how long a defector may have brooded over his plan, the actual break always unleashes emotional demons, among which acute anxiety and depression are the most common. The fact that Vienna was ninety miles inside the Soviet zone of Austria did little to quiet the defector's anxiety.

Defector interrogation, which can go on for months, is a job for specialists. The most that could be done in Austria was to make sure the person was who he claimed to be, to assess the strategic intelligence he might be able to impart, and try to siphon off any perishable information he might have on the security of the American forces in Austria.

The first question asked each defector was strictly prescribed: Did he have any information (called "early warning") of a pending attack on the United States or NATO? That the station absolutely had to give this first priority was a reminder that the Pentagon did not want to be as surprised by World War III as the commanders in the Pacific had been by the attack on Pearl Harbor. Unfortunately, the defectors handled in Vienna had no more idea when the war might start than the station did and, rather than being flattered by such a weighty question, usually considered the interrogator a fool for asking it.

By the time Skachkov had identified himself and written a request for asylum, the KGB knew he was missing and the SK—the *Sovetskaya Kolonia*, or Soviet colony, the element of the KGB *rezidentura* responsible for policing the loyalty of the Soviet colony abroad and protecting it from Western penetration—was investigating his disappearance.

Skachkov had little operational information of interest to the station, but as an economist with inside knowledge of Soviet economic policy in Austria, he would be a valuable source for interrogation by specialists. For Skachkov, the most exciting part of his defection must have been the flight from Vienna to Salzburg.

For regular air traffic, the American garrison in Vienna had requisitioned Tulln, a former Luftwaffe airfield, capable of handling four-motor aircraft. But Tulln was in the Soviet zone, several miles from Vienna—and to get there one had to drive through a Soviet checkpoint. This was no problem for properly documented U.S. personnel, but was obviously out of the question for defectors.

To provide a limited access to the city for small liaison aircraft, the air force had made a makeshift airstrip—actually an L-shaped parking lot—in a downtown area of the American sector of Vienna. Small aircraft lifted VIPs, agents, or others in a hurry from the strip to Tulln or to the American military headquarters near Salzburg in the American zone. To take off or land, pilots had to maneuver around apartment houses as if they were driving a taxi.

On Booth's first flight from the strip, he had forced his eyes open to find himself looking over the shoulder of an Austrian munching breakfast in his third-floor flat. The headlines of the morning paper propped against the coffee pot were clearly visible. After that Booth used other transportation.

With Skachkov's plane safely airborne, Booth had scarcely begun to pick at his in-box when Peter Todd burst through the door—even when things were quiet, he rarely had time to knock. A Soviet major, claiming to be a KGB man, had requested asylum at the American military police post at the *Stiftskaserne* and was now being driven to CIC headquarters in the American sector. This was big news.

Except for a Soviet code clerk on the run with a bag of cipher material, a KGB major was potentially as valuable a defector as the station could hope for. Not only might he have inside information on Soviet operations against the station and other U.S. installations in Vienna—penetration agents, surveillance, bugs, phone taps—but he might know something about Russians whom the KGB regarded with suspicion. He might even know something about Popov.

When Fred Gordon, a nervous young case officer, pulled a yellow pad from his briefcase and began to take notes, the Russian broke into a broad grin.

"Aha, Captain Olson," he laughed. "I've been wondering when we would meet." Major Peter Sergeyevich Deriabin, KGB, had established his bona fides in one sentence: he was well enough informed about American intelligence to know the pseudonym of the only case officer in Austria who spoke Russian and took notes with his pen cradled between the first and second fingers of his right hand.

This was a blow for Gordon. Only six months in the field and he had been identified by the first KGB officer he had ever met. He rose from the table and tottered out of the room to give Todd the news. It only took a moment to reconstruct how Gordon had been blown to the KGB.

A few weeks earlier, Gordon, using the pseudonym "Captain Olson," had recruited Sergey Feoktistov, the Russian manager of a small Soviet-controlled factory in the Russian zone. At least Gordon thought he had recruited Feoktistov. The fact that Deriabin knew Gordon's *nom de guerre* could only mean that Feoktistov had been singing to the KGB.

When Gordon returned to the interrogation room, Deriabin politely explained that as part of his counterintelligence program he had decided to establish a few double agents in the American camp. Feoktistov was the first bait he cast.

Feoktistov was an émigré, a former colonel—he called himself a general—in the czarist army, who had settled in Czechoslovakia. In 1945, when the Red Army overran the country, the Russians found Feoktistov was a qualified engineer. Rather than repatriate him at once, they gave him an "external" passport and made him manager of a factory near Vienna. (External passports are the documents given repatriation candidates who are permitted to remain abroad at the convenience of the Soviet government.)

When Deriabin came across Feoktistov's file in the KGB's Vienna archive, and learned that he had close contacts with the emigration, he instructed the engineer to write a letter to an old chum who was affiliated with the NTS, a Russian émigré organization in West Germany. The NTS—the Union of Russian Solidarists—was known by the KGB to maintain contacts with CIA and other Western intelligence services. To bait the hook, Deriabin ordered Feoktistov to indicate he was fed up with his Soviet supervisors. Deriabin sat back to see if CIA would strike.

As he had reckoned, NTS promptly informed its CIA liaison of the letter and Feoktistov's apparent disaffection. CIA headquarters, always more enthusiastic about émigré-related activity than Booth could be, directed the station to get up an approach to Feoktistov. Booth did so and, with a degree of ease that, as he reflected later, should have caused some doubt, Gordon "recruited" Feoktistov.

Headquarters enthusiasts for émigré operations were delighted; now maybe the Austrian station, and particularly Booth, would see that émigré organizations had a real role to play in operations. On the other side of the fence, Deriabin was also pleased.

A few days after his defection, Deriabin quietly told Booth that he had tried to use Feoktistov to put himself directly in touch with Gordon. His approach must have been too subtle for, if Gordon had perceived the offer, as presumably relayed by Feoktistov, and mentioned it in his reports, the station might have been able to make contact with Deriabin in time to head off his defection and to keep him in place as an agent. It was a grievous loss, but already in the spilt milk department; the station was more than lucky to have Deriabin as a defector.

Peter Deriabin, then thirty-three, was a strange choice for assignment to Vienna. Not that his career had been less than impeccable. On the contrary, he was such a trusted State Security officer that, after three years in counterintelligence, he had been promoted to the KGB's elite Guard Directorate, the body responsible for the security of the Kremlin and the communist dignitaries who work there. To Booth's knowledge, no other member of the Guard had ever been posted abroad—they knew too much.

A native of Lokot, a remote area even for Siberia, Deriabin was almost a communist paradigm. Like Popov, he had been born in a wooden cabin. But Deriabin's parents were relatively well off in a prosperous area and, unlike Popov, he received the best education the region had to offer. From the first, Deriabin was a good student and fascinated by books. His education ran parallel to his political development. When he was nine he moved from membership in the October Cubs to the Young Pioneers, the children's political group that prepared its members for the Komsomol, which Deriabin joined at fifteen.

By the time he was nineteen Deriabin was a history teacher and, in his own words,*"the Siberian equivalent of that energy phenomenon in capitalist society, the go-getter president of the Junior Chamber of Commerce who always finds time, somehow, to pump a hand, make

*Peter Deriabin and Frank Gibney, *The Secret World* (New York: Doubleday, 1959, paperback, Ballantine Books, 1982). One of the most revealing books written by a former Soviet intelligence officer.

a speech, or launch a civic improvement drive." He ran the school Komsomol unit and directed Komsomol work in a number of communist organizations—the most colorful of which must have been the "League of Militant Godless."

Called for military service in 1939, Deriabin was co-opted to work with a political commissar and became editor of the regimental news bulletin, a propaganda sheet, most often used by the troops for rolling cigarettes. A month before the Nazi invasion, he applied for party membership. When his party card reached him, his battalion was en route from the Chinese border to the front near Moscow. A month later he was in a military hospital with severe leg wounds.

Released from hospital, Deriabin was assigned to an infantry division then on its way to Stalingrad. Although he was a junior political commissar (the equivalent of a junior, or second lieutenant) he was also second in command of a mortar company—in the fury of Stalingrad, politics took second place. By the time he was wounded again, Deriabin had been promoted and was assistant to the regimental operations officer.

Deriabin saw his last combat in April 1944, when his regiment crossed the Bug River, the last barrier to the Soviet thrust toward Odessa. When a German counterattack cut off the advanced units, Deriabin fell—a bullet in the back had broken both his shoulders. Conscious, but unable to move, he watched as a German soldier pulled off his new American combat boots and unstrapped the wristwatch Deriabin had taken from a dead German. His looting completed, the German pumped two bullets into Deriabin's chest.

Deriabin lay in the mud for twelve hours before he was found by a squad of retreating Russians and ferried back across the Bug. Red Army regulations forbid able-bodied soldiers to leave a combat area even to transport wounded: Deriabin was left on the riverbank, bleeding from the mouth, unable to move his arms and with a punctured lung. Somehow he struggled to his feet and, still under heavy fire, began staggering to the rear—barefooted, a living specter from a Goya drawing. When his erratic path took him past an advance observation post, Deriabin's division commander recognized him and ordered an officer to escort him to the division aid station.

Deriabin's combat service was over. Even before he was released from hospital, he had been recommended for an army counterintelligence school in Moscow. After three years of combat and four wounds Deriabin knew his luck was spent. It was time to go to the rear.

After graduating first in his class, Deriabin was assigned as an aide to the commanding officer of naval counterintelligence. By 1946 Deriabin had been in Moscow long enough to begin to master the office politics that governed assignments in Soviet intelligence and the party. Eager to return to teaching, he maneuvered his release from the NKVD and made his way back to Siberia. Had it not been for the confusion of the postwar period, his resignation would never have been permitted. An officer may be relieved of a secret police job, but he does not simply ask for a change.

Like many combat veterans, Deriabin soon found that civilian life had lost much of its appeal. He also felt a financial pinch. As a teacher, starting again at the bottom, his wages plummeted to a mere six hundred rubles, a quarter of his NKVD pay. The solution was obvious: he applied for readmission to the NKVD. A few weeks later Captain Deriabin was reinstated and assigned to Barnaul in the Altai Kray. Here again he was disappointed. The routine of secret police work involved little but the surveillance of the townspeople—none of whom was guilty of anything more sinister than complaining about Soviet bureaucracy—and was no more to Deriabin's taste than teaching school. After an appeal to a friend, Deriabin was transferred to Moscow.

Experience as a peacetime secret police officer stiffened his growing suspicion that the Soviet communist system might be a gigantic lie, and the goal and the ideals he had so earnestly huckstered to his students and military comrades perhaps only a cynical cover for a vicious dictatorship. But it was not for Deriabin to change the system. In the absence of an alternative, he reasoned, it was wisest to make the best of it.

For five years Deriabin worked as a senior counterintelligence officer in the Moscow headquarters of the MGB (later to become the KGB). His job was to screen military personnel guarding the Kremlin and to select the officers and men who might be qualified for additional training. The assignment gave him a unique insight into the political infighting in the Kremlin and the security and intelligence services.

Despite the pressure of his work, Deriabin enrolled in the Institute of Marxism-Leninism and began to attend lectures at the Political Science Academy. At the library reserved for advanced political science students, he got his first glimpse of the forbidden Western press and the proscribed works of fallen Soviet political leaders like Radek and Bukharin. Slowly, he began to document his case against Stalin and the system he had created. Books by non-Russian writers fanned his interest in the possibility of a better life somewhere—anywhere—outside the Soviet Union.

Even as his motivation slumped, Deriabin was rising in the Soviet hierarchy. The perquisites were exceptional—although only a captain, he was given a two-room apartment, his income jumped, and he had access to the special commissaries reserved for the Kremlin staff. But this luxury came at a price. In the Byzantine atmosphere of the Kremlin, he would inevitably risk becoming identified with one of the factions contesting for political favor. When the odds tipped against his crowd, Deriabin would be a candidate for a dreary assignment far from Moscow. Without such luck, there was always the Gulag, at the side of many of his predecessors. Quietly, Deriabin began scouting for another, less exposed job.

In 1951 Stalin cashiered Victor Abakumov, the minister of state security. As the tumbrels carried Abakumov's favorites into exile, the secret police and intelligence services began a series of personnel shifts and reorganizations. Deriabin was offered a choice of assignment in the Guard Directorate personnel section or in offices of the Kremlin guard. Either job placed Deriabin's head above the political parapet, an easy target. It was now time to leave. With the help of a friend, he was assigned to the Austro-German section of the Foreign Intelligence Directorate of the MGB. For more than a year he worked closely with Colonel Evgeniy Kravtsov, chief of the Austro-German section.

When Kravtsov was named KGB *rezident* in Vienna, he asked Deriabin if he would accept an Austrian assignment. For the first time he saw the possibility, if not of escaping from the USSR, at least of freeing himself from Moscow's political atmosphere. When Kravtsov assured him the problem of his earlier service in the Kremlin's Guard Directorate could be set aside, Deriabin agreed. He would be deputy chief to the *Sovetskaya Kolonia*, the SK, in Vienna. He arrived in Vienna in September. In the absence of his chief, he was responsible for the security of the Soviet community in Vienna.

As Deriabin began to investigate Skachkov's disappearance, his mind turned to defection—not Skachkov's, but his own. The contrast between life at home and what he had seen in the last six months in Austria had destroyed whatever vestiges of faith he might have harbored in the Soviet system. He had already made one effort to make contact with American intelligence, but the offer had apparently gone unnoticed. Maybe it was time to force the issue, to make a complete break. So, on the afternoon of 15 February the man from Siberia climbed out of a taxi, approached the MP at the entrance of the *Stiftskaserne,* an American military police office near the *Innere Stadt,* and asked to speak to an American officer. He noticed that it had begun to snow. Before breakfast it turned into a blizzard.

The first hectic hours of questioning were enough to convince the station that Deriabin was an important catch—possibly the most valuable intelligence defector since the war. Not only did he have detailed data on the KGB organization in Vienna, but his inside knowledge of the Kremlin and the intrigue that had swirled through the KGB headquarters since Beria's downfall was unique. Interrogation would come later; the immediate problem was to get him safely out of Vienna.

By midnight it was clear that the Soviets knew Deriabin was missing. Despite the snowstorm, American military police were informed by the Austrian police liaison officers that armed Soviet patrols could be seen combing the streets of the *Innere Stadt.* With little regard for cover or the sensibilities of the few Austrians out on such a stormy night, KGB officers in civilian clothes pushed through bars and nightclubs, scrutinizing each male patron. By morning the Russians had rallied a posse of lightly disguised surveillance agents and posted them at the Westbahnhof, the railroad station from which trains left Vienna for Linz and Salzburg in the American zone. Another team of agents prowled through the snow, eyeing the two Piper Cubs parked alongside the American airstrip.

This was the most barefaced KGB surveillance the station had detected in Vienna, chilling proof of how vigorously Colonel Kravtsov was reacting to the disappearance and probably defection of one of his most trusted subordinates. As Deriabin disclosed details of his background, the more certain it became that, even if the weather cleared, the station could not risk flying him from Vienna to Salzburg or even Tulln. When the Soviets balanced the possibility of recapturing Deriabin against a major diplomatic incident, their choice would be clear. If an American aircraft "strayed" out of the approved air corridor and was shot down or forced to land in the Soviet zone, the diplomatic furor could be dealt with. As soon as Deriabin, dead or alive, was in their hands, the Russians could apologize. If the State

Department made an issue of it—and no one would be able to prove that the plane had not strayed out of bounds—the Russians could generously offer restitution for the aircraft.

With escape by air ruled out, there was no alternative but to smuggle Deriabin out of Vienna on the U.S. military train, the famous Mozart Express. It would be more than a ninety-mile trip through the Soviet zone, and chancy enough. If the Russians had any reason to think Deriabin was on the train they could stop it as easily as if it were rolling through the Ukraine. Nor would it matter that the occupation agreements specifically exempted the daily train from search; the same statutes also specified that only official U.S. personnel could ride the Mozart. Fortunately the rules did not apply to freight.

Masters made a quick tour of the CIC building in which Deriabin was being held. In the cellar "he discovered a hot-water tank that had just been replaced by a newer model. Six and a half feet long, it was about thirty inches in diameter. The bottom had a small joint to which a pipe had been fitted and a spigot. The top was bare except for a pressure gauge and emergency valve and the fitting for the intake pipe. With a hacksaw, Masters cut along the seam joining the top to the body of the tank. Inside, the tank was coated with what seemed to be moss, about the thickness of flannel. After two hours of frantic work, Masters had scoured the tank clean and fitted handles on the inside. He bored a series of holes in the top and bottom and fitted a panel which, if air became a critical problem, Deriabin would be able to pull free. The end product looked depressingly like a makeshift coffin, something that might be used for a burial at sea, but it would be big enough for one passenger and a bottle of water. With a stencil, Masters addressed the tank to a quartermaster unit at Camp Truscott, Salzburg. Camp Truscott was the headquarters of the American forces in Austria and in the western corner of the American zone.

A CIC captain, outfitted in a sergeant's uniform—Booth assumed that an NCO would be less conspicuous in the baggage car—was detailed to ride with the shipment and to make sure that the baggage handlers loading the other freight did not cover the air holes. He had another job. If the train was boarded in the Soviet zone, he was to resist, if necessary to shoot, any Russian who attempted to force his way into the baggage car. It was not an enviable assignment. Early in the occupation an American sergeant had been shot by Russians when he resisted their attempt to board the train.

Like most defectors, Deriabin was now suffering a severe post-defection trauma. The impact of his decision to escape and the knowledge he had forever turned his back on the only culture and society he knew had shaken his self-control. Speaking only Russian—he did have a good reading knowledge of German—and without friends, he could have little idea how he would be treated or what would happen to him when the interrogation was finished. He had stepped into the unknown.

As he wrapped himself in a GI blanket and began to ease himself into the tank, Deriabin managed a slight grin. "Will it be all right if I smoke?"

"As soon as we've passed through the Soviet checkpoint at Enns," the CIC captain said, "I'll give the tank three kicks. Then you can smoke." Gordon translated.

Deriabin folded his hands across his chest and closed his eyes. Booth got the point—all Deriabin needed was a lily to make the picture complete.

With more confidence than Booth could muster, Masters welded the top shut. After a few anxious moments, Deriabin's muffled voice assured Masters that the air supply was adequate.

As Booth threaded his way through the bustling station to the platform reserved for the military train, the Soviet surveillance agents were clearly visible. Outfitted as Austrians, they were the only non-Americans on the platform alongside the train.

From the window of his compartment in a passenger car behind the freight wagon, Booth glimpsed the baggage cart with the tank as it was trundled to the front of the train. From another passenger car at the rear, Todd watched to see if the tank triggered the attention of anyone on the platform. But the Russians were only interested in the travelers—perhaps they thought the station would be bold enough to disguise Deriabin and try to slip him out as a passenger.

Only one passenger interested the Russian surveillance team. A portly woman, wearing heavy boots and bundled up against the snow, was actually jostled as she strode alongside the train. Only when she began a loud conversation in English with the sergeant who was checking passengers onto the train did the Russians lose interest. Fortunately, none of the other travelers even remotely resembled Deriabin.

Although the Mozart was supposedly an express train, the Soviet officials insisted that it make way for any other train along the route, a routine harassment. The ninety-mile trip to the Soviet checkpoint on the Enns River, the border between the Soviet and American zones, took almost three hours and was the longest train ride Booth ever experienced. He could only imagine what it was like for the man in the tank.

Finally, a few minutes late, the Mozart bumped to a stop at the checkpoint, two hundred yards from the bridge across the Enns. The train commander, a military police lieutenant who had no idea of the cargo he was carrying, stepped onto the quay. Saluting smartly, he handed a sheaf of papers to the Soviet major in charge. With rifles slung across their backs, a platoon of Soviet enlisted men ranged alongside, carefully inspecting the train and probing under the carriages as if they expected to find a stowaway clinging to a brake box.

In a futile attempt to control his nerves Booth tried to recall how long it usually took for the train to clear the checkpoint. He could not remember. Nor could he turn a page of the paperback thriller on his lap. Finally, Booth decided that if it took more than fifteen minutes it would be a sure sign of trouble. As he stared at his watch, Walter Mitty fantasies whirled through his mind. If the Russians tried to board the train, he would rush to the engine, put a gun to the head of the engineer, and order him to crash through the barriers and cross the bridge to the American zone. By the time he remembered there was no way to get into the engine from the passenger cars and that he didn't have a gun, the train commander had stepped back on board. He offered another snappy salute to the Russian major and signaled the engineer. The train began to inch forward. As it picked up speed on the bridge, Booth stepped from the compartment into the corridor and spotted Todd hurrying forward toward the front of the train.

"What's the matter?" Todd asked. "Too hot in your compartment?" Booth's shirt was soaked with sweat.

When they got to the baggage car, the grinning CIC officer pointed to the tank. Sure enough, smoke had begun to filter through the air holes. Major Deriabin was a tough customer.

Todd cut Deriabin out of the tank in Linz, the first stop in the U.S. zone, and drove him through the blizzard to Salzburg and the safe house that army intelligence had provided. It was a small chalet, isolated in an open area some three hundred yards up a steep slope from the bachelor officers' quarters, a small hotel on the outskirts of Salzburg. On first glance it seemed to be a well-selected spot, snug, almost cozy. As a safe house, it was a welcome change from anything Booth and Todd were accustomed to. Meals—always a problem in a safe house—could be brought up from the officers' mess. To cut down on housekeeping during the initial interrogation at the chalet, Booth and Todd would bunk at the BOQ.

After an early breakfast, they struggled uphill through the fresh snow to the chalet. In the pressure of getting Deriabin out of Vienna there had been no time to change clothes and both were still in proper diplomatic dark suits, somber overcoats, and hats. In the fresh snow the hill seemed steeper than it had the night before and their city shoes and overshoes made walking difficult. In the early daylight the chalet appeared to be an even better place to stash Deriabin for a few days than it had the night before. It was small, but roomy enough for Deriabin and Gordon, now functioning as an interpreter, and the guards that G-2 insisted be on duty inside the building at all times. Certainly it would suffice for the few days it would take to finish his initial questioning and for headquarters to make arrangements to transfer him to the United States. Important defectors, and Deriabin was clearly a very important defector, were usually brought to the Washington area for detailed interrogation and eventual resettlement.

There was only one hitch: the chalet had been rented in summer. The CIC officers who had set it up could not have known that it was in the middle of the best ski slope on the outskirts of Salzburg.

By noontime when Booth started back down the slope to the BOQ whence a car would take him to an office in Salzburg where he could begin drafting cables for Washington, the scene outside the chalet looked like an advertisement for an Austrian ski resort. Scores of skiers, all determined to make the most of the fresh snow and brilliant sun, were hurtling down the hill.

If Booth had been wearing a leotard and pink tutu, he could not have been more conspicuous than slipping and sliding down the slope in business garb. Nor could he fathom what the Austrian skiers thought could be going on in the shuttered chalet—formally dressed civilians, serviced by uniformed GIs stumbling up the hill with heavy aluminum food containers. There was one advantage; the scene was so strange that none of the skiers was bold enough to come within a hundred yards of the safe house.

*   *   *

After lunch, Todd and Gordon continued questioning Deriabin on the KGB in Austria. By nightfall he had identified some seventy KGB officers, sketched the organization of the KGB *rezidency*, and pinpointed KGB offices and safe houses scattered throughout the Soviet sector of Vienna. Deriabin's knowledge was comprehensive and, even in the strained atmosphere of the safe house, his ability to recall details was phenomenal. The information he gave tallied with what Todd had collected and expanded on the data already provided by Popov.

There was every reason to believe that Deriabin was a straightforward ideological dissident who had made an irrevocable break with the Soviet Union. But in the hectic forty-eight hours he had been in CIA hands, there had been little opportunity to probe into his motives and character. Until this could be done, Deriabin would be handled as if he were an unknown quantity. It would be essential that he not discern the station's special interest in the GRU or any military intelligence officer, least of all Popov.

That night, as Deriabin began to unwind from the long day of questioning, Booth joined Deriabin and Todd for an after-dinner drink. Had Deriabin, who possessed an acutely sensitive understanding of counterintelligence, not been exhausted by the day-long interrogation and the emotional turmoil of his defection and escape from Vienna, he might have spotted the apparently superficial queries they casually posed on the organization and staffing of the GRU in Vienna. It was only when Deriabin's head began to nod with fatigue that Booth dared to be specific.

Popov had frequently reminded Domnin that the KGB had agents in every Soviet office abroad and stressed the point that the GRU was not immune to penetration by its sister service. He was convinced that the KGB had recruited GRU officers as informants on the work and private lives of the military intelligence staff. In response to one of Booth's questions, Deriabin began to cite the KGB agents in the Soviet high commissioner's staff and among the administrative personnel at the Grand Hotel. What about the military? Deriabin shook his head. Penetrations of the officer corps in Austria were handled by KGB officers assigned to the various military formations. He knew nothing about their work.

What about the GRU, did the KGB have any agents within the GRU *rezidency* in Vienna? Deriabin paused for a moment and then listed a trio of field grade officers he knew to have been recruited by the KGB. Were any GRU officers suspected of loose living, insecurity? No, Deriabin said, he knew of no security cases pending against any GRU officers in Austria.

Later, as Deriabin sipped a nightcap, Todd asked about GRU personnel. Were they all graduates of the Military Diplomatic Academy, blue-stripe officers? Most were graduates, Deriabin said, but there were a few infantry men and some line officers. Peasants? Deriabin thought for a moment and recalled "Petro" Popov, a peasant working on the Yugoslav line. How did he get along with the GRU hotshots? He was an amiable fellow, well liked and an enthusiastic fisherman. There was another fifteen minutes of small talk before Booth suggested that the exhausted Deriabin drop into bed.

A peasant, a fisherman, amiable and well liked, Popov was not a security case. It was little enough, but it had come from a KGB officer responsible for the security of the Soviet colony in Austria.

A few days later, Deriabin was slipped across the border and to an airfield near Munich where an unmarked plane was waiting for its sole passenger.

In March 1959 *Life* magazine published excerpts* from Deriabin's forthcoming book. At that time, one short passage in the article brought Deriabin's comments on Vasili Sitnikov, the experienced and wily chief of the KGB's Anglo-American section in Vienna, vividly back to Booth.

"Well, Peter," Sitnikov had said. "Old Allen Dulles has fixed us in Austria. But in Berlin. . . ." That was the whole quotation, and Deriabin's reference to Sitnikov ended on that odd, equivocal note. What was it, Booth wondered, that Sitnikov had stopped short of saying?

Years later he realized that if Sitnikov had finished that one sentence, Popov might have been saved. Possibly, Sitnikov was referring to George Blake, a KGB mole then buried in the British intelligence service in West Berlin. It was Blake who would play a key role in Popov's exposure.

Three days after Deriabin defected in Vienna, Nikolai Khokhlov rang the doorbell of Georgi Okolovich's apartment in Frankfurt, West Germany. Okolovich was a senior member of NTS, the Russian émigré organization. After introducing himself, Khokhlov calmly stated

*Peter Deriabin and Frank Gibney, "Red Agent's Vivid Tale of Terror," *Life* magazine, 23 March 1959.

that the Central Committee of the Communist party of the Soviet Union had decided to liquidate Okolovich and that he, Captain Khokhlov, had been sent from Moscow to do the job. Having won Okolovich's undivided attention, Khokhlov explained that he had no intention of going through with the murder, but wanted NTS help in arranging the flight of his wife and child from Moscow.

Khokhlov had been recruited by the *Spetsburo,* as the Bureau of Special Tasks was known, in 1942. In Soviet intelligence, special tasks or "wet affairs" are any murder, assassination, or kidnapping the Central Committee ordains be done. As a *Spetsburo* operative in World War II, Khokhlov went behind the German lines in Nazi uniform and organized the assassination of Wilhelm Kube, the administrator of Belorussia and one of the most vicious of the Nazi satraps. It was a brilliant operation, but unfortunately for Khokhlov it made a lasting impression on General Pavel Sudoplatov, the *Spetsburo* chief. When the war ended, Sudoplatov refused to release the young agent. Unable to wriggle free, Khokhlov determined to defect the moment he saw any chance to arrange for the escape of his wife and young son. Rashly, he assumed that NTS could make the necessary arrangements.

When Okolovich explained that NTS could not possibly arrange for the flight of Khokhlov's family from Moscow, Khokhlov and Okolovich went to CIA for help. Although an effort was made to pressure the USSR into releasing Khokhlov's family, it was impossible for CIA to arrange for their escape.

Following up on the information Khokhlov had disclosed, a CIA case officer contacted Pierre Bragin,* a long-time Department Thirteen officer who was living in Vienna under cover as a Rumanian refugee and businessman. The son of Russian émigré parents, Bragin had grown up in France. He was recruited by Soviet intelligence while serving in the International Brigade during the Spanish civil war. When Loyalist resistance collapsed, Bragin escaped to the Soviet Union. During the war, he also operated behind German lines in Nazi uniform.

When the case officer introduced himself to Bragin in fluent Russian and said he had come "from headquarters" to talk to him, Bragin misunderstood and assumed that the CIA man had come from Moscow. Before he realized his mistake, Bragin had disclosed so many details of his situation in Vienna and projected assignment in

---

*A pseudonym.

Western Europe, he had completely compromised himself. Faced with the prospect of returning to the Soviet Union and the loss of any possible chance of ever returning to Western Europe, Bragin chose to defect. He was whisked out of Vienna the following day.

Seldom had the KGB gone through quite such a bad patch. In some three weeks, Major Deriabin, Captain Khokhlov, Captain Bragin, the economist Skachkov, and two East German agents had been lost. When Khokhlov appeared at a press conference in West Germany, details of his murder mission and photographs of the weapon concealed in a cigarette case were given sensational treatment in the world press. Not since Ignaz Reiss and Walter Krivitsky defected during the Stalin purges had Soviet intelligence suffered such losses.

15
AUF WIEDERSEHEN WIEN

No one could be sure what cumulative impact the defections of Skachkov, Deriabin, Khokhlov and Bragin would have on the KGB in Austria, or how they would affect the Popov operation. Nor was anyone certain that the KGB even knew Bragin had defected. Because he had not been "surfaced"—jargon for publicized—as a defector, the KGB might have reasoned that the station had broken the rules and kidnapped him.

Hollywood and a few former intelligence operatives notwithstanding, the secret world bears little resemblance to the OK Corral. Spying is too productive an activity to be jeopardized by case officers turned gunslinger. Mistakes have happened, but the unwritten covenant that intelligence services do not kidnap or murder the opposition staff personnel is rarely violated. But from the Central Committee's viewpoint, the convention does not extend to any of its own agents who might have strayed, or Soviet defectors. Both are fair game and the KGB has a long string of scalps to prove it.

Now for the first time Booth began to wonder if the station could rely on Moscow's restraint. Lest Department Thirteen be tempted to square things, CIA personnel were directed to avoid the *Innere Stadt*. Operations in which case officers were most exposed to possible kidnapping were throttled back. A handful of recruitment operations would be tabled until it was possible to get a reading on the KGB's reaction.

The military intelligence units of G-2 were bolder. A CIC officer on street surveillance near the Soviet headquarters at the Hotel Imperial—and almost within range of the camera still occasionally operating from the toy tiger in the rear window of the parked sedan—was grabbed by three KGB officers, beaten, and thrown into a telephone kiosk. His backup team dragged him into a getaway car, but the KGB had shown the flag. Surveillance would be suspended until the dust settled.

It was almost two weeks after Bragin had been shipped out of Vienna before the Max telephone rang. By that time tentative plans had been made to put Popov on ice until it was known what form the KGB countermeasures would take.

Popov was unruffled. Not only had no new security restrictions been imposed on the Soviet community, but, incredibly, the KGB was actually going out of its way to improve relations with its GRU colleagues and the Soviet military and diplomatic staffs. Even the surliest KGB types had begun to pass the time of day with their compatriots. The smiles were forced and the greetings less than sincere, but the message was clear. The secret police was so embarrassed that a public relations campaign had been mandated.

"Skachkov was not such a loss," Popov reported. "But when Deriabin left, it was as if the KGB had lost a front tooth."

"Now the bastards are trying to convince everyone that they are only here to protect us from the terrible imperialists." Popov laughed. "It may be a while before they hit back, but they will. Right now, there's no problem."

It was a year before Popov's prediction came true, and Skachkov was found dead on a back street in Frankfurt. He had slipped out of the safe house for a night on the town and had been seen drinking heavily. The official cause of death was a "heart attack." It was not until a KGB assassin defected in 1961 that CIA got another inside look at Soviet murder techniques.

Bogdan Stashinsky was a nineteen-year-old student at Lwow University when the KGB recruited him. By the time he was twenty-five he had shown so much promise that he was transferred to Department Thirteen for further training. On his first foreign assignment, Stashinsky intercepted Dr. Lev Rebet, a prominent Ukrainian émigré, on the steps of his Munich apartment. Thrusting a metal tube about the size of a cigar toward his victim, Stashinsky triggered a device that broke a glass ampule and blew prussic acid vapor into Rebet's face. The Ukrainian's blood vessels contracted exactly as if he had suffered a coronary spasm. Death was instant. By the time Stashinsky had inhaled the antidote—amyl nitrate, a specific for heart attack victims—and rushed down the stairs, the vapor had begun to evaporate. When the autopsy was performed all evidence of the murder had vanished. As far as the coroner could tell, Rebet had died of coronary disease.

Two years later Stashinsky murdered Stefan Bandera, another Ukrainian émigré leader. This time a slight malfunction blew bits of impregnated glass into the victim's face. There was no doubt that Bandera had been murdered. In 1961 Stashinsky defected and told West German officials about the KGB murder technique. He knew nothing about Skachkov, but the coincidence of a healthy Soviet defector with no record of heart trouble dropping dead of a heart attack was strong evidence that there was more than one assassin in the KGB stable.

Domnin had five more meetings with Popov before Popov's scheduled home leave in July 1954. This time he would not visit Solnechnaya. With Gallina, his daughter, and infant son, Popov would spend his vacation at Kaliningrad, formerly the capital of East Prussia, in the area ceded to the USSR after the war. There, the Russians had taken over a plush resort the Nazis had built for vacationing Gestapo personnel as well as high-ranking officers from the Soviet atomic and guided missile programs. The Kaliningrad resort, Popov pointed out, was a veritable hunting preserve for strategic intelligence. On vacation, senior officers were even more prone to flaunt their accomplishments than in the restrictive Moscow atmosphere.

Popov's absence would give the station a chance to catch its breath. Domnin returned to Washington to brief Helms and the few senior personnel who had knowledge of the Popov case. He would also deliver a personal message from Popov to Allen Dulles, who had replaced Bedell Smith as CIA director in February 1953.

"You can tell Mr. Dulles for me that there's a CIA cow grazing on the bank of the Volga," Popov said. The wad of rubles Domnin had given Popov on his previous home leave had bought a cow for the Popov family in Solnechnaya. The milk would be a useful supplement to the family diet.

Mike Andenko, Domnin's backup man, would use the respite to wrap up the seemingly endless paper work involved in keeping headquarters informed of every detail of Popov's handling. By the time Domnin returned, the reporting would be up to date.

Booth hoped the trip would give Domnin a chance to unwind. As far as anyone in the station knew, Popov was still CIA's best in-place source of Soviet military developments and a unique window on Soviet intelligence. Every minute that could be spent with him was precious and it was the station's responsibility to make the most of the time Popov had available. As long as Popov was in Vienna, Domnin was on duty literally twenty-four hours a day. This meant that on the chance that Popov might have a few free hours, or call for an emergency meeting, Domnin could not leave the city, nor could he *ever* be out of contact with the station duty officer. Andenko did his best to buffer Domnin's occasional flare-ups, but even the poker games Booth arranged with other case officers did little to relieve the nerve-racking tension of his circumscribed existence. Domnin was an enthusiastic poker player, but chess was his best game and he played at tournament level.

That summer Vienna seemed suddenly to burst into life. Perhaps it was the weather, possibly the slight indications that the Russians might at last agree to the State Treaty that would restore Austria to full autonomy. Certainly that sun-drenched summer helped the city to shake off the last of the blight of the Nazi period and to soften the grim face of Soviet occupation. Even the armed guards patrolling the entrance to the Hotel Imperial caught some of the new spirit. As they shouldered their submachine guns, the stolid enlisted men could be seen stealing admiring glances at the Viennese girls bold enough to use the shaded sidewalk in front of the forbidding headquarters. Museums, concert halls, restaurants, and the wine-gardens of Grinzing bustled with tourists. For most of the station, it was the first glimpse of Vienna as it may have been before the First World War had torn the Hapsburg Empire apart.

It was lost on Domnin. When Popov failed to telephone on schedule, Domnin began to fret. By the time Popov was three weeks overdue, Domnin's nerves had begun to crumble. The delay was more than his ingrained optimism could rationalize. Using any pretext, he would ease into Booth's office. Could a surveillant or two circulate around the Imperial? Perhaps they would spot Popov, then at least the station would know that he was back in town. No—the last thing

Booth wanted to do was to brief an agent to look for him. How about cranking up the tiger-camera again? No—there were too many cars parked along the Ringstrasse to get the vehicle into position.

"Maybe," Domnin said, "I could make a few turns around the Imperial. If Popov's lost the phone number, I could slip it to him?"

This, it was agreed, would be the last resort.

When Popov was more than a month overdue, the chief of station, as worried as Domnin and Booth, finally agreed. It was time to make a reconnaissance. There was enough tourist traffic along the Ringstrasse to give Domnin cover. If Popov had lost the phone number, maybe Domnin could do something.

"Goddamn," Domnin said as he pushed through the door to Booth's office. "He was right there, crossing the Ring. He saw me and made a sign."

On his first pass by the Imperial, Domnin had spotted Popov crossing from the headquarters to the officers' mess at the Grand Hotel. With more sang-froid than Booth would have wished, the cheeky agent had lifted his hand to his head as if he were holding a telephone.

"He's just got back, I know it," said Domnin, babbling in his excitement. "If he hasn't forgotten the number, we're back in business."

Popov was five weeks late, but he hadn't forgotten the number.

The information Popov had dredged from his three weeks at the Kaliningrad rest center ranged from atomic submarine data to information on guided missiles. This was high-level intelligence—the report on the new submarines was the first inside data CIA had disseminated on these craft—but for the Austrian station it was less important than the reason Popov had been so late in returning.

Popov's first interview at GRU headquarters was with the major handling administrative matters for the Germany/Austria branch. Comrade Khrushchev—then engaged in smoothing relations with Tito—had ordered a cutback in Yugoslav operations. High-level penetration agents in the Yugoslav army and government would, of course, continue in place. But in Vienna, and other European posts, Yugoslav operations would be put on a target-of-opportunity basis. If a likely-looking spy presented himself, he would be recruited. But for the present at least, the GRU would give up its program of seeking out recruitment candidates in the Yugoslav community. This, the administrative officer said with a smirk, meant that the GRU staff in

Vienna would be reduced—Comrade Popov's slot was the first to be cut. (Only a few GRU administrative personnel are ever posted abroad and those who are not that lucky resent case officers whose assignments take them to the capitalist fleshpots.)

After telling Popov to enjoy his holiday at Kaliningrad, the major instructed him to report for reassignment in Moscow as soon as his vacation was over.

Like his colleagues, Popov had been careful to cultivate friends in the GRU's Moscow hierarchy. Colonel Kishilov, chief of personnel for the European Directorate, had been in Popov's class at the Military Diplomatic Academy and Popov had not let their relationship lapse. Before leaving for Kaliningrad, Popov had stopped by Kishilov's office. All things considered, Popov explained, he thought he would be more useful to the GRU in Vienna than harnessed to a desk job in Moscow. Without a glance at the two bottles of perfume—which Popov had thoughtfully brought from Vienna as *blat*—Kishilov told Popov to drop by his office on his return from vacation. Perhaps something could be worked out.

Three weeks later, his holiday over, Popov hustled into Kishilov's office. There *was* an opening in Vienna. If Popov made the right impression on Colonel Khlysov, he might be assigned to the Vienna *rezidency* of the GRU's Operational Directorate.

At the time, Soviet military intelligence, the GRU, was organized in two separate "lines" or divisions. The Strategic Intelligence component was senior and, as its name suggests, was concerned with high-level—strategic—operations. On form, officers in Strategic *rezidencies* recruit and operate high-level agents, many of whom live and work in countries far from the *residency*. For security reasons, Soviet intelligence prefers to handle some agents on what it calls a "third country" basis—an agent operating in Bonn is less likely to be spotted by surveillance if he meets his case officer in Vienna rather than anywhere in West Germany. It is the Strategic Intelligence staff that handles most of these operations.

The operations directorate of the GRU, sometimes referred to as the "Cross Border Directorate," recruited and worked local agents, usually of a lower level of interest than those run by the Strategic *rezidency*. In practice, Western counterintelligence experts found little difference in the activity of the two GRU units. Each *rezidency* ran the best agents it could find and recruit, bureaucratic niceties notwithstanding.

Considering his peasant background and weak language skills, Popov had been lucky to be assigned to the Strategic Intelligence Directorate when he finished the Military Diplomatic Academy. "Strat" officers considered themselves a notch above their comrades in the operations directorate and were usually one grade higher in rank. As a rule these officers were all graduates of the Military Diplomatic Academy.

Popov was wise enough in the ways of the GRU to know that the last thing he should do would be to give the crusty Khlysov the idea that he really wanted to return to Vienna. In the best tradition of officers desperately anxious for a field assignment, he confined himself to laconic responses to the colonel's questions.

As he leafed through Popov's service record, Khlysov scowled. "You've been in Vienna—how'd you like it?"

Popov shrugged. "Duty is duty."

"How's your German?"

"Not perfect, but I speak it."

Khlysov closed Popov's dossier. "You want to go back?"

"Not particularly," Popov lied.

After four weeks of orientation in the operations directorate, Popov and his family returned to Vienna.

In Vienna the operations *rezidency* was primarily concerned with the recruitment of Austrians to infiltrate the defense forces Austria would establish as soon as the occupation ended, officials with access to the foreign or economic ministries, and Western military personnel. Although priority was given to officers, almost any soldier was considered worth recruitment. Enlisted men could supply training manuals, photographs, and samples of new equipment as readily as officers, were more amenable to direction, and usually worked for lower wages.

It was in November 1954 that Popov stumbled into an opportunity that was to shape the rest of his intelligence career.

Goaded by Domnin, Popov had begun serious work on his German. This study, amplified by his informal tutorials at Lyuba's side—a well-recognized means of mastering a foreign language, but scarcely approved of by Soviet security—had so improved his competence that he could now carry on German conversations with some fluency.

On the prowl through the *Bierstuben* of the *Innere Stadt*, Popov made a place for himself beside a morose, middle-aged Viennese. As the beer flowed, Popov painstakingly elicited his companion's name and the fact that he was a *Polizei Beamter,* a middle-level police official. Strictly speaking, police penetration operations are a counterintelligence matter and fall within the province of the KGB. But Colonel Nikolsky, the GRU operations chief, was an old hand. As far as he was concerned, finders-keepers was the rule when there was a spy to be recruited.

The Austrian had made no objection to Popov's buying the beer. Nor did Popov's unmistakable Russian accent keep the policeman from discoursing on the problems of supporting a family on a cop's wages. Popov sympathized—a policeman's lot is a hard one. He had struck gold and he knew it.

The following morning, still reeking of stale beer, Popov went to the office of Colonel Alexei Kriatov, chief of the GRU illegals support section in Vienna. After describing his new contact, Popov added the frosting. The Austrian was in charge of a district bureau responsible for issuing documentation papers to Austrian citizens. Identification cards, birth certificates, resident permits, all manner of the extensive documentation needed by Austrian citizens, were lodged in his office.

Kriatov was impressed. This was exactly the material required by Soviet agents who would be sent abroad documented as Austrians. If the policeman could be recruited, the GRU would have its own source of documentation. The KGB had recruited police officials through the Soviet zone of occupation and had good access to Austrian documents. Now Kriatov saw the opportunity to document GRU agents on his own. No longer would he have to go to the KGB, cap in hand, and put up with their humiliating questions every time he wanted to document a spy.

Kriatov congratulated Popov and directed him to cultivate his new friend. When the time came, he said, one of the illegals support case officers would make the recruitment. If it was successful, Popov would get credit for the coup. A few weeks later, the recruitment was made. Before the occupation ended, the Austrian had supplied Kriatov with dozens of identification papers, passports, and the rubber stamps, seals, and copies of the signatures necessary to complete them. Kriatov was not to forget Popov's help.

Early in the postwar period, Stalin had probably thought to divide Austria as he had done Germany and to separate the Soviet zone of occupation from the Allied area by a barricaded border, with Vienna compartmented as discretely as Berlin had been. But as the Russians were to discover, this was not a practical notion. Only twenty-seven percent of the Austrian population lived in the Soviet zone and many would certainly flee at the first sign that a border was being constructed. If the Soviet zone were to be cut off from the rest of Austria, the truncated area would become an economic desert.

By 1953, when the Russians reluctantly bowed to Austrian pressure and agreed to begin paying the costs of the Soviet occupation forces (the United States had been paying its own way since 1947), the occupation of some one hundred and forty-four thousand square miles of Austria had become expensive. And, try as they might, the commissars had yet to win either the hearts or minds of the stubborn Austrians. The inhabitants of the Soviet zone remained staunchly anticommunist, even anti-Russian.

The occupation did offer one advantage for the USSR. The need to provide secure lines of supply and communication to the Red Army units in Austria was the de jure reason for maintaining large armies in Hungary and Czechoslovakia. But other rationalizations for that could be found. Perhaps the time had come to play the Austrian chip. With a show of reluctance, the Russians agreed to discuss the Austrian peace treaty at the Four Power Foreign Ministers' meeting in Berlin in January 1954. As the conference wound down in February, Molotov abruptly proposed that the Allied Commission for Austria be abolished, but that the occupational troops remain in place. This was slightly encouraging but a diplomatic dud—it made no sense to abolish the commission while the troops remained encamped in Austria. The Western powers rejected the proposal.

With this, the post-Stalin "new course" seemed to harden, at least in respect to Austria, and the prospects for ending the occupation appeared as remote as ever.

It was not until February 1955—on the day Soviet Premier Malenkov asked to be relieved of his duties as chairman of the Soviet Council of Ministers because of "inexperience"—that Foreign Minister Molotov made an unexpected concession. If a State Treaty were to be signed, the occupation troops could be withdrawn. All that would be needed were ironclad guarantees to ensure that there would be no new *Anschluss* with Germany: Since the last thing anyone but the most unregenerate Austrian Nazis could want was another *Anschluss*, the Western powers quickly agreed. For the first time there seemed to be some real hope for the occupation-weary Austrians.

A month later, dawn broke and the Austrian government accepted a Russian invitation to Moscow. On 15 April the Austrian and Soviet governments signed an agreement on which the State Treaty could finally be based. Austria would forswear any future military alliances and agree not to permit any foreign military bases on its territory. It would also provide the USSR with ten years' production of crude oil from Austrian fields and pay Moscow for the "German assets" left in Austria when Nazi Germany collapsed. The occupation would end and, ever generous, the Soviet Union would release the Austrian prisoners held in the USSR. In the circumstances, Austria had bought a bargain.

Even before the April agreement was signed, the GRU had begun to prepare for postoccupation operations. Methodically, Soviet intelligence began to collect background data—city directories, telephone books, maps, city plans, documentation of all kinds, clothing and photographs of future dead drops for agents. Radio sets were buried. The only task taking precedence over the collection of operational support material was the recruitment of Western military personnel and Austrians who would remain in place.

As the occupation soldiers began dismantling the military installations and prepared to pack their duffel bags, the intelligence agencies faced the grim task of cutting back their bloated rosters and finding new cover for those members who would remain in Austria. During the ten years of occupation, the various intelligence outfits had battened on the cover offered by the proliferation of occupation offices and were blubbery with excess personnel.

In the last three years of the occupation the CIA station had doubled in size. When Ed Masters put the first audio system into the Popov safe house he worked alone. His replacement, dubbed "Dr. Zoomar" by the case officers, had two assistants. They could draw electronic schematics as well as the best RCA engineers, but when it came to improvising in a safe house, Masters was badly missed.

By the time the new organization was shaken out, Popov had reported on the slots the GRU and KGB had won in the new Soviet embassy. With these agents added to those in TASS, Aeroflot, Intourist, and the Trade Mission, Russian intelligence had an impressive three-to-one advantage over its CIA antagonists. It might have been worse. In most countries forty to sixty percent of the Soviet official community are committed to intelligence work.

*   *   *

As Popov's departure drew near, headquarters assumed increasing control of the operation. CIA's capabilities in the USSR were a tightly held secret; no one in the Austrian station knew—or had reason to know—what the agency could do in Moscow. On the basis of what Deriabin had reported, and the stories the station had heard about the surveillance that blanketed Western diplomats in Budapest and Prague, Booth guessed that the Moscow embassy could not have been under closer scrutiny if it had been pressed between glass slides and put under a microscope.

The first indication of headquarters' plans for Popov came when a new secret ink was sent from Washington. After testing, Domnin was to train Popov in its use.

The new ink was impressively simple. All the agent had to do with incoming messages was to expose them to sunlight for a few minutes. No activating agent was necessary, sunlight would do the trick. Following headquarters' instructions to the letter, Domnin prepared a test message and thumbtacked it to the window sill in Booth's office. For an hour they watched. The papar remained blank. Two hours passed—three hours—still nothing happened. Obviously there had been a mistake. Domnin went back to the drawing board and prepared another message. Still nothing happened.

On the chance that headquarters had skimped on the original formula, Domnin doubled the strength of the solutions. Three days and innumerable tests later, Domnin had still not been able to raise even a trace of a message. As far as the station was concerned, headquarters had indeed come up with a secret ink.

A polite query brought an abrupt answer from headquarters. Of course the formula worked—just follow the instructions. Domnin repeated his experiments. Not a trace.

Could there, Booth asked headquarters, be some difference between the quality of sunlight in Washington and in Austria? Vienna was gloomy, but surely the climate was no worse than Moscow? Irritably, headquarters announced it was dispatching an expert to teach the station how to use this ink, the simplest one on the laboratory shelf.

After fiddling with the formula for three days the expert cabled headquarters. Perhaps a different ink would be best. What had worked so effortlessly in Washington was a bust in the field. As it turned out, the effort had been wasted. A few weeks later, headquarters decided to put the operation on ice while Popov was in the USSR.

In June 1955 Amos Booth left Austria for an assignment in Washington. Domnin would leave a few days after Popov's departure, scheduled for early September.

Driving through the Vienna suburbs and into the Soviet zone for the last time, Booth slowed the car. There were still traces of the Soviet checkpoint at which Otto, the Austrian agent, had been kidnapped, almost five years earlier. He had not been among the prisoners released by the Russians.

It was a wrench to leave but Booth did not look back. Vienna was already yesterday.

16
ASSIGNMENT EAST GERMANY

A few weeks before Popov left Vienna for Moscow, Domnin learned there would be no attempt to communicate with the agent in the USSR and that he would not be encouraged to contact the agency. Someone had made a tough decision—with Popov on the shelf, CIA would lose its best inside source on Soviet military matters and the GRU. The KGB's growing ability to monitor the activity of foreigners in Moscow made it clear that, for the present at least, an interruption in Popov's reporting would be less dangerous for him and more tolerable than the possibly fatal risk of contact in Moscow. Technically, at least, it would have been possible to handle Popov in the Soviet Union. The agent could cache secret-ink reports in a dead drop—despite the fiasco with the first ink sent to Austria for Popov, excellent secret writing systems were readily available and it was within the capability of almost any service to reconnoiter possible dead drops in the Moscow area. Instructions to the agent could be hidden in a drop or mailed to him in a letter posted in the USSR. Coded messages, which could be picked up on one of the commercial radio sets readily available in Moscow, could be beamed to the agent from abroad. In most parts of the world, such communications would have been pretty tame stuff, standard espionage procedure. But Moscow was the big league. If there had been any doubt about this, a NATO report had to be considered. According to this information, the best counterintelligence officers in the KGB had spent weeks analyzing how opposing intelligence operatives might communicate with spies in the USSR and had taken the trouble to test their elaborate surveillance systems in espionage war-games. When a team of experienced KGB field personnel failed to crack the security cordon, the KGB was satisfied it could spot any illicit communication between foreigners and Russians.

For years Western intelligence had referred to the USSR and the Eastern European countries as "denied areas," an expression that gained currency in the late 1940s when travel into communist countries was severely restricted and few tourists, businessmen, or journalists were allowed through the iron curtain. The only spies bold enough to try had no alternative but to cross the border "black," illegally. Few survived.

At the request of the security services, the Soviet and satellite foreign offices insisted that the staffs of the Western embassies and consulates be held to a minimum. Embassy slots were so scarce that secretarial and administrative work was routinely parceled out to the diplomats' wives. All diplomatic personnel were kept under close, even repressive, surveillance.

It was not until 1954 that the USSR began to ease Stalin's restrictions. Tourism revived slightly, a few businessmen were given grudging welcome, and some cultural exchange was initiated. But the expression "denied area" lingered in intelligence parlance. Loosely defined, it was applied to any country with tightly sealed borders and efficient secret police authorized to operate outside the law. The definition fitted the USSR, the Eastern European countries, China, North Vietnam, and North Korea. There were other police states, but without the tutelage of the KGB, the security services of the noncommunist dictators rarely achieved a level of competence to justify denied-area status.

As far as the Second Chief Directorate, the KGB's internal counterintelligence component, was concerned, the Western intelligence services would never have reason to think of the Soviet Union as anything but a denied area.

Like most institutions of its size—some twenty-five thousand staff employees and more than a hundred thousand uniformed border guards—the responsibilities of the various KGB directorates are subject to bureaucratic shifts and administrative realignment. In 1955 the Second Chief Directorate had two primary tasks. It monitored the political activity of all Soviet citizens and suppressed any that did not have the approval of the Central Committee. It was also responsible for intelligence and counterespionage operations against all foreigners—diplomats, journalists, businessmen, and tourists—within the USSR.

The Second Chief Directorate was organized in six geographic, and a number of functional, departments. Department One, responsible for the United States and Latin America, had the best staff. With more than fifty case officers on permanent assignment, it could also call on the formidable resources of the entire KGB staff in the Moscow area. In Department One, the First Section concentrated on recruiting embassy personnel as agents. The Second Section engaged in counterespionage, penetrating and neutralizing any intelligence operations mounted from the U.S. embassy. The investigation of every Russian discovered to be in contact—official, social, or casual—with any American, was the responsibility of the Third Section. The Fourth Section directed and, as John Barron* has put it, "stage managed," the contacts American officials had with Russians in Moscow and throughout the Soviet Union. To support these operations, Department One had a corps of some three hundred highly trained surveillance agents exclusively committed to following every American official and clerk on duty in Moscow. Department One also operates against Latin American diplomatic installations and their personnel in Moscow, but less than twenty percent of its resources are devoted to these targets.

Other Second Chief Directorate departments have precisely the same responsibilities for the British Commonwealth, for Germany, Austria, Scandinavia and other Western European countries, for developed non-European countries and underdeveloped non-European countries.

Department Seven, with more than one hundred case officers, works exclusively on tourists.

Foreign newsmen are such treasured KGB recruitment targets that Department Ten is solely devoted to foreign journalists in the USSR. One of the best case officers from the American department is known to have been transferred to "Grub Street," as Department Ten is known by its English-speaking case officers.

In the West, no one could be sure how efficient the First Department was, but Deriabin's observations and those of Yuri Rostvorov, a KGB officer who defected in Japan in 1954, seemed conclusive. Until the agency had more experience in the USSR, it would not risk contact with Popov in Moscow.

*   *   *

*John Barron, KGB (New York: Reader's Digest Press, 1974). Readers interested in the organization of the KGB and a documented study of its activity will find this an excellent text.

In August Domnin began to drill Popov in the communication plan. Because Popov's only other languages were German and Serb, it seemed certain that his next foreign assignment would be to East Germany or possibly Yugoslavia. The East German assignment seemed most probable. To make up for the cover positions they had lost in Austria, the GRU was expanding its staff in East Germany. There were relatively few GRU slots in the Belgrade embassy and Popov's blunt manner did not make him a likely candidate for diplomatic cover.

As soon as Popov learned of his foreign posting, he was to chalk the initial letter of the country of his assignment on one of the numbered posts carrying electric wires on the outskirts of Moscow. A contact man would check the post regularly.

Once he was abroad, and could safely write, Popov was to mail an innocuous letter to one of two widely separated letter drops in Western Europe. This would alert the agency to his arrival and a secret-ink message would give Popov's views on how he should be contacted.

James Bond may not have gotten his start handling live letter drops, but many young case officers have cut their operational teeth on these mundane but vital support agents. Live letter drops, or LLDs, are agents who have been recruited to receive letters and pass them along to a case officer. Persons who rarely travel and get so little mail they are not likely to confuse a personal letter with operational correspondence are favored for recruitment. Because operational mail rarely comes more often than once a month, sometimes once a year— or, as in Popov's case, only when the agent wants to renew contact— case officers often mail dummy letters to make sure the drop is alert.

Because no one could be sure how long it would be before Popov was posted abroad and could write, the first law of operations had to be taken into account—if things can go wrong they will. No one could recall such an unfortunate occurrence, but if the live drop were to drop dead before Popov left the USSR, the agent would be up a rope. Popov was given two letter drops, both in good health.

As a prop for his memory, Popov's Russian/German dictionary was borrowed and a technician inscribed the addresses on pages 19 and 22—the year of his birth—in secret ink. Unless Popov were to be smitten simultaneously with a loss of memory and a headache—the developer for the ink had been put up in pill form, exact replicas of Soviet aspirin tablets—he should be able to write.

In the event Popov could not use the letter drops, Domnin also gave him the telephone number of a CIA office in Europe. All Popov had to do was to call and say that "Max" wanted to speak to Colonel Grossman. The station would alert headquarters and within a week Domnin would be at hand to answer Popov's next phone call.

As a final bit of insurance, Domnin coached Popov on another fall-back contact possibility.

"Just remember this," he said. "On the chance that you are transferred so suddenly that everything comes unstuck and you can't write or telephone, you can still make contact."

Popov smiled, remembering the letter he had dropped into the American car in Vienna.

"I know what you're thinking," Domnin said, "but it worked and you had no trouble making contact. If everything goes wrong the next time you're posted abroad, I want you to take your time and study the local situation. Even without asking any questions, you ought to be able to identify someone in the American community, in the embassy most likely, who looks as if he or she is bright, who might even be in the business. Sometimes your own counterintelligence people brief the Soviet embassy staff on which Americans to avoid. But don't take this at face value—they're often wrong. Make your own decision."

Domnin paused to be sure Popov understood the briefing. "Once you've picked the person, find a safe way to hand him an envelope. Write 'For CIA Only' on an inside envelope and put your message in the inside envelope. All you have to say is 'Tell Grossman that Max is in Copenhagen.' The message will be in Washington within hours. It will take a few days for me to get to you, but I will be able to make contact. The best thing is that the communication will be absolutely secure and you can use that method in any country."

Popov nodded. "I'll remember."

"But don't forget that this is the last resort—if you can, use the letter drops or telephone number."

It was not the most professional re-contact arrangement; a more secure plan could have been fashioned, but it would have been complicated and thus more easily confused. The plan was a reasonable compromise. When Popov failed to use it, he made a mistake, possibly a fatal mistake.

Booth's Washington assignment was not unlike the job in Austria, the big difference being that it was thousands of miles away from the action. He was an operations officer in a division responsible for Germany and several Eastern European countries, but not the Soviet Union—the USSR warranted a division of its own. Under the rules of compartmentation, this meant that unless a Soviet operation was based in one of the countries for which Booth was responsible, he would not see any cable or dispatch traffic concerning it. Only a few members of the Soviet division were cleared to read the Popov traffic. After having wrestled with the case for three years, it was not easy for Booth simply to forget it. Still, there were compensations. The division in which he worked was the biggest and certainly the most productive in the agency, and it was as much as Booth could do to keep up with the important activity that fell within his responsibility. Not the least item on the plate was an operation that became known as the Berlin Tunnel.

The tunnel was almost six hundred yards long, six feet high and some fifteen feet underground. It ran from a mock U.S. Army "radar station" near Rudow, in the American sector of West Berlin, beneath the border separating East and West Berlin, and for some four hundred yards within the Soviet sector. It terminated ten feet below a telephone cable buried alongside the Schoenefeld road, leading to the Soviet-controlled airport serving East Berlin. The master cable contained three smaller cables servicing 432 separate telephone lines. These lines connected the Soviet high command in East Berlin to the General Staff and foreign office in Moscow and to all major Red Army units in East Germany, Soviet diplomatic installations, and the Russian intelligence headquarters in Karlshorst, East Berlin.

Spliced into these telephone lines was another cable leading through the tunnel to the "radar station" a few hundred feet from the fence marking the demarcation line between East and West Berlin. In the station, 432 tape recorders—one for each phone line—consumed hundreds of feet of tape, recording every call made on these lines.

The Berlin Tunnel was the creature of William King Harvey, chief of CIA's Berlin office. He had conceived the operation, directed the elaborate engineering project involved in digging the tunnel, bracing it with steel supports and disposing of the more than three thousand tons of spoil removed from the site. He contrived the radar station cover for the buildings at the tunnel head that provided space for the amplifiers, whirling tape recorders, and the technicians who oversaw the tunnel and delicate tap.

It was an immense clandestine undertaking, one of the most ambitious and productive technical operations CIA had ever sponsored. The tunnel provided the agency and NATO forces—who with the exception of the British had not the slightest notion of the source of the data—with the complete order of battle of the Soviet Group of Forces in East Germany. Along with this came the unvarnished comments of senior Soviet officers and the directives Moscow showered on its troops in the field.

Soviet generals tend to be bigger than life, or to think they are, and the restraints binding lesser mortals have little effect on these bemedaled mandarins. Sometimes, the general who signs the orders proscribing loose talk on the telephone is one of the monitors' favorite chatterboxes. In East Berlin the generals' comments on Herr Ulbricht's government and the social life and sexual preferences of their colleagues added a bit of zest to the thousands of meaty but boring transcripts that poured from the translators' desks. Generals were not the only indiscreet Russians.

The telephone is just impersonal enough to free some solitary souls from whatever it is that inhibits their social lives; the lonely are a great satisfaction to tap-monitors. In Berlin the scuttlebutt provided by these forlorn gossips often provided the glue the analysts used to stick the East German mosaic together.

One favorite was a dedicated quidnunc someone had christened the Town Crier, a lonely clerk in the headquarters of the Soviet Group of Forces. Late in the afternoon, possibly after his superiors had left for the day, the Crier would call another solitary, a clerk in a division headquarters some distance from Berlin. After transacting enough business to justify the call, the Crier would settle down for a cozy chat. His comments on the wife of General Grechko, then commanding officer in East Germany, would have impressed Cholly Knickerbocker. The Soviet *grande dame* regarded East Germany as a gigantic mall established for her shopping—more accurately, looting—convenience. Scarcely a week passed without the Town Crier regaling his friend, and the monitors, with a new story of Comrade Grechkova's foraging for another fur coat or grand piano. The monitors also eavesdropped on General Grechko when he made arrangements for shipping Grechkova's loot back to Moscow.

Not surprisingly—because so many case officers had personal experience with telephone taps—the best discipline was kept by the GRU and KGB personnel; little of operational interest was ever discussed on the intelligence telephone circuits. But operations were not all that was of interest. In East Germany the bulk of Soviet intelligence personnel were under military cover, only a few had diplomatic camouflage. As nearly mute as the operations officers were, the military administrative staffs responsible for providing logistical support, housing, and transportation, handled the intelligence personnel exactly as if they were military. Thus the loose-lipped administrators provided ample grist for the counterintelligence analysts. As these specialists studied the telephone transcripts, they began to piece together tables of organization of the various intelligence cover offices and to a degree to keep track of departing officers and their replacements.

Like all high-risk activity—four hundred yards of the tunnel were in the Soviet sector—the Berlin phone tap was strictly compartmented from other operations. Only personnel on the tunnel BIGOT list had any knowledge of its existence. "BIGOT" is a code word coined in World War II when special security clearances were required for personnel planning Operation Overlord, the cross-channel invasion of France. Officers with a need to know where the invasion forces would land were given a BIGOT clearance. The term came from a rubber stamp—"TO GIB"—used on orders of officers being sent to Gibraltar in connection with Operation Torch, the invasion of North Africa. When planning for Overlord began, "TO GIB' was simply reversed to read BIGOT.* Years later, sensitive operations were still said to have been *Bigoted* and all personnel with knowledge of them were inscribed on the BIGOT list. The Popov BIGOT list was one of the shortest in headquarters.

Rigid compartmentalization is meant to restrict the information a penetration agent, or possible defector, might be able to get his hands on. The system works but it is not without problems. When strictly enforced, it can be responsible for some of the apparently simpleminded blunders that come to light and amuse the press and other

*Anthony C. Brown, *Bodyguard of Lies* (New York: Harper & Row, 1975), p. 529.

intelligence critics. In secret operations the fact is that one hand does not necessarily know what the other is doing. Computers have simplified the problems of information control, coordination, and document retrieval from central registries—names can be flagged and automatically brought to the attention of persons who need to know—but at best it is an imperfect system. Sometimes memory works faster.

When Popov was recruited, notation was made in the central registry that any document mentioning his name—painfully common in the USSR—should be referred to the chief of the Soviet division. When the system worked perfectly, this would be done—as soon, that is, as any analyst fed the name into the computers. But there was always a filing backlog and it was often weeks before routine documents were processed for the computers.

It was December 1956 when Paul Hopkins came into Booth's Washington office. He was an old hand and had replaced Peter Todd in Austria a few months before the occupation ended. As chief of the Soviet section, he worked closely with Domnin in the closing weeks of Popov's Vienna assignment. Now in Washington, one of his responsibilities was checking tunnel traffic for clues that might be of operational interest.

"I don't know how much you know about this, but you'd better take a look at this report," Hopkins said as he shoved a single sheet of paper across the desk.

It was a routine bit of intercept from the tunnel, a telephone call from a personnel officer in the Soviet Group of Forces headquarters to a Soviet rifle division headquarters near Schwerin, East Germany. Lieutenant Colonel Pyotr S. Popov had completed his processing in East Berlin and would arrive in Schwerin by train the following morning. He was to be met and provided with quarters.

The Soviet personnel officer had been taken in by Popov's military cover. Had he known Popov was an intelligence officer, the message would have been sent by enciphered cable.

Every week, Hopkins scanned a hundred or more pages of transcript for any information possibly bearing on CIA operations in Germany. Scores of Russian names, some garbled in transmission, were included in the reports crossing his desk. Only a handful of officers outside the Soviet division knew Popov's name or might conceivably have spotted it in the flood of tunnel material. If Hopkins's attention had wandered, it might have been weeks before the transcript was processed for the computers.

That afternoon an *Eyes Only* cable flashed to Harvey in Berlin. Gregory Domnin was assigned to the Berlin office and would arrive within ten days' time. Harvey was to cable headquarters immediately, recommending an innocuous but plausible job that would explain Domnin's sudden assignment to other members of the office. Domnin would carry a message from Helms and the chief of the Soviet division explaining his sudden transfer.

Harvey was an old-timer, a former FBI man and a counterintelligence specialist. Despite this, he had had no need to know about the Popov case and had never been cleared for it. But Harvey kept up with agency scuttlebutt and knew that Domnin was a senior Russian-speaking case officer who had been in Austria for three years. He had also deduced that the only reason an officer with Domnin's language qualification could have been there for such a long time would be to handle an in-place agent. Chances are that he rubbed his hands as he scribbled a reply to Helms.

Within the Berlin office, Domnin's cover job would be to research the voluminous Soviet files for operational leads and to determine which files should be shipped back to Washington. It was not an assignment many officers would have welcomed. On the face of it, Domnin was being put out to pasture. Only those on the Popov BIGOT list knew better.

17
TREFFPUNKT SCHWERIN

Harvey was impatient. He had set up a high-security safe house, furnished it comfortably, and bugged it with the highest fidelity recording equipment the agency could provide. Now there was nothing to be done until Popov made a signal. He was not a patient man and the waiting wore at his nerves.

Domnin kept busy setting up files and familiarizing himself with West Berlin and the operational ground rules, quite different from what he had known in Austria.

Unlike Vienna during the occupation, Berlin was a divided city. There was no *Innere Stadt* administered on a rotating basis by each of the four occupying powers. Instead, there were two city administrations—one in East Berlin, the capital of the German Democratic Republic, the other in West Berlin, an outpost of the Federal Republic of Germany and occupied by American, British, and French forces. But, at least until the Berlin wall was built in August 1961, there was no physical barrier separating the two parts of the city. Any Berlin resident, member of the occupying forces, or visitor was free to circulate as he wished. One could walk, take a taxi, or drive from West Berlin to the Soviet sector. For a few *pfennig* the S-Bahn, the elevated tram system, or the U-Bahn, Berlin's celebrated underground railway, would whisk travelers from sector to sector. Only occasionally would a sudden East German control impede travel between the sectors.

Tens of thousands of Berliners made the trip every day—about sixty thousand of those coming from East Berlin were *Grenzgaenger*, border-crossers, who held regular jobs in West Berlin. Others made the trip to visit open libraries, the uncensored theater, or simply to sample the standard of living offered by the capitalist enclave, one hundred and ten miles behind the iron curtain. Some West Germans crossed into East Berlin to visit relatives, to attend the theater, or simply to buy fresh vegetables that came into the communist sector from the surrounding farmland. Tourists, piqued by the opportunity to inspect a glum communist capital, took guided tours of East Berlin. Others, possibly titillated by the sensation of rubbing elbows with spies, took the S-Bahn.

East and West Berlin were rightly known as espionage centers. In Karlshorst, a suburb of East Berlin, the KGB and GRU were lodged discretely in the huge Soviet compound. Nearby were the offices of the East German security service, the MFS. Each of the Eastern European countries maintained an embassy in East Berlin and the staffs were well salted with intelligence officers.

Official East German studies claimed to have identified some eighty Allied intelligence agencies in West Berlin. There were not quite that many, say two score. But in Berlin in 1957 spying was still a growth business and platoons of spies scurried back and forth across the sector boundaries.

Not all of the travelers from East Berlin made a round trip. In 1956, 139,745 East German refugees streamed into West Berlin. A year later, 110,005 East Germans fled. In the sixteen years before the border was sealed, more than three million East Germans "voted with their feet." One-fifth of the population of East Germany opted out. If Popov could get to Berlin, he would have no trouble slipping across the sector border.

Lieutenant Colonel Kirkland and Captain Wickham were tired. They had driven one hundred and forty miles north from Berlin to Rostock, East Germany's largest seaport, on a commonplace bit of "liaison" business. The city had been badly bombed, and although partially rebuilt, it had little to offer the two British officers. Rather than spend the night there, they would eat at a *Gasthaus* a few miles to the south and then drive on to Berlin. As members of the British Military Liaison Mission to the Soviet Group of Forces headquarters in Potsdam, they were authorized to travel on official business in East Germany. Authorized that is, as long as they obtained approval in advance and provided Soviet headquarters with a detailed itinerary of their trip.

The liaison missions had been established early in the occupation to deal with the snarls that frequently arose between the military forces in the two Germanies. The Russians had set up an office in West Germany. The British, French, and American offices were in Potsdam. Along with untangling routine military problems, the liaison officers had also come to function as de facto military attachés. Like military attachés, they were occasionally invited to military maneuvers and it was understood they would report on what they saw. When suitable excuses could be found, these officers traveled in the zone. Although not operational in the sense of running agents, the liaison personnel took care to arrange their excursions into the Soviet zone to give the best possible glimpses of Soviet military installations and airfields. Their sightings were a useful addition to agent reports and the data pouring out of the tunnel. The Russian officers stationed in West Germany played by slightly different rules. Whenever they could shake the light surveillance the West German security forces attempted to keep on them, they would service dead drops for agents operating in West Germany.

It was a hybrid arrangement, but tolerated because each side profited from it.

By the time Kirkland and Wickham had finished a bowl of *Bohnensuppe* and were waiting for a plate of *Bratwurst* and potato salad, the locals had begun to tuck into huge glasses of the strong local beer, and the restaurant was smoke-filled and noisy. With a long drive still before them, the British officers had no enthusiasm for mixing with the regular guests who would be more than glad to vaporize over the East-West political scene with the only capitalists they had seen for years. They hurried through the meal.

Leaving Wickham to settle with the waitress, Kirkland stepped out of the restaurant and walked down a dark corridor to the men's room. A few minutes later, as Kirkland was trying to soap his hands under the single spigot of cold water, the door opened and a stocky man wearing civilian clothes and a hat pushed his way into the room and pulled the door shut behind him.

When Kirkland had dried his hands on the limp towel hanging on the wall, the stranger took off his hat and pulled an envelope from his pocket. With a wary glance at the door, he approached Kirkland and whispered in accented German, "*Bitte, diesen Brief Oberst Grossman, amerikanische Geheimdienst Berlin, uebergeben. Bitte, so schnell wie moeglich.*" He thrust the thick, letter-sized envelope into Kirkland's hand.

Not sure Kirkland had understood that he was to give the letter to Colonel Grossman at CIA Berlin as quickly as possible, the man repeated the message.

Like all diplomats and military attachés stationed in communist countries, Kirkland had been briefed not to accept unsolicited documents from strangers. No matter how earnest the appeal, nor how enticing the documents seemed to be, experience had shown that such offers were often the first step in a counterintelligence provocation—possibly the excuse for a *persona non grata* action.

In the 1940s, before the KGB had consolidated its hold on the Eastern European countries, dissident citizens had begun to slip embarrassing documents to foreign diplomats and journalists. Realizing that it could not possibly hope to surveil every potentially disaffected person all of the time, the KGB hit upon another means of plugging the leaks.

In what was to become almost a routine exercise, a furtive stranger would thrust a packet of papers into the hand of a diplomat. Seconds later, police would materialize, arrest the stranger, seize the documents from the diplomat, and charge them both with espionage. In the ensuing brouhaha, the diplomat would be offered the chance to save himself embarrassment by agreeing to sign on as a spy. When he refused, a diplomatic protest would be filed and the diplomat declared *persona non grata*. When word of these provocations spread, diplomats, like wise children, learned to spurn candy from strangers.

Kirkland had only a moment to make up his mind. The obvious decision would be to obey his instructions and send the visitor packing. Yet there was something authentic about this nervous man with his hair combed so oddly across his head. Kirkland hesitated and then pocketed the letter. After repeating his message a last time, the stranger clapped on his hat, opened the door, and disappeared down the hallway.

Kirkland waited a few moments and walked slowly out of the men's room and along the corridor to the restaurant. To Kirkland's relief, the stocky man was not in the room. With Wickham leading, Kirkland made his way out of the restaurant and to the official car with its conspicuous military mission licence plates. Kirkland eased himself behind the wheel and maneuvered the car back onto the highway. As they picked up speed, he kept an eye on the rear-view mirror.

"Did you see anyone follow me into the loo?" he asked.

"No, did you have a romantic adventure?" Wickham asked.

"You'd better take a look at this," Kirkland said, and handed Wickham the sealed envelope.

"What the hell is this?"

"The chap who followed me into the toilet handed it to me."

Wickham whistled and turned to look through the rear window. There were no cars in sight. Holding the envelope in the light of the dashboard, Wickham said, "It's addressed to '*Oberst Grossman, amerikanische Besatzung, Berlin.*' He a friend of yours?"

"No, damn it, I've never heard of him. But you'd better open the envelope."

Wickham tore open the letter. Inside were six sheets of ruled note paper. Bending forward, Wickham could see that each page was covered with meticulous handwritten notes.

"Blood," he said.

"What is it?"

"I can't make it out, but it's written in Russian." Wickham paused for a moment. "You've just agreed to courier six pages of Russian script to Berlin—about enough to land us both on the front page of every newspaper in Germany. That's the last time I let you go to the toilet alone."

"Oh dear," said Kirkland, and stepped on the accelerator.

Despite Wickham's foreboding, there was no surveillance along the way and they were passed quickly through the Soviet checkpoint on the outskirts of Berlin.

The state of liaison between foreign intelligence services is a barometer of foreign relations—when foreign policy objectives coincide, intelligence liaison flourishes. Since William Stephenson, a British intelligence officer stationed in New York City, began to help General William Donovan organize an American intelligence service in 1940, the British and American services have enjoyed a special relationship. Only occasionally have things gone askew. The exposure of Kim Philby and his friends Guy Burgess and Donald Maclean and the British invasion of Suez in 1956 taxed the relationship, but it survived.

But no matter how close, or how special, a relationship, no intelligence service will ever refuse the opportunity to look over a liaison partner's shoulder and to peek at any cards he may be holding close to his chest.

In Berlin the following morning Kirkland drove directly to the British intelligence offices. The station chief listened to Kirkland's story and scanned the pages of the letter. There was no Colonel

Grossman in the American telephone book, nor could the station chief recall having heard of anyone named Grossman in Harvey's office. Considering the risk Kirkland had taken in accepting this curious document, it was not something he could let pass through his hands without examination.

For all its reputation, British intelligence is no more immune to the first law of operations than CIA. When Kirkland delivered the letter to MI-6 in Berlin, the Russian translator was on leave. A case officer with some knowledge of Russian was summoned and told to scan the letter.

The surrogate translator had been sweating over the document for an hour when the case officer who shared the office opened the door and tossed a briefcase onto the adjoining desk. In response to a light question—possibly "How's trade?"—the case officer pushed aside the Russian-English dictionary.

"It looks as if Bill Harvey's got a good GRU case, somewhere out in the zone." That, as far as is known, is all he said. It was quite enough.

George Blake, an MI-6 officer with ten years' seniority, was too discreet to ask his colleague any more questions about the letter he was translating. As a KGB mole in place in British intelligence, Blake had learned not to appear too curious. Besides, if there was anything to it, he might learn more about it in the days to come.

When the translation was finished, the letter was hand-carried to Harvey.

With Harvey at his shoulder, Domnin began to read aloud from the letter. Brushing past the notes on the GRU and the fragmentary comments on Popov's time in Moscow, he found the proposed *Treff* on the last page. *Treff*, German espionage slang for rendezvous or meeting, is commonly used by both Russian and Western intelligence officers who have served in Germany. (*Spravka*, Russian for file, is sometimes used by Western intelligence officials. In Moscow, even non-English-speaking case officers affect to greet one another in English.)

Had Popov been making a date to take his wife to the movies, he could not have proposed a less artful meeting arrangement than the one he made to the Berlin office. At six-thirty every Wednesday evening Popov would loiter for fifteen minutes in front of the German-Soviet Friendship Society rooms in Schwerin. He would keep this schedule until he was contacted by CIA.

Harvey shook his head. "Couldn't he at least have given us a recognition signal? How the hell does he think a courier will recognize him? We'll probably give the meeting plan to the first Russian who comes out of the Friendship Society."

Domnin continued reading. Popov could make an occasional trip to East Berlin and assumed he would have no trouble crossing into the U.S. sector. What he needed was Grossman's telephone number.

Harvey checked the map behind his desk. Schwerin, a small city on the Berlin-Rostock railway line, was about fifty miles southwest of Rostock and some ninety miles northwest of Berlin. It would be an easy run for the right courier.

"Karl" had never been used by the Berlin office. He was an East Berliner, a retired postal worker. His only son and family had fled to West Germany in 1953. When a case officer on the prowl encountered Karl in West Berlin, and learned he lived in East Berlin, the office had checked him out. Karl had been in the Nazi party for a few months in 1930, but had never taken an active part in Nazi politics. As far as the record showed, his party membership had lapsed before Hitler came to power in 1933. He was an ardent and, at least in West Berlin, outspoken anticommunist, with a passionate, almost racial hatred for Russians. Aside from this, Karl's politics were quite old-fashioned. He was "Kaisertreu," a royalist, a rare political persuasion in Berlin in 1956.

Karl was convinced that if the Allies had left Kaiser Wilhelm II on the throne after World War I, Germany would have been spared Hitler. Without the Fuehrer to botch things, the Imperial General Staff would have made short work of the Red Army and the world would have been saved from communism. A bit primitive, but heartfelt.

Like housewives remembering to stow odd buttons in the family sewing box, good station chiefs are careful to keep a few potentially useful contacts on the shelf. Unless a station has something in reserve, it is usually impossible to respond to an urgent need for a clean courier, letter drop, or safe-house keeper. The only agents that can be presumed to be clean—unsuspected by anyone—are those who have been thoroughly investigated but never used operationally. Some of these high-security support agents are recruited and given a small retainer against the day—usually night—they will be needed. Others are kept warm by case officers—an occasional bottle of wine, a meal, or, as in Karl's case, a chess game. When needed, they can be formally recruited. Many are used only once.

Karl was not a political philosopher, but he did keep up with the daily press and, like most Berliners, was aware of the intelligence battles raging in the city. When the American failed to proposition him, Karl volunteered. He was ready for anything that would put a spoke in the Russian wheel. Karl wore glasses but, as he said, could still handle a rifle or throw a grenade. He was seventy-four.

As an East Berliner, Karl would have no trouble buying a roundtrip ticket to Rostock—he would step off the train in Schwerin. If anyone asked, he was making a nostalgic trip to the city where he had courted his wife before the war. After making the "pass"—slipping the message to Popov—he would take the next train back to Berlin. There was only one hitch. The case officer was not sure Karl could bring himself to shake hands with anyone he knew to be a Russian.

It was a brief message. A terse sentence instructed Popov to cross into West Berlin on the S-Bahn and gave the telephone number he was to call once he was across the sector border. Inscribed on a small bit of gray rice paper, it was rolled into a pellet no larger than a pea. Karl would carry it loose in his overcoat pocket. If he encountered a police control on the train and thought he was going to be searched, he would drop the pellet on the floor. If he could not do this, he would leave the message in his pocket. Only a thorough search by a trained counterintelligence officer could bring it to light—a policeman looking for contraband would not notice it.

Karl also had the option of swallowing the pellet, but this could be conspicuous and was not recommended. Intelligence services have what is called "edible" paper for such contingencies, but edible really means "water soluble" and although a mouthful will eventually disintegrate, it often turns into an unpalatable mess, the consistency of the plastic dentists use to fit false teeth.

That Tuesday night Karl was introduced to Domnin, who briefed him on the *Treff* and described Max, the man he was to meet in Schwerin. Rather than risk Karl's jibbing at the prospect of actually shaking hands with the enemy, Domnin was careful to note that Max looked rather like a Russian. Karl was less interested in this than why he had to make the meeting in front of the German-Soviet Friendship Society.

"Look at it this way," Domnin said. "It's better than doing it in front of the police station."

Friday night flights from Tempelhof in West Berlin are crowded with businessmen heading for home, Berliners going to West Germany for the weekend, and refugees. Karl was traveling light, only one bag and a shabby briefcase. He looked like any other refugee from East Germany.

When Karl returned from Schwerin, Harvey had decided it was time for him to join his son in West Germany. With a bonus to make up for the furniture he would leave in his East Berlin apartment, Karl was glad to leave, but only after he had made a final visit to his apartment. This posed some risk and Domnin could have done without the final visit to the apartment, but Karl was adamant. He would not leave without the photograph of his wife. She had been killed when the Red Army swept into Berlin in the last days of the war.

Karl wasn't sure what he had done to deserve such favored treatment, certainly the trip to Schwerin had been uneventful. He had hopped off the train and killed an hour strolling around the city. Then, after stopping for a bowl of potato soup and a beer, he had found Max right where Domnin had said he would be. Karl palmed the pellet and shook hands. Max had acknowledged the pellet with a wink and invited Karl for a beer. But the courier had a train to catch, there was no time for any more beer.

"That fellow not only looks like a Russian, he talks like a Russian," Karl said. "If you ask me, he is a Russian. Are you people sure you know what you're doing?"

Domnin admitted that Max looked like a Russian and even talked like a Russian. "We know what we're doing, but we couldn't have done it without your help," he said.

Karl swore on the Kaiser's honor that he would never tell anyone what he had done. As he said goodbye to his case officer at the passenger gate at Tempelhof, Karl paused for a moment. "Look," he growled. "Darmstadt is not so far from Berlin. If you need someone for another trip, you can call on me. You won't even have to pay for the next one."

18
OPERGRUPPE KARLSHORST

When the Max phone rang, Popov was in West Berlin, at the S-Bahn station Am Zoo. Still not trusting Popov's accent in German, Domnin instructed him to take a taxi to the Hotel Kempinski on the Kurfuerstendamm in the American sector. He would have no trouble pronouncing Kempinski in German or Russian. Domnin would be standing across the street from the hotel.

It would take fifteen minutes for Popov to get to the *Treff*; enough time, Domnin reasoned, for him to get there first. He was worried that the Russian might not have West German currency and would have to negotiate payment of the cab fare in *Ost* marks. If Popov spoke more than a few words, the driver would know his passenger was Russian. The Kempinski is a fine hotel, but not the sort of place a Russian in civilian clothes would necessarily seek out. Or so a street-smart Berlin cabby would think. If he was an informer, and many cabdrivers were, he would tip the West Berlin police. As far as Domnin was concerned, the fewer people who knew that a Russian, any Russian, had been in the vicinity of the Kempinski, the better.

By the time the case officer detailed to drive Domnin to the meeting had pulled up on the far side of the Kurfuerstendamm, Popov was paying his taxi fare. When he turned and spotted Domnin, his discipline melted. With a wave, he bolted across the sidewalk and, oblivious to the risk, plunged into the stream of rush-hour traffic. For a moment Domnin wondered how he would phrase the cable telling headquarters that Popov had been run down before his eyes. When Popov had negotiated half the distance, Domnin stepped in front of the parked car, determined to pull his agent the last few feet to safety. As he grasped Popov's outstretched hand, Domnin heard a shouted warning from over his shoulder. With brakes locked, a German cyclist slued into them. Slammed against the car, Domnin saw Popov, feet in air, hit the greasy pavement on his backside. The German catapulted off his bike and rolled to a stop a few yards away.

Anxious to avoid an incident, Domnin pulled Popov to his feet, but before he could push the Russian into the car, the bellicose German had picked up his bicycle and briefcase and, shouting at the *Idioten* who had chosen the bicycle path for a chat, was limping toward them.

After four years of combat, Popov was not one to be intimidated by a German civilian in occupied Berlin. Shaking free of Domnin's restraining grasp, he turned to face the outraged German. "Fascist," he shouted. The unmistakable Russian pronunciation—"Fasheest"—stopped the German in his tracks. Muttering an imprecation, he remounted and wobbled off on the bicycle path alongside the busy street.

At twenty miles an hour, the shaken case officer chauffeur drove a circuitous route through the swarm of evening traffic to the safe house at Litzenseestrasse.

It was a busy evening; Popov had a lot of ground to cover. Recounting his stay in Moscow, Popov was surprised to learn Domnin had not known he was in Schwerin. Had the Moscow man missed the signal on the post?

"We spotted a chalk inscription but it meant nothing—we weren't even sure you had made it," Domnin told him.

"Impossible," Popov said. "I put an 'S' for Schwerin and a 'G' for Germany. How could you have missed it?"

"Damn it—you were supposed to put one letter on the post. 'G' for Germany would have been quite enough. We couldn't figure out what 'SG' meant."

Popov was contrite.

"Why didn't you write to the letter box when you got to Germany? Did you lose the address?"

Popov shrugged. "I was going to write. Then I saw the British car. I thought it would speed things up. But you got the letter, so it really doesn't matter."

"Sure, we got it. So did the British. Now they know CIA is in contact with a GRU officer somewhere around Schwerin."

But Popov had no time for second thoughts, he was bubbling with news. The GRU was making a change in its organization in East Germany. Lieutenant General Feodor Federenko, the deputy chief of the GRU in Moscow, was being transferred to Karlshorst, East Berlin. He would direct all GRU operations based on East Germany and would establish a new strategic operations group. With a staff of ninety GRU case officers, the *Opergruppe,* as it was called, would operate throughout Western Europe. "It's as if a section of the GRU headquarters were transferred from Moscow to Karlshorst," Popov said.

"Do you remember Colonel Kriatov from Vienna?" he asked.

"Of course, he was head of the GRU illegals support section. You turned the Austrian policeman over to him."

"That's right. He got all the Austrian documentation the GRU will need for the next ten years from that guy," Popov said.

Domnin remembered that when Khokhlov arrived in West Germany, he traveled with an Austrian passport, ostensibly issued to "Josef Hofbauer." In the investigation that followed Khokhlov's defection, Austrian authorities learned that the passport was genuine. It had been delivered by the Austrian police on orders from Soviet occupation authorities. The idea that the KGB would give Khokhlov a passport that the Austrian police knew had been obtained for illicit use, baffled Domnin. In a way it was typical of Soviet intelligence operations. The most painstaking security precautions and elaborate operational tradecraft on the one hand and, on the other, flagrant violations of the most commonplace practices.

"For once it seems," Popov continued, "I've gotten lucky. Kriatov is still grateful. When he heard I was assigned to Schwerin—it's a pretty city, but aside from the fishing, it's boring as hell. There's not a damned thing to do there at night—"

Domnin interrupted. "Maybe that's just as well. Is Gallina here yet?"

Popov's eyes flashed. "No, not yet. But she's coming to Berlin with the children. That's what I'm trying to tell you. When Kriatov heard I was in Schwerin, he told Federenko what I had done for him in Vienna and asked for my transfer to the illegals section in Karlshorst." Popov leaned back to watch the impact of this news on his case officer.

Domnin was impressed, more impressed than he wanted Popov to know. Soviet illegals were highly trained agents—often staff officers—dispatched from Moscow under the deepest possible cover.

Documented with false papers, they remain abroad for years. Illegals have their own communications and are rarely, if ever, in contact with the legal *rezidency*, the case officers under diplomatic cover. After the war, when Western counterintelligence intensified surveillance of Soviet embassies, the GRU and KGB began to increase their reliance on illegals to handle the most sensitive agents. A few Soviet illegals had been uncovered in the West, but most had been tipped by an agent in place or a defector.

Aside from penetration agents, Soviet illegals were the most important counterintelligence targets. Popov had hit the jackpot.

For an hour Domnin questioned Popov about the new job—it would be weeks before the transfer became effective—about Moscow, changes in the GRU and political developments under Khrushchev. Finally, Domnin noticed that Popov had become restless under the fusillade of questions. He pushed aside the clipboard with the lined yellow pad and leaned back in the heavy, overstuffed armchair. Popov took a deep swig of vodka.

"If you're not still mad about the letter, I've brought a little something more for you," Popov said.

"I'm not mad, Pyotr Semyonovich, just worried. By now you ought to know better than to take chances like that. You were damned lucky with Lyuba. But you can't count on luck, you've got to use your head. Have you heard anything about her?"

"No, I wrote to tell her I was in Germany, but I didn't give any return address."

Domnin exploded. "What in hell are you thinking of? You're damned well crazy. You had a perfect chance to drop her. For all she would know, you were back in Russia for ever. Now she knows you're here. I don't know what you're thinking of."

Popov bristled. "It's just that she counts on me. She'll never let me down, I know that. But she's probably having a bad time of it. Maybe sometime I can do something for her."

Domnin was angry and depressed. Popov had been in contact with CIA for four years. As far as Domnin could know, there had been no security breaks on the CIA side. The agency had taken every possible precaution in disseminating Popov's material—it had been attributed to a variety of notional sources and never pinpointed as coming from an in-place agent or originating in Austria. Scores of reports had been disseminated, some so sensitive they had been sent under an *Eyes Only* rubric to the White House and the secretaries of state and defense. Even after four years, the Popov BIGOT list showed only a handful of persons were fully informed of the details of the operation.

Despite his GRU training, his experience as a CIA agent, and Domnin's coaching, Popov continued to take avoidable chances and to cut security corners. Only a bullheaded peasant, Domnin thought, would carry on with Lyuba, hand a devastatingly revealing letter to a stranger, and dash across the street to embrace his case officer in public. Popov was stubborn, he reflected, and sentimental as well.

Across the coffee table, Popov was sulking, stung by his case officer's rebuke. For a moment, Domnin took stock of his agent. Always thickset, Popov was heavier than he had been in Vienna. His face was puffy. Obviously he had found something to do in Schwerin. Domnin suspected Popov had been drinking heavily.

"Okay, Pyotr, enough recrimination for today." Domnin smiled. "What else is it you've got on your mind?"

The tension broken, Popov managed a slight smile. The GRU transborder, or operations directorate, had five "operations points," or bases, in East Germany, he explained. Under command of General Romanovsky, the headquarters were in Stossen-Umsdorf, East Berlin. Colonel Yegerov, who had been Popov's first chief in Vienna, was Romanovsky's operations chief. Now Yegerov was being transferred from Berlin to Moscow. Before he left, Yegerov toured the bases to say goodbye and to allow the base chiefs to check the data that would be included in the comprehensive operations report Yegerov was required to prepare before turning his job over to his successor.

Schwerin was the last stop on the farewell tour and Yegerov had spent most of the day closeted with Colonel Ivanov, chief of the Schwerin base. There would be a farewell dinner that night but, because he was duty officer, Popov would miss it. Not that he minded. Popov disliked the fat and pompous Yegerov who he felt had ridden him too hard in Vienna. As far as Popov knew, the only black marks in his dossier were the fitness reports Yegerov had written in Vienna.

By the time Yegerov finished his conference with Ivanov, Popov was already seated at the night-duty officer's desk outside Ivanov's office. Yegerov stopped at the desk and asked brusquely how security was at the base. Surprised, Popov explained that the GRU offices in the headquarters of a Soviet infantry division were protected by the perimeter defense of the entire division. In that case, Yegerov said, perhaps he could leave his briefcase in Popov's care. Yegerov was not popular with his case officers, but the occasion of his departure was an excellent excuse for a celebration. From his experience at other bases, Yegerov knew the dinner would be a wet one.

With ostentatious concern, Popov took the briefcase and, holding it at arm's length, delicately slipped it into the safe reserved for the duty officer. Yegerov smiled, gave Popov a mock salute, and strode out of the office, Colonel Ivanov hustling along at his side.

It was after midnight before Popov locked the door of the office and opened the briefcase. There was only one document of interest. A large sheet of graph paper contained Yegerov's notes and a schematic presentation of each of the five transborder intelligence bases.

Yegerov's chart listed the case officers assigned to each section within each unit in East Germany. Alongside the table of organization, the intelligence collection tasks assigned to each section and case officer had been carefully typed. Although the case officers were referred to by workname, or pseudonym, on the chart, Yegerov had not trusted his ability to remember the true names. In the upper corner of the schematic, he had clipped a sheet of note paper giving the true name of each of his case officers and supervisors.

It took two hours, Popov said, but he had made an exact copy of the chart on five sheets of flimsy paper filched from a secretary's desk. He handed Domnin an oblong packet of tightly folded papers.

"How'd you conceal this?" Domnin asked.

"That wasn't any problem. When I finished copying, I opened the seam in the lining of my jacket—in the left armpit—and slipped the packet into the sleeve, between the lining and the cloth. In the taxi, I cut a slit in the lining at the wrist and pulled the papers out. It wasn't difficult."

"At least it worked," Domnin sniffed. He knew agents had to improvise, but Popov's matter-of-fact account of having smuggled the potentially lethal papers into West Berlin irritated him.

As they studied the details on the creased papers, Domnin continued to ponder Popov's casual story. Before they were through, Domnin knew that even if Popov had had the time to discuss the problem, Domnin could not have improved on Popov's solution.

By the time Domnin and Popov had finished the night's work and climbed into the car, it was almost midnight. As the car slowed, a few blocks from the U-Bahn station where the agent would be dropped, Domnin turned to Popov.

"Pyotr Semyonovich," he said. "Now more than ever you've got to be careful. No more risks. We can't take these chances. Unless you've got an ironbound excuse, I don't want you to come in from Schwerin until you are transferred to Berlin. It's too tricky for you. We can wait until you get here."

Popov stared out of the rear window. A light rain had begun to fall and the dark streets seemed deserted.

"You're right. I just wanted to give you something to make up for the time we lost while I was back home. I don't know what Yegerov did with that briefcase while he was at the other bases, but if you take any action on the basis of that chart, it could kick back on me. Chances are no one else had it overnight."

"Don't worry about that," Domnin said. "It will take weeks before we have sorted it all out. We won't take any action that could possibly be tracked back to you."

Popov pushed the car door open and bent over to shake hands. Domnin hesitated for a moment and pulled the Russian to him in a clumsy embrace. *"Gib acht auf dich,* Pyotr Semyonovich," he whispered. "Be careful."

Popov pulled his coat collar up and strode down the dark street.

The GRU transborder bases had never impressed Western counterintelligence as much of a security threat. Most of the transborder agents detected in West Germany were of a uniformly low level. Only a few were in a position to report intelligence that might not almost as readily have been clipped from newspapers and military publications. It was impossible to tell from the chart which targets the GRU had penetrated, but based on Popov's comments on his session with Yegerov, there seemed to be a wide gap between the GRU's objectives as spelled out on the chart and the actual achievements of the GRU bases.

Still, as one counterintelligence officer studied the papers, doubt flickered in his mind. How could Yegerov, an experienced operative, be so foolhardy as to entrust an unlocked briefcase with such a document to a case officer, *any* case officer? The briefcase could have been rigged to show if it had been opened. If the document had been brushed with "tell-tale" (a powder used by private detectives and quite invisible on white paper), examination under ultraviolet light would immediately show if been handled.

If it was a trap, Popov had been taken in. But no such trap would have been laid unless he was under suspicion. If Popov was suspect, would the GRU have given him an assignment in Germany, whence he could presumably escape to the West? Would the GRU have been willing to sacrifice quite so much merely to snare a mole? Years later, some counterespionage specialists who studied the case thought that even such a hecatomb would not have been too high a price to pay for the discovery of a penetration agent and his destruction.

19
THE CATBIRD SEAT

When Popov was assigned to the illegals support section of the GRU *Opergruppe* in East Berlin it was as if he had stepped into another dimension of operations, into a clearing house for the most sensitive agents in the GRU stable. His job would be to process illegal agents transiting East Berlin en route to their assignments abroad.

Soviet illegal operations are based on one of the most casually accepted privileges of life in an open society—the free movement of individuals from one country to another. Millions of tourists, business people, immigrants, and refugees annually stream across the borders of noncommunist countries. In the United States today, seven million visitors and more than four hundred thousand immigrants are admitted annually. The camouflage offered by this migratory mass is the essential ingredient of Soviet illegal operations.

Once past the customs barriers of his unwitting hosts, a Soviet illegal disappears like a diamond dropped into an inkwell.

Soviet foreign intelligence was born in 1921, when Lenin charged the Fourth Department (*Glavnoe Razvedyvatel'noe Upravlenie*, the Chief Intelligence Directorate, or GRU) of the Soviet General Staff with responsibility for espionage and counterespionage abroad. (Although the Cheka, the great-grandparent of the KGB, was formed in 1917, it was at first an internal security organization and did not begin formally to collect intelligence abroad until the 1920s.) The first GRU operatives sent from the USSR were picked from among the most competent of the young activists who had grown up in the European underground communist movements and who immigrated to the Soviet Union on the heels of the Russian revolution. These men and women, few of whom were Russian by birth, had learned conspiracy in the later days of the communist fight to overthrow the Russian regime. Smuggling, illegal border crossing, and the use of false documents were skills they had learned as adolescents.

At the outset these operatives, more nearly agents than intelligence officers, lived with their families in the USSR and conducted their operations like traveling salespeople on long clandestine business trips through their territory. As Soviet spying became more extensive, these commuters found they were spending more time traveling than they were in Moscow. This, and the risk of repeated border crossings, mandated a change. A cadre of illegals, some with their families, quietly took up residence abroad.

Utilizing forged identity papers and passports, these agents avoided open contact with such Soviet diplomatic and trade offices as were in existence. The sympathy that the various national communist parties, labor movements, and liberal well-wishers had for the struggling Soviet Union motivated scores of well-placed persons to play a quiet role in the Soviet experiment by contributing intelligence and scientific data to the shadowy, but romantic illegal representatives of "the future." Such men as Walter Krivitsky, Ignaz Reiss, Alexander Ulanovsky, and Richard Sorge—only Ulanovsky was born in Russia—were gifted intelligence organizers and created spectacularly successful agent operations in the countries bordering the Soviet Union, in Western Europe, China, and Japan. Operations in the United States came a little later. It was 1927 before two illegals, Alfred Tilton, a Latvian, and Lydia Stahl, a Russian émigrée, began seriously to organize espionage in the United States.

As the USSR gradually began to normalize its relations with the capitalist powers and to establish embassies and other official installations abroad, the GRU and KGB undertook to assign personnel to these offices under official or "legal" cover. A careful distinction was made between the legal, or embassy-based *rezidenturas*, and the "illegal" apparat staffed by operatives using false papers and having no apparent contact with the Soviet Union.

Between the two world wars, Soviet illegals were widely deployed and highly successful. Many remained in place when World War II broke out, but the attrition was high. Leopold Trepper, a Polish Jew, was sent to Belgium on the eve of the war. Although Stalin had planned for him to organize an agent network in Great Britain, he was belatedly directed to work against Nazi Germany. After recruiting spies who reached the upper levels of the Nazi war machine, Trepper was betrayed and captured in France in 1942. While under arrest this wily agent engaged in a sophisticated counterespionage struggle with his captors. After ingratiating himself with the German intelligence officers who thought they had doubled him against the Soviets, Trepper contrived to pass the Moscow center a detailed message describing his arrest and the fate of the members of his network. He continued to play this double game until, after almost a year in captivity, he escaped. He remained at large in Paris until the city was liberated in August 1944. Then he made his first serious mistake: he returned to Moscow.

There was no hero's welcome for this dedicated anti-Nazi in Moscow. Stalin could not forget that Trepper had been sent to Belgium by General Jan Berzin, an old Bolshevik and one of the Soviet Union's great masters of espionage. Berzin and most of his staff were among the senior intelligence officers struck down by Stalin in 1938. Trepper survived ten years in Soviet labor camps before he was "rehabilitated" by Khrushchev. He returned to his native Poland, but could not tolerate the anti-Semitic policies of that government. After a long struggle—at one time his two sons engaged in hunger strikes, one in front of the United Nations building in New York, the other in Copenhagen—Trepper was finally permitted to emigrate to England in 1973. This authentic hero of the wartime underground died in 1981.

Sandor Rado, a Hungarian cartographer who settled in Switzerland in 1936, established three clandestine radio transmitters which were used to send to Moscow the highest level military intelligence smuggled into Switzerland from Germany. In 1943 Swiss federal police arrested the radio operators and Rado was forced to run for cover. With the illegal net wiped out, the Soviet General Staff lost access to its single most precious source of intelligence on the German armies in the East. Rado survived the war and left Paris for Moscow on the same plane with Trepper. In Cairo, however, Rado had second thoughts and sought asylum with the British. A few days later he changed his mind again and went on to Moscow. He too served a long stretch in Soviet labor camps, but was eventually rehabilitated and died recently in Budapest.

In Japan, Richard Sorge, who operated under his true name, accurately predicted the German invasion of the USSR in 1941. His subsequent reporting on Japanese military planning was sufficiently precise to convince the chronically paranoid Stalin that the Japanese did not plan to attack the USSR, a fact that permitted the General Staff to move enough divisions from the China border area to stem the German invasion before Leningrad and Moscow could be taken.

With few of its illegals having survived the war in place, and those who did under suspicion of having collaborated with the Nazis or—even worse—the Western Allies, Soviet intelligence began slowly to reorganize its illegals program in 1945. In the early postwar period, illegals were selected from among the most capable Soviet intelligence officers—Colonel Abel being an outstanding example. But as Western counterintelligence began to focus on the work of the Soviet legal apparatus and to impede the activity of embassy-based *rezidenturas,* the Russians, feeling the pinch, began to expand the illegal apparat. It soon found that it needed more illegals, particularly operatives who had some previous knowledge of the areas in which they were to be assigned, than could be found among Russian-born staff-personnel. The GRU and KGB had no choice but to use trusted foreign-born agents as well as native officers for illegal assignments. Today, as in the pre-World War II era, a Soviet illegal can be either a Soviet intelligence officer or an agent of any nationality who is sent from the USSR under a false identity and with forged documents to support his cover legend. In England, Conon Molody posed as Gordon Lonsdale, a Canadian businessman. Morris and Lona Cohen, both Americans, ran his elaborate signal center while documented as New Zealanders.

Whatever their status within Soviet intelligence—agent or intelligence officer on special assignment—illegals follow the same pattern of operation. After the requisite months—more often years—of training, the illegal is issued a forged passport and the documents necessary to support it. This first set of documents, called "traveling papers," is used only to permit the agent to slip through the communist curtain and into the West. Once abroad, the illegal moves cautiously through one or two European countries, getting his feet on the ground and satisfying himself that he has not attracted any suspicion. When this first phase of the assignment has been completed, some illegals trigger a prearranged meeting with a member of an official cover *rezidentura*—France, Switzerland, and Italy are the favored areas of these meetings. At this rendezvous the agent swaps his traveling papers for a passport and a packet of documents that establish his permanent identity and will permit him to take up residence in his target area. Some agents enter their assigned countries

before exchanging their travel documents for their permanent identity papers.

Once in place the illegal quietly settles into a modest and inconspicuous occupation, usually a form of self-employment which will
give him the maximum freedom of movement. As soon as he is hun-
kered down and has a plausible source of income, he is ready to go to
work.

Protected by this all but unbreakable cover, illegals are frequently
used to handle agents too sensitive to risk placing in contact with
case officers under legal cover in an embassy. Other illegals serve primarily as communications experts, conduits for information being
funneled to Moscow from agents in place. Occasionally illegals
whose cover gives them natural access to potential candidates are
permitted to make recruitments, but this is rare. Each illegal is
unique and represents too much of an equity to risk in anything as
chancy as a recruitment that might go wrong. Official cover intelligence officers, on the other hand, are easily interchangeable if compromised.

The Soviet investment in each illegal agent is immense. Most are
subjected to years of training in conspiracy, clandestine communications, and the language and customs of their area of assignment. Illegals must also learn a trade or skill at which they can work while
abroad. Employment is not only for cover—Moscow prefers its illegal operatives to pay their own way. In England, Gordon Lonsdale
bought into a pinball machine business. His communications man,
Morris Cohen, was a rare-book dealer specializing in Americana
and, ironically, books on locks.

Agents who have not lived outside the USSR are often given experience under illegal cover in one of the countries that will figure
in the legend they will use when finally they reach their target area.
Khokhlov lived in Bucharest for four years, immersing himself in
the Rumanian scene, shedding his Russian mannerisms and learn-
ing to keep cover. Bragin was getting business experience in Vienna. Another illegal, Yuri Loginov, spent more than seven years
prepping for what was to have been an assignment in the United
States. After mastering a brace of disparate skills—bookkeeping
and welding—he was also tutored as a travel writer. Longinov was
then sent on a trip to Egypt and South Africa to flesh out his cover
and to acclimatize himself to Western life. Despite his training,
Loginov stubbed his toe in South Africa, where he was uncovered
and arrested.

But time and money are not all that is at risk when an illegal begins work. If an illegal is detected, careful surveillance can lead counterintelligence operatives to the agents in place he may be controlling.

Since there is no easy means of sifting illegals from the millions of tourists, aliens, and immigrants—not to mention native and naturalized citizens—the detection of these agents is one of the most taxing counterintelligence problems. In some cases an uncovered agent will lead counterintelligence investigators to an illegal—just as the Austrian took case officers to Bragin in Vienna. Other illegals have defected, as did Reinno Hayhanen, Colonel Abel's radio man.

The arrest of Colonel Abel in New York in June 1957 had finally alerted J. Edgar Hoover to the threat posed by illegals. But like other Western security agencies, the FBI had no ready means of spotting illegals. There were hundreds of thousands of aliens circulating legally in the United States at any given moment and estimates of the number of *illegal* aliens today ranges from six to a staggering twelve million. Not that aliens, legal or otherwise, are the problem—Soviet intelligence is known to prefer its illegal agents to pose as naturalized or native citizens of the country they are working in. It seemed likely that most of the Soviet illegal agents operating in the United States were documented as recent immigrants, or, like Abel, as native citizens. Without a tip, or lead, there didn't seem to be any means of identifying suspects. FBI counterintelligence specialists needed only to step into a New York taxi to be reminded that the accents which in some areas might trip up an impostor were a big-city commonplace. Half the cabdrivers in the city seemed to speak with thick, Eastern European accents.

Hoover would not admit it, but the fact was that he had to rely on CIA for tips on Soviet illegals.

Popov's assignment put him in the catbird seat. If there had been any doubt about the importance of his new job, it was resolved when he called Domnin for an emergency meeting in West Berlin. The first agent he was assigned to handle was headed for a permanent assignment in New York City.

20
THE WOMAN FROM MOSCOW

Even if she had not been the only woman on the Soviet military transport plane from Moscow, Popov told Domnin, he would have recognized Margarita Tairova anywhere. She was about thirty-five and unmistakably Russian in appearance.

When Popov learned that he was to be her escort officer while she was in East Berlin, he had made an unscheduled visit to West Berlin to alert Domnin. All he could report was that he had been assigned to escort and dispatch Magarita Nikolievska Tairova, a GRU illegal who was going to New York to join her husband, also an illegal. As escort officer, it would be Popov's job to shepherd Tairova through the last-minute briefings, give her documents a final check, and even to inspect her clothing once again to make sure that there were no tell-tale labels. He would also audit and inspect the cash she would be carrying.

Tairova's travel documents, Popov explained, would be brought to East Berlin by her Moscow case officer, who would travel separately. In Berlin, a few hours before her departure, a "cobbler" would apply the various entry and exit stamps necessary to document her story—that she was an American who had been in Europe on a brief vacation—to the passport. In the early days, Soviet intelligence referred to false passports as "shoes." Since then, documents technicians have been known as "cobblers."

As soon as Tairova's final briefings were complete, Popov told Domnin, he would escort her to Tempelhof airport in West Berlin. There, from a discreet distance, he would watch her embark on a Pan American flight to Frankfurt, West Germany. Only Tairova's Moscow case officer would know the name she would use in New York and the role she would play in GRU operations. Unless someone broke security, he added, all that he might be able to report would be the name on her travel papers.

Tairova had been in East Berlin several days before Popov could free himself for a second session with Domnin in West Berlin.

As yet, neither Domnin nor Popov had become accustomed to the meeting arrangements in West Berlin. In Vienna, an open city, all Popov had to do was to telephone Domnin and indicate the time he would appear. Then, he could take a streetcar or taxi to a spot near the safe house and walk a few blocks. In Berlin he had to travel on the S-Bahn from East Berlin, get off at the first stop, and call on the "Max" telephone to announce his presence. Then, he would take another train to the See Ufer Bahnhof, where Domnin would pick him up in a German-plated car driven by a case officer. Domnin was not yet used to the lively driving of the West Berliners and the last thing he wanted was an accident with Popov in the car. Even though the case officer was an old Berlin hand, Domnin would not let him drive more than twenty-five miles an hour.

This complicated procedure took time, and the trip across the sector boundary bothered Popov. The differences between East and West Berlin were more obvious than anything Popov had seen in Austria. Unlike the Soviet sector in Vienna, East Berlin was a separate city, a communist city, administered by the East German government operating in the shadow of the Soviet occupation forces. Although the East German and Russian security police rarely checked documents on the S-Bahn—and Popov could have slipped through a control by flashing his GRU credentials—the passage made him nervous. In East Germany the Russian presence was deliberately obvious, even threatening, a reminder that any more outbreaks such as had occurred in 1953 would be put down with as much force as might be required. It seemed to underline the risks Popov was taking in meeting his case officer.

Domnin had sensed this, but he was not prepared for Popov's mood when he came to give his second report on Tairova.

A moment after Popov had eased into the back seat of the car beside Domnin, he glared at the back of the case officer-driver and mimed a question.

"He's an American, one of our case officers," Domnin assured him. "He doesn't speak a word of Russian, but he's okay. Don't worry."

"Sure," Popov said. "That's just what they think about me in Karls-horst. They think I'm all right, that there's no security problem. That's what Tairova thinks too. But not everybody is what they seem to be. You know that just as well as I do."

It was the first time since Popov had complained about Alex, the émigré agent first sent to meet him in Vienna, that he had questioned CIA security.

"How do you know anyone is straight?" Popov asked, staring at the driver's back. Popov slumped back in the seat and pulled his hat down over his forehead. It was after 7 P.M. and there was little traffic on the dark streets.

"What's the matter, Pyotr Semyonovich? Has something happened?" Domnin asked.

"Nothing's happened. Maybe nothing will. But if it does, it'll be too late for me." Popov laughed. "If they catch me, they'll need a squad of lieutenant generals to sort it out. Not to decide if I'm guilty, just to figure out how many pieces to cut me into."

"We can talk about it when we get inside," Domnin said as the case officer turned off the street into the open garage beneath the safe house. It was a comfortable villa on the Litzenseestrasse.

Domnin had never seen Popov so jumpy and decided not to ask about Tairova until Popov brought up the subject. They had settled down to a cold supper before Popov began to talk about the agent. She was, he said, a long-time GRU office employee in Moscow, a clerk in the central archive. In 1948 she had married Igor Arsentiye-vich Tairov, a GRU officer about to begin training as an illegal. From what Tairova had said, Popov thought Tairov had already been on an illegal assignment in England, but had no idea what name or cover had been used. He did know that Tairov's pseudonym was "Zhakob" and that Tairova was worried about him—not that he might be ar-rested but that without her calming influence he might find big-city life too much to his liking. Zhakob was a good agent, she assured Popov, but he drank too much and couldn't keep his hands off other women. As worried as she was about her own safety, Tairova's pre-occupation seemed to be keeping her husband on a short tether.

As escort officer, Popov explained, one of his responsibilities was to quiet the anxieties of nervous agents. "I don't know how much Zhakob drinks, but the only nerve balm Tairova uses is vodka. She drinks like a sergeant on payday."

The GRU operations plan, Popov said, called for Tairova to enter the United States posing as Mary Grodnik, an American tourist returning from a month's vacation in Europe. After a few days at a New York hotel, Tairova would shed the Grodnik identity and become Florence Grochowska, ostensibly the daughter of a Polish American family in Cleveland. As soon as she had assumed the Grochowska identity, Tairova was to start looking for a job as a manicurist.

According to Tairova, Popov said, she had spent several months in Vienna, posing as a Polish refugee while she completed a course qualifying her as a manicurist and beautician. Tairova's Moscow-based case officer assumed that Tairova would readily find work in a New York beauty salon. Popov was less certain.

"She can't even put on her own makeup," he said. "She looks like a Kiev housewife in Leningrad for the first time. I'd spot her in a minute."

The final step in Tairova's settling down in New York would be her meeting with Tairov, her husband. According to Popov, the meeting was prearranged. Ostensibly it would be a casual encounter, but romance would blossom and they would "marry" as soon as plausible. Although the Tairovs had been man and wife for almost ten years, the new marriage license would be a useful document to support their legend.

Popov had examined the passport Tairova would use for the trip to the United States. It had been issued to Mary Grodnik, an American from Chicago. Popov did not know whether it was a valid passport, obtained by an agent posing as Grodnik, or one that had been lost by a tourist and "washed" in the GRU documents laboratory in Moscow. Technicians can remove all traces of writing in a passport and in effect "reissue" it with a new photograph and the particulars of the agent who will use it. "It's a good job," Popov said. "It would probably pass anything but a laboratory test."

The Grochowska passport, Social Security card, and other documents would be hidden in a concealment device built into Tairova's luggage. Packed in a separate concealment device behind the mirror in her cosmetics case were Tairova's emergency funds, twenty thousand dollars.

Domnin was surprised. Usually Soviet intelligence forbade an agent to cross a border while carrying—no matter how carefully concealed—two sets of identification documents. If Tairova's concealment device was spotted, the large sum of money might be explained. There could be no explanation for two sets of documents. For all of Kriatov's concentration on security, the GRU cut corners in illegals' work just as it did in the low-level cross-border operations Popov had been working on in Schwerin.

"That money is supposed to last her for a year," Popov said. "What I can't understand is why they gave it to her in one-hundred-dollar bills. I don't know how much money people carry around New York, but I don't think too many people use one-hundred-dollar bills every time they want to buy a bottle of vodka."

Domnin nodded. "Your people are just lazy. Big notes are easier to conceal, but they could be conspicuous in New York."

Russians prepare currency for concealment by ironing the notes flat and leaving them in a book press for a few days. A wad of ironed and pressed bank notes half an inch thick could be a small fortune, four times the amount of cash Tairova was carrying.

That was all Popov could tell about Tairova. "She drinks too much, but she's all right. All she wants is to be with her husband. From the way she talks, I think she'd rather be back in Moscow than going to New York. She said the first time she sees Tairov look at another woman, she'll grab him by the hair and drag him back home, no matter what the GRU thinks."

Popov paused for a moment and pushed at the food on his plate. Looking up at Domnin across the coffee table, he said, "I don't know why they have to mix simple people like her up in this business. It's bad enough for the rest of us. But at least we know what we're involved in. She's a simple woman. If she hadn't married Zhakob, she'd be typing in an office somewhere and worrying about getting on the list for a decent apartment."

He took a forkful of smoked sturgeon and washed it down with a long swallow of vodka.

"There's one other thing," Popov told Domnin as they prepared to leave the safe house. "You've got to promise me there won't be any surveillance of Tairova along the route. When she leaves Berlin she's going to Frankfurt. Then to Paris for a few days. This is just part of her legend—an American tourist who has been on a European trip.

She won't be doing anything at all, just sightseeing. Then she'll take a plane to New York. It's her first assignment. She thinks New York is like Berlin during the war and that your people are the Gestapo. She'll be seeing surveillance everywhere. If you try to follow her she'll spot it for sure."

"We won't do anything in Europe," Domnin said, "but how can we identify Tairov unless we follow her in New York? If we don't have a tail on her when she leaves the airport, we might lose her altogether and never spot Tairov."

Popov shook his head. "I don't know. But whatever you do you've got to be careful. Maybe you can follow her to the hotel. But you've got to be discreet. If she spots anything it could blow back on me. Aside from Kriatov and the case officer from Moscow, I'm the only one who could have warned you."

"Okay," Domnin said. "I can promise that we won't take any action in Europe. But we'll have to follow her in New York, at least until we can identify her husband."

"I guess that's all right. But tell your people that my head's in a noose. It's one thing talking about military equipment. But these damned illegals are too sensitive. Sometimes I think I'd have been better off to stay in Schwerin. This may be too much for me."

As they finished supper Popov turned again to Tairova. There was a question that he had not wanted to raise with her. He had scoured a map of the eastern United States but could not find the city where Tairova was to rendezvous with Tairov.

"Where," he asked, "is this *Jonkers*?"

Yonkers, Domnin explained, is a suburb of New York City.

It was almost midnight before they left the safe house and climbed into the back seat of the car.

"I take it," Domnin said, "that Lyuba doesn't know you've come to Berlin?"

Popov jumped; Domnin had touched a nerve. "Not exactly. I told you I had written her from Schwerin to say I was in Germany. The other day I wrote to say I was being transferred to Berlin."

"You're out of your mind, Pyotr. Is she still working for the *rezidentura* in Vienna?"

"I don't know. They dropped most of the agents on the Yugoslav line. But if she's still working, Maximenkov will be her case officer. He's a mean bastard."

"What are the chances she'll tell him that she's heard from you?" Domnin asked.

"She wouldn't do that. She's clever enough to keep quiet about us. She wouldn't even work for them at all if she could get a job as a secretary."

Domnin remained silent as the car wove through the streets leading to the See Bahnhof.

"You know," Popov said, "if *you* gave her a job in Vienna, there wouldn't be any more trouble. She's a good secretary if she could only find a job. Can't you take her on in the embassy or some office?"

"You damned well can't be serious," Domnin expostulated. "How do you think it would look if the embassy hired a Yugoslav refugee who can't speak English and is a GRU agent? Don't you think Maximenkov might smell something if she just walked into an embassy job?" Domnin paused. "Does anyone suspect you were sleeping with her?"

Popov shook his head. "Maybe there was some talk about it. But I'm not the only one; plenty of case officers have girl friends on the payroll."

"You know what I've told you, Pyotr. You've had plenty of chances to drop her," Domnin said. "You've got problems enough without keeping up with that woman. Sooner or later they'll find out. Now it's more important than ever that you keep your nose clean. There's no telling what will happen if they get wind of her."

Popov shook hands with Domnin and stepped quickly out of the car. Without looking back, he hurried along the side street, retracing for a few hundred feet the route the car had taken. It would lead him to Muellerstrasse and then to the station where he would take the U-Bahn back to East Berlin. By walking back along the route they had driven, Popov could satisfy himself there had been no surveillance behind them.

As the driver pulled the black sedan away from the curb, Domnin turned and looked back down the street. The soft illumination from the overhead street lamps cast heavy shadows under the rain-drenched trees. The street was empty. Popov had vanished.

It had been the most difficult meeting Domnin could remember. Now that Popov had given the details on Tairova, the FBI would have no choice but to tail her from the moment she arrived in New York until she met her husband. If the jittery woman spotted the surveillance, Popov would be in jeopardy. But the Bureau was a professional service—operating on its own terrain, it should be able to tail an inexperienced Russian agent without being detected. This, he reckoned, might even be less of a problem than Popov's heedless relationship with Lyuba. Bad enough that he had made a mistress of an agent—but he had remained in contact with her. Just by keeping Lyuba informed of his whereabouts, Popov was risking his future. A flicker of indiscretion on her part could cause Popov's recall and probably his expulsion from the GRU. Although the agent had not admitted it, Domnin assumed that Popov might even have invited Lyuba to visit him in Berlin.

Slumped in the back seat, Domnin pulled off his hat and closed his eyes. If Popov had not looked so bad, he mused, he might have felt better about the meeting. But the agent was puffy with fat. His flushed face and blotched complexion could have come from the alcohol he was consuming. Certainly the boozing could account for the tension, possibly even for the high blood pressure that Domnin guessed plagued his agent. But, as he had reassured Harvey, Popov was physically tough. Life in the village and four years of combat had hardened him enough, Domnin thought, to cope with these pressures. And Popov had had a lifetime of practice in pushing unpleasant facts to one side.

The immediate problem, Domnin realized, was the new job. When Popov moved from Schwerin and the easygoing life of the Tactical Intelligence officer, he had been thrust into the inner sanctum of Soviet operations in East Berlin. Although it was ostensibly easy for him to cross into West Berlin to meet Domnin, the trip obviously created new tension and reminded the agent of the gulf between safety there and the risks he was running in East Berlin. The work in the illegals section was more intellectually demanding than anything he had known and the augmented security precautions fretted him.

Popov was accustomed to the security practices in the *rezidentura* in Vienna and at the base in Schwerin. Once mastered, these cumbersome and time-consuming procedures had become a habit. The few pages of notes that constituted the only record he was allowed to retain on his cases and the leads he was pursuing were kept in a steel workbox, boldly labeled with his pseudonym "Panev." The workbox was about the size of an attaché case, with a hinged top and built-in-lock. Whenever a case officer left the office, he locked the box and carried it to the windowless, vaulted signal center and file room where the code clerks worked. After ringing for a clerk, he pushed the heavy box through a shuttered slot cut in the heavy steel door of the vault. It would be kept in the vault until his return. A busy case officer might go through this routine six times a day.

There was another tiresome precaution. Before leaving Moscow each officer was issued a heavy brass seal. Like the gold and onyx signets that dangled from the watch chains of Victorian gentlemen, each one was engraved with a unique, cabalistic design. Before an officer left his desk for the night, he smeared the lock on the workbox with melted wax and authenticated it with his personal seal. Only then could the box be passed through the slot for overnight safe-keeping.

When an officer prepared a dispatch or cable he wrote it by hand and carried it to his section chief for release. All scrap paper and drafts were attached to the final copy and destroyed by the communications center personnel as soon as Moscow had acknowledged receipt of the document. No copies were kept in the *rezidentura*. If a cable or dispatch were needed for review, a précis would be telegraphed to the *rezidentura* from Moscow. The security precautions which forbid case officers to keep detailed records in the *rezidentura* may account, at least in part, for the gross mistakes Soviet intelligence frequently makes.

Popov was accustomed to these routines, but in the illegals section, security was even tighter. In Vienna and Schwerin he had shared an office with other case officers. Although shoptalk was theoretically forbidden, the atmosphere was easy, there was always time for a joke, an opportunity to ventilate the frustrations of operational work. Scalding hot tea, sweetened with jam, and coffee were always available.

In East Berlin, Popov, like the other illegals support officers, had a private office and worked alone, the door always shut. No one but Kriatov was authorized to enter without knocking and allowing time for him to put all of the paper on his desk into the workbox and snap it shut.

In Schwerin, Popov seldom saw his chief more than once a week. In Berlin, Kriatov bobbed into the office four or five times a day. He was as familiar with the work and knew the details of each operation as well as any of the case officers. Popov had reason to be jittery.

"Take a roundabout route, but let's get back to the office," Domnin said. "I've got to brief Harvey."

21
INFORM THE FBI

For the first time since he had been chief of the Berlin office, Bill Harvey had drafted an urgent cable that he did not want to send to Washington. When he released the cable on his desk and Popov's latest report reached Washington, CIA would have to pass it to the FBI. Harvey knew this could mean trouble. J. Edgar Hoover ran his own show and nobody, not even a president, could tell him how to do it. Almost everyone who had tried to work in liaison with the FBI knew that Hoover was a cop, a law-enforcement man with little understanding of intelligence, and even less of counterespionage. The fact that Popov was an agent of CIA, the outfit Hoover blamed for thwarting his ambition to have the FBI made responsible for foreign espionage as well as internal security, only made matters more complicated.

If Hoover did not appreciate the importance of keeping Popov securely in place, he might act unilaterally and simply arrest the two illegals. Russian agents in the United States were the FBI's exclusive responsibility. CIA could recommend to Hoover how the Tairov case should be handled, but the ultimate decision would rest with the unpredictable FBI director.

Still, the cable had to be sent. As Harvey pored over the draft, he remembered a story he had heard early in World War II about the trouble Hoover had caused for another agent. The irony was almost incredible: that agent's name was also Popov.

Dusko Popov, a well-born Yugoslav, was a key double agent in the British operations against German intelligence in World War II. In 1940, when he realized a German intelligence officer was maneuvering

188

to recruit him, Popov approached the British embassy in Belgrade. A British case officer, impressed by the deep anti-Nazi conviction beneath the man-about-town exterior of the young Serb, told him to accept German recruitment. Popov's first assignment for the Nazis required him to develop business cover in London. Once there, the Germans assumed his social connections—not quite as good as the Germans thought, but he had put the Duke of York up for membership in a Yugoslav yacht club—would give access to the upper brackets of the British establishment.

With the help of both the British security service and MI-6, Tricycle, as the British came to call him, went to work. Within a few months he had established himself as one of the most productive German agents in England and had "recruited" a number of subsources—all supplied by the security service (MI-5).

Tricycle so impressed his German case officers that in 1941 he was ordered to move to the United States. As the Germans explained, the *Abwehr*—German military intelligence—had recruited a number of agents in the United States. The hitch was that all the agents were known Nazi sympathizers, many were members of the German-American Bund. Several spies had been arrested and Admiral Canaris, the *Abwehr* chief, expected more arrests to follow. It would be Tricycle's job to recruit a *new* network of spies, each carefully compartmented from the others and none having any connection with the American Nazi movement. In effect, Tricycle was to duplicate his successful mission in England.

When the Germans were unable to suggest a plausible cover, Tricycle used his connections to wangle a position in the Yugoslav propaganda office in New York.

British intelligence representatives in Washington had explained Tricycle's mission to J. Edgar Hoover and attempted to show him how a double agent could deceive and confuse the Germany spy masters. Whether Hoover understood this or not was moot—he had agreed grudgingly to Tricycle's coming to the United States. Once he was in the United States, Hoover specified, Tricycle would operate under FBI control.

At Tricycle's last meeting with his German case officer in Lisbon in June 1941, he was given a long list of Nazi intelligence requirements. Included was a page of detailed questions on naval and air force installations at Pearl Harbor. Before he settled down in New York, the case officer said, Tricycle was to go to Hawaii. Tricycle protested. Not even a well-heeled playboy could explain a sudden decision to take a holiday quite so far from New York. He would make the trip in the fall.

Tricycle's German control was adamant. The *Abwehr* had accepted an urgent request from the Japanese to supply as much information as possible after his arrival in the United States. Tricycle had no choice but to agree with the case officer's demand.

Before leaving for New York, Tricycle gave the list of German requirements to his British case officer for transmission to London. It was in London that British intelligence blundered.

Instead of sending a representative directly to President Roosevelt or to the State Department, they assumed that, when Tricycle gave the questionnaire to Hoover, the message would be clear. Certainly the pointed questions, and the urgency with which the *Abwehr* insisted that Tricycle go to Hawaii, should have convinced any competent intelligence analyst that the Japanese were planning an attack on Pearl Harbor.

As Sir John Masterman, chief of the British deception planning organization, has said,* Tricycle's questionnaire contained a "sombre . . . warning of the subsequent attack on Pearl Harbor." He added, "Obviously it was for the Americans to make their appreciation and to draw their deductions from the questionnaire rather than for us to do so. Nonetheless, with our fuller knowledge of the [Tricycle] case . . . we ought to have stressed its importance more than we did." A considerable understatement, and a brave admission, but the fact remains that the questionnaire was given to Hoover by Tricycle on 20 August 1941, almost four months before the Japanese attack on Pearl Harbor. The original text is in British records and a photocopy appears in Tricycle's book.†

Tricycle arrived in New York with forty thousand dollars supplied by the *Abwehr*. In keeping with the style of life he had always enjoyed, he rented a penthouse apartment on Park Avenue, bought a flashy red convertible, and picked up with a former girl friend, a fashion model he had known in Europe.

Hoover was aghast. Not only had perfidious Albion saddled him with a Nazi agent, but the man was a moral delinquent as well.

---

*Sir John Masterman, *The Double-Cross System in the War of 1939–1945* (New York: Ballantine Books, 1982).
†Dusko Popov, *Spy/Counter Spy* (New York: Grosset & Dunlap, 1974). An exciting spy story by one of the most remarkable agents of World War II.

Following the orders given him by the British before he left for the United States, Tricycle did his best to impress the FBI with the importance of the Pearl Harbor questionnaire and the trip to Hawaii the Nazis had insisted he make. Once he had been there, Tricycle explained to an FBI contact man, he could send the Germans, and their Japanese clients, whatever deceptive reports American intelligence wished. All very well, said the FBI man, but until you have talked with Mr. Hoover personally, you are not to do anything at all. Hoover, he said, would visit New York in two or three weeks.

Unable to move his FBI case officer, Tricycle packed his girl friend into the convertible and left New York for a vacation in Florida.

Tricycle and his girl had securely stretched out on the sand before an FBI agent in a dark suit, white shirt, and snap-brim hat—the uniform Hoover required for all FBI personnel—strode across the beach. Taking Tricycle aside, the FBI man announced that in registering as man and wife at the Miami hotel, Tricycle had violated the Mann Act. If he did not send the girl packing, he would be prosecuted for having taken a woman across a state line for immoral purposes. Tricycle had heard stories of American puritanism, but could scarcely credit this announcement. Still, there was a war on in Europe, and Tricycle did not want to endanger his double-agent mission in the United States.

Okay, he said. He would drive the girl back to New York in the morning. Not at all, responded the FBI man. If Tricycle crossed one more state border with the young woman, he would face a year in prison. Tricycle bought an airline ticket for his furious paramour and drove back to New York alone.

Ten days later Tricycle was ushered into Hoover's presence in New York. It was an explosive meeting. Hoover charged Tricycle with trying to wheedle information from the FBI which he could sell to the Germans for the funds he needed to support his dissolute life. Tricycle responded by pointing out that he had been sent to the United States to establish an important German espionage network and that he had brought with him an intelligence questionnaire that seemed to show where and when the United States was going to be attacked by the Japanese. Moreover, he said, he had been vouched for by the highest echelons of British intelligence.

As Tricycle tells the story, Hoover snorted and reminded him that as yet no German agents in the United States had contacted him.

After trying once more to explain that he had been sent to establish an entirely *new* spy net, Tricycle left Hoover, still enraged. It would be up to his British friends to try to show Hoover that there was more to counterespionage than arresting low-level agents.

When the Japanese attacked Pearl Harbor on 7 December 1941 Tricycle was at sea returning from a German-sponsored espionage assignment in Latin America. After docking in New York, he asked an FBI man how the United States could have been taken by surprise at Pearl Harbor. He was told that "It shouldn't be on your mind. . . . You are a soldier. You don't ask questions. Do your job and let others do theirs." And then the FBI man told Tricycle he had "better learn to walk in step with us." As far as Tricycle was concerned, it was Hoover who was responsible for the success of the "surprise" Japanese attack on Pearl Harbor.

With the clandestine support of his British contacts—the FBI refused to supply the intelligence necessary to feed the *Abwehr*—Tricycle managed to retain the confidence of his German sponsors until, with a not very plausible excuse, he was able to return to Europe in October 1942. There he met with his German case officer and before long was again active in England. Until the German collapse in 1945, Tricycle was the *Abwehr*'s "best agent in England"—and played an important role in the Allied deception of the German high command.

When Ian Fleming worked as a headquarters staff officer in British intelligence during World War II, he learned something of Tricycle's operational exploits. He also had the good fortune to spend a night on the town with him in Lisbon, where Tricycle had gone to meet his German control. Tricycle's attraction for women, his urbane manners and casual courage, impressed Fleming. Years later, when Fleming began to write, he chose well when he modeled James Bond on the real-life Dusko Popov.

But Dusko Popov had long since retired. It was another Popov that Harvey worried about as he scrawled his signature at the bottom of the cable that would bring the FBI into the Popov operation.

AUTHOR'S NOTE:

Rumors and gossip about Tricycle's difficult relations with the FBI and the reasons for the failure of his mission in the United States were known and generally accepted by some of the intelligence officers involved in World War II deception operations. The publication of Tricycle's autobiography in 1974 seemed to lend truth to the scandal. Only since the first publication of *Mole* has fresh scholarship poked holes in Tricycle's account of his activity in the United States.

In *A Thread of Deceit*,* Nigel West helps to put Tricycle's aborted mission in the United States into *operational* focus. Along with noting some of the serious distortions of the Tricycle story as parroted by various historians, West points out that no matter how successful Tricycle was in the later stage of his espionage career, he was from the outset kept under close surveillance by the British. His apartment was bugged, and the apartment above his residence occupied by MI-5 officers. An extra bit of caution in dealing with double agents is rarely misplaced.

Thomas Troy, a CIA veteran and intelligence historian, has plowed through some thirty-one books which deal, in part at least, with Dusko Popov's relations with the FBI. In *The British Assault on J. Edgar Hoover: The Tricycle Case*,† Troy cites convincing evidence from FBI records that Popov's lurid account of his meetings with Hoover were imagined and that the FBI did in fact circulate the famous Abwehr questionnaire to the appropriate ONI and G-2 offices. There is no record of Hoover ever having met Tricycle, nor is it plausible that Director Hoover would under any circumstance have done so. Sadly, for those who like a good story, Troy notes documentary proof that the FBI took the trouble to give the sophisticated but unsuspecting Tricycle advance warning that transporting his mistress from Manhattan to Florida would be a violation of the Mann Act and might well land him in the pokey. Thus the picture of two somberly dressed, snap-brimmed, FBI puritans struggling across the sand to correct Tricycle's morals also appears to have been imagined.

Tricycle died at his home in the south of France in 1982.

*Nigel West, *A Thread of Deceit: Espionage Myths of World War II*, (Random House: New York, 1985).
†Thomas Troy, "The British Assault on J. Edgar Hoover: The Tricycle Case," International Journal of Intelligence and Counterintelligence, Vol. 3, No. 2, Intel Publishing Group Inc, Stroudsburg, Pennsylvania.

22
WALTER AND MARY

It was the first time anyone in the FBI's New York field office could remember a case being handled this way. Usually in an important operation a deputy director in Washington headquarters would telephone on a special, high-security line to alert the special agent in charge of the responsible branch in New York and to supply any background that might not have been included in the teletape message. The enciphered teletape would follow in an hour or so. In what the FBI was to call the Walter and Mary case, the coded message came first.

There was another odd thing. The teletape began with a cryptic warning: *Source Protect*. Then, wrapped in the customary jargon, the message gave the essential story. Suspect Soviet intelligence agent Margarita Nikolievska Tairova, Soviet national; aka Mary Grodnik, U.S. citizen; aka Florence Grochowska, U.S. citizen; arriving New York International Airport from Paris, France, sometime after 23 October 1957. Suspect probably traveling as Mary Grodnik. After arrival New York, suspect will meet Soviet agent, code name "Zhakob," at Broadway and Post Road, the Bronx. Tairova was to be kept under "discreet twenty-four hour surveillance." After Tairova's rendezvous with Zhakob, he was also to be put under around-the-clock observation. It was of utmost importance that Zhakob, a Soviet illegal, be identified. The teletape ended with another warning: *Source Protect*.

The FBI agent in charge of surveillance had already begun to block out a plan to cover Tairova when a senior officer in the Internal Security section telephoned to ask if the teletape message was clear. After being assured it was, he said that Mr. Hoover had instructed him to advise the New York field office that Tairova was not to be allowed out of sight of the surveillance team at any time. It was equally important, he added, that neither Tairova nor Zhakob "make"—detect—the surveillance. If the New York office needed additional surveillance support, agents could be assigned from other field offices. It was to be a maximum commitment.

When the chief of the Bucket Brigade asked how long the surveillance was to be continued he was told that from the way Mr. Hoover had reacted, Zhakob might be as important as Colonel Abel. Because it might take a long time to learn what Zhakob was doing, the surveillance could go on indefinitely. (The Bucket Brigade is FBI slang for the New York surveillance team. Any mobile surveillance is known as a "bucket job" and any agent on such a surveillance is said to be "in the bucket.")

"If it's that important," the surveillance chief said, "you'd better tell Mr. Hoover that we can spend twenty-four hours a day with the suspect for a week. Maybe a month. After that, we'll be crowding our luck. No matter how many men we use we can't keep it up indefinitely. After a while, any target will sense something—even if they don't make a single tail. They just feel it. It's even worse if they're jumpy. One tourist with a camera is all they need to be convinced they've made a tail."

After listening to a few words of sympathy from Washington, the surveillance man spoke up again. "It's worse with Russians," he said. "They've had experience. You remember it was touch and go with Abel and we were only on him for a few days."

This, he was told wryly, was a field problem.

"Okay, damn it, I'll promise you a month. But if it's really so hot, you'd better tell Mr. Hoover that there's no way in hell we can go around the clock with a suspect indefinitely and not get made."

After reminding the New York office that if Tairova was lost, there would be no way of identifying Zhakob, the caller promised to inform Mr. Hoover. There was one more thing, he added. At the first chance, a bag job was to be done on Tairova's quarters. She was known to be carrying a large sum of money and a second set of ID papers. With luck, there might be something in her luggage that would give a clue that would help to pinpoint Zhakob. Bag jobs are illegal entry operations in which a suspect's living quarters, or office, are clandestinely entered and "tossed"—searched. Compared to an around-the-clock surveillance, the bag job would be easy.

As a parting shot, the surveillance chief asked if he could be told what source it was he was supposed to protect. He could not be told, but the woman was coming from France, the information was solid, and the source was hot—he could draw his own conclusion.

"I might have known," said the surveillance man. "It could only be CIA."

"How come?"

"There's no Broadway and Post Road in the Bronx. That address is in Yonkers. Do you suppose they got any of the names straight?"

Somewhere between Hoover's office and New York, Popov's "Jonkers" had been transposed to the Bronx.

That afternoon, one of the men from the Bucket Brigade arranged for copies of the passenger manifests of all incoming flights from Europe to Idlewild International Airport to be delivered to him at the airport. For almost six weeks he studied the passenger lists, searching for Grodnik, Grochowska, Tairova, or any possible variation of these names. Passenger manifests are frequently garbled in transmission by the airlines and despite the CIA report that Tairova would travel as Mary Grodnik, the FBI would copper its bet. In a case where the Bronx got confused with Yonkers, other mistakes might have been made.

It was not until 27 November that the passenger list for Air France flight 077 from Paris to New York listed "M. Grodnik, USA." She was traveling tourist class. If flight 077 was on schedule, it would arrive at Idlewild at 8 P.M. There would be plenty of time for the Bucket Brigade to get into position.

For centuries surveillance was practiced as an art, its techniques passed from one generation of gray men to another. It was not until the twentieth century that the shadowy craft became a science employing the most advanced—usually referred to by the technicians as "state of the art"—forms of photography, electronics, radio, and all types of transportation. Today, the nondescript, gray men come like sorrows, not singly but in battalions.

New York is a pigeon's paradise. A "pigeon," or target, on the move in Manhattan can choose among subways, buses, taxis, rental cars, private vehicles, elevators, escalators, and stairways. He can scurry along crowded or empty sidewalks, duck into alleys, cross vacant lots, loiter in parks and prowl through as complex a variety of buildings, department stores, shops, museums, and churches as exists in any city.

When a tail-smart spy is trying to spot a possible surveillance, he may appear to act indecisively, even implausibly. Suddenly and without any apparent reason, he will whirl and double back on his tracks, looking into the faces of those behind him and making eye contact with as many of the crowd as he can. Any foot surveillant within a hundred feet of a clever spy who makes a series of these moves is likely to have to drop the chase. Another tactic is to seek sparsely traveled sidewalks, or open areas, where the spy can isolate himself and thus cut down the number of people he must scan if he is to glimpse a familiar silhouette or a face he has seen before.

After doubling, redoubling, and doubling his path again, an agent may board a subway at the last minute, step off at the next stop, walk slowly along the platform toward the street exit, and, at the last moment, jump back onto the train. Leaving the subway, he might enter a tall office building, take an express elevator to the first stop, step out and walk away as if headed for an office. The moment the elevator door closes behind him, he returns, pushes the button for another car, goes up two floors, steps out, and hurries to the emergency stairway. Then, he might walk ten floors down, take yet another elevator to the ground floor and adjacent subway. There he may repeat his on-again, off-again subway technique. For measure, he might stop for an hour of browsing in Macy's, Bloomingdale's, or any store with escalators, elevators, a good choice of exits, and easy access to a subway station.

The Russians call this "dry cleaning." Sometimes it works. But when the surveillance is all-out, the pigeon cannot isolate himself. The surveillance team makes its own crowd. Agents dressed as businessmen with briefcases, as messengers, tourists, idlers, housewives with easily discarded shopping bags combine to make a cross-section of the crowd to be found on any busy street, in a department store or office building. On the move, a pigeon may be convoyed by a score of surveillants, with an equally large reserve team positioned in the rear and ready to leapfrog forward if summoned.

Laid back behind the foot-soldiers is a motorized brigade, prepared to pick up the chase if the target opts for a taxi or is picked up by a passing car—a "floating contact." (Not for thirty years has a tail leaped into a taxi, flashed a badge, and told the driver to "follow that car.") In a full court press or "all skate"—as many as ten vehicles, shabby but fast and well-maintained passenger cars, taxis, trucks, motorcycles, and in good weather, a bicycle or two—might be on the street. (Now that skateboards and roller skates are common in New York, a flighty pigeon may have even more to keep an eye on.)

The coordination of this intricate activity requires a communications network almost as complex as that of a motorized battalion moving cross-country. More than one radio channel might be required to link the pocket radio sets, walkie-talkies, and the larger, more powerful radios concealed in the surveillance cars.

Tairova didn't have a chance. Spotted when she handed her passport to the immigration officer, a description flashed over the radio even before she had passed through customs. Subject is white. Height approximately five feet, four inches. Build stocky. Hair blonde. Eyes blue. No visible scars. Wearing gray tweed coat with fur trim. Black leather gloves. Beret-type hat.

Surrounded by agents toting suitcases, Tairova took an airline bus to the midtown terminal. There, after a struggle with her two bags and cosmetics case, she took a taxi to 14 East Twenty-eighth Street, the Prince George Hotel. As she walked in, an innocuous van pulled to the curb across from the hotel. On Twenty-seventh Street another vehicle was positioned to allow a clear view of the hotel's rear entrance. Backup agents waited in radio-equipped sedans spread out through the area.

Although CIA had suggested that "Grodnik" might become "Grochowska" the day after her arrival in New York, Tairova did not seem to be in a hurry to change her identity. She rose late in the morning, had breakfast in the hotel coffee shop, and strolled slowly up Fifth Avenue, apparently window-shopping. After buying a city street map at a drugstore at Grand Central Station, she took a Lexington Avenue bus back to Twenty-eighth Street.

Although Tairova appeared to be nervous, she was no more so than many American tourists encountering the bustle and traffic of New York for the first time. Oddly, she did not appear to be taking any countersurveillance precautions. Not once did she double back in her tracks. She did not appear to loiter in front of shop windows that might reflect a person behind her. Nor did she change her pace as she strode along the crowded sidewalks.

That afternoon Tairova walked to Macy's where, after considerable deliberation, she bought stockings, cosmetics, and underwear. By late afternoon when she returned to her room, the telephone had been tapped and a bug installed. Posing as out-of-town business-men, two FBI agents had established a "plant"—a listening and ob-servation post—in a room near Tairova.

Before dinner, Tairova ordered two old-fashioneds, a drink which the KGB instructors in Moscow consider to be strong but typically American, in the hotel bar. By nine o'clock she was back in her bed-room. In the plant, the agents listened as Tairova opened the bottle of Remy Martin she had brought through customs and poured herself a lonely nightcap.

For three days Mary Grodnik busied herself in New York. She took long walks, shopped casually in big department stores, and went to the movies. She saw Frank Sinatra and Rita Hayworth in *Pal Joey* at the Capitol and Glenn Ford in *Don't Go Near the Water* at Radio City Music Hall. On Saturday, the thirtieth, she bought a quart of domes-tic vodka at a liquor store a block east of the Prince George on Twenty-eighth Street.

On her second day at the Prince George, and only after Tairova had entered the Capitol theater, an FBI agent slipped into her hotel room. Both suitcases and the cosmetics case had been left unlocked. A quick search of the luggage revealed nothing, except perhaps that Mary Grodnik, unlike other American tourists returning from a va-cation in Europe, had brought no gifts or souvenirs with her. Nor did she appear to have an address book, photographs, letters, or post-cards. If, as CIA had reported, she was carrying twenty thousand dollars and a change of identity documents, they were well con-cealed. The agent speculated that if the documents were not con-cealed with the money behind the mirror in the cosmetics case, they were probably in the frame of the American Tourister bags she trav-eled with. Certainly there was nothing in the room to indicate where or when Tairova would rendezvous with Zhakob. The newspapers and magazines in the room had all been bought in New York.

On Friday, 30 November, Tairova strode out of the hotel at ten-thirty. For the first time, the surveillance team sensed she had a specific destination. After walking along Madison Avenue to Forty-second Street, Tairova took a crosstown bus to Times Square. There, she walked a few blocks north, and took an uptown bus to Eighty-second and Broadway. She crossed Broadway and after walking south to Seventy-ninth Street, paused briefly to look behind her be-fore buying a newspaper. It was the first time the surveillance team had noted even this rudimentary precaution. Then, after crossing

Broadway again, she walked directly into the Manhattan Towers Hotel at Broadway and Seventy-eighth Street.

After a brief conversation with the room clerk, a bellhop escorted her upstairs. A few minutes later, she returned, signed the register, and paid the room clerk a week's rent in cash. Tairova left the hotel and, after walking several blocks south on Broadway, took another bus to Twenty-eighth Street and walked across town to the Prince George Hotel.

An hour later, she paid her bill, tipped the bellboy who had helped with her luggage, and stepped into a taxi.

In the course of the fifteen-minute taxi ride, Mary Grodnik became Florence Grochowska. As she had told the room clerk at the Manhattan Towers, she had come to New York from Chicago, was looking for a job, and would remain at the hotel until she found an apartment.

For a week Grochowska continued her apparently aimless sightseeing and moviegoing. Then, on 4 December, she took a taxi to Grand Central Station at Forty-second Street. After picking up a train schedule at the information booth, she walked slowly to the tracks from which trains left for Ludlow, Yonkers, and Glenwood. Apparently satisfied with her reconnaissance, she returned to the Manhattan Towers. In Yonkers, FBI agents had already familiarized themselves with the area of Broadway and the Post Road.

On Sunday, 6 December, after a leisurely breakfast, Grochowska took a crosstown bus to Fifth Avenue. Despite the cold weather, she walked to Saint Patrick's Cathedral. After strolling slowly around the church, she entered through the enormous doors. After a few moments, she walked out of the cathedral and made another tour around it. Then she went to the movies.

That night, when the surveillance chief made out his daily report, he speculated that this might have been a "walk-past." When illegals are dispatched, they are usually instructed to make appearances at a specific time and place in one or more countries along the route to their permanent assignment. This permits an officer from the illegals support staff in the area to confirm that the agent has arrived safely at each important stage of his journey. If an emergency has occurred and new instructions must be passed to the agent, the support officer has the option of making contact. It is likely that Tairova made a walk-past in Paris as well as in New York.

On Monday the seventh, Grochowska, bundled in her tweed coat, left the Manhattan Towers at 4:30 and went directly to Grand Central Station. There, she climbed aboard the 5:19 Hudson Line train to

Yonkers. Half an hour later, when she stepped off the train in Yonkers, the Bucket Brigade was in place. After loitering in the station for a few minutes, Tairova slowly made her way to Broadway and the Post Road. After checking her watch, she crossed the street and at precisely 6:30 entered the Park Hill Cinema. Three FBI agents fanned out behind her.

At the rear of the theater, Tairova paused to allow her eyes to adjust to the dim light. After scanning the nearly empty movie house, she walked down the aisle on the left. In the half light flickering from the screen, the surveillance agents could see that she had taken a seat directly behind a lone man, his coat folded over the back of the seat beside him. Tairova slipped out of her coat and adjusted it across her shoulders. For a few minutes she seemed engrossed in the film. Then, after a casual glance around the theater, she leaned forward and tapped the man on the shoulder. He turned, whispered a few words, picked up his coat, and walked slowly up the aisle and out of the movie. Tairova waited a few moments and followed.

On the street, the man buttoned his black double-breasted overcoat and adjusted a snap-brim hat, incongruously small for his puffy, round face. He was about five-feet-eight and stocky. Probably about one hundred ninety pounds.

Moments later Tairova hurried up and, forgetting security, embraced him. After a long kiss, she stepped back. To the surprise of the surveillance team, she opened her coat and, imitating a fashion model, spun slowly in front of him. Only later did the FBI men deduce that Tairova had been on a diet and was proudly showing off her new figure.

It had been a classic, high-security *Treff*, but Tairova had been reunited with her husband and the FBI had made Zhakob.

Escorted by another convoy of FBI agents, the Tairovs took the train back to Manhattan. Arm in arm, they strolled across town to the McGuiness Sea Food Restaurant at 47th and Broadway. As FBI agents filtered into the bar—a noisy Broadway joint with a moving panel of risqué cartoons above the bar—the bartender casually greeted Tairov, obviously a regular customer. After several drinks, the Tairovs took a taxi headed north. At the corner of West 105th Street and Central Park, Tairov paid the cabdriver and escorted the unsteady Tairova to a shabby five-floor apartment building at 70 West 105th Street.

The following morning a posse of agents tailed Tairov to an office building at 22 West Thirty-eighth Street. There, as the FBI was to learn, he was known as Walter Anthony Soja and worked as a book-keeper for a wholesale supplier of women's accessories. Zhakob had been positively identified.

West 105th Street had once been part of a well-kept, middle-class neighborhood. But in 1957, when the FBI began the surveillance of Walter Soja's apartment at number 70, the area was on the skids, a slum in the making. The buildings were poorly maintained and the streets littered with trash.

The most that could be said for the apartment that an FBI agent posing as a narcotics detective on a stakeout had rented as a plant was that it gave a clear view of the modest entrance to Tairov's apartment building. No one could leave the building without FBI knowledge. The plant—one room with a rusty hot-plate and toilet—was filthy. The least brush against the wall was enough to send a troop of cockroaches scuttling for quieter quarters. It was the worst plant any of the agents could remember and it was two days before they learned that by hanging their sandwiches from a string tied to an overhead light fixture, the cockroaches could be kept at bay.

Tairova kept her room at the Manhattan Towers, but in effect moved in with her husband. Despite Moscow's plan that she find work in a beauty shop, Tairova made no attempt to do so. After sleeping late, she would move casually around New York, shopping and attending occasional movies. As a rule, she would meet Tairov at the Beacon Bar at about six-thirty, when he had finished work. After a few drinks, the couple would eat in a nearby restaurant and return to West 105th Street.

Surveillance continued, but there was not the slightest indication of what the Tairovs' intelligence assignment could be. By mid-February it seemed possible that both the Tairovs were members of a sleeper, or reserve, Soviet network that had not yet been activated. Their only task seemed to be building cover. At no time did either agent appear to be surveillance-conscious, or to take any countersurveillance precautions.

To the casual observer, the Tairovs appeared to be a rootless, lower-income couple, apparently content to spend their money and free time in bars and restaurants. Although Tairov worked out regularly at Al Roon's Health Club at Seventy-third Street and Broadway, neither Russian appeared to have any hobbies, or intellectual or cultural interests beyond an occasional movie. Closer observation showed that the couple spent more money than Walter Soja was earning and that there was no apparent source for the money Florence Gro-chowska was spending for her room at the Manhattan Towers. She rarely slept there and was seldom seen by the staff. A regular patron of a beauty shop near the hotel, Grochowska tipped appropriately and talked casually with the hairdresser.

It was an empty existence for two people five thousand miles from home.

23
NEW YORK EXIT

It was the tension in Popov's voice that alarmed Domnin. The agent had telephoned for emergency meetings in the past, several times in Vienna and once in Berlin. Each time he had urgent intelligence to deliver, or something special like the Tairova case to report. This time Popov had sounded nervous and abrupt, with no hint as to why he had called.

It was early on a Tuesday evening in March 1958 when Domnin sped toward the S-Bahnhof where he and Harry Schubert, the case officer driver, were to pick up the agent. In the back seat of the sedan, Domnin leafed through the briefing notes that had been prepared against the possibility that Popov might have to flee. The busiest crossing points, the best times of day, and as always, the worst case—how to escape if being pursued—were all considered.

If Popov had blundered it might be days before the GRU security staff learned of it, Domnin rationalized, plenty of time for Popov and his family to scurry out of East Berlin. With a minimum of luck, Popov would have no difficulty crossing into West Berlin with his wife and two children. Even if there was a snap control on the train, his GRU credentials would get him through. Unless, of course, Popov was already under suspicion. If so, the chances for escape would be narrowed, possibly nonexistent.

Popov was walking slowly along Muellerstrasse, when Harry Schubert spotted him, alerted Domnin, and slowed down. As the car approached the agent, Domnin pushed the door open and Popov tumbled into the back seat. Pulling the door shut, Domnin spoke to the driver in English. "Let's move it, we may have a lot to talk about tonight."

Schubert hunched forward and stepped on the gas. As he turned off the Muellerstrasse, he muttered in English. "The street's clean. Nobody on foot and not a car in sight."

Throughout his meetings with Popov, Domnin had kept their relationship on a formal basis. Occasionally, he used the reassuring "Pyotr Semyonovich," the first name and patronymic customary in Russian conversation. Only rarely did he call Popov the Russian equivalent of Pete.

"What's the matter, Petro? You sounded upset on the telephone."

"Something important has come up. I've got a real problem."

"If you've got time, let's wait until we get to the house, otherwise tell me about it now."

Popov looked uneasily at the driver.

"It's the same fellow. He still doesn't speak any Russian," Domnin said.

"It's all right," said Popov. "There'll be time enough to talk about it at the house."

"There's one good thing about it, at least I got Ivanov's permission to write her."

Domnin leaned forward in the heavy chair and picked up a yellow pad from the coffee table. "You'd better start from the beginning," he said.

It started, Popov said, in Schwerin when Ivanov, the colonel commanding the transborder point, was pestering him about agent recruitment. It was one thing, Ivanov told him, for Popov to handle the agents he had taken over from his predecessor at the base. But that was something anyone could do. What really counted was making recruitments. Popov had been given a quota of six for the year and as yet had not come up with a single candidate, let alone a recruited agent.

It was then, Popov said, he had remembered a friend of Lyuba's, an Austrian woman who had married an American sergeant in Vienna. He remembered meeting the woman once in Vienna and vaguely recalled that the sergeant had been transferred to Germany a few months before the Austrian occupation ended.

"She's more of a communist than Lyuba, but apparently your army doesn't check on things like that," Popov said.

"They try to, but unless the man's in a sensitive job, I guess they haven't time enough to do a very thorough job of it," Domnin said.

Popov proposed to Ivanov that he write to his former agent, Lyuba Bielic, and ask if she could give him the address of her friend in Germany.

"As I remember it," Popov said, "the sergeant was a drunk and always broke. I figured that if I could get the woman to come to Berlin, I could ask her to sound out her husband. With any luck, I might have been able to get him to come here and proposition him. It probably would have worked. I don't know what job the guy had, but as far as Ivanov was concerned, anyone in your army is worth recruiting. Anyway, you never can tell—even if his job wasn't important, he might get a better one later on. We've done that plenty of times—recruit some drunk and then try to maneuver him into a place where he will have access to training manuals and stuff like that."

Domnin nodded. Both the GRU and KGB had milked low-level military spies of good intelligence.

"I thought that having Ivanov's permission to write her would be good cover for the letter I had already sent to Lyuba," Popov added.

But what he had not known, Popov explained, was that Maximenkov, who was responsible for Yugoslav operations in Vienna, had found Lyuba's name in the *rezidentura* archive and was himself trying to re-recruit her. Kremlin policy on Yugoslav operations had changed.

"Maximenkov is a drunk, stewed half the time. With my luck one night when he had been drinking and it was almost midnight, he decided to go to her apartment." Popov paused for a moment. "Maybe he had something else on his mind. I wouldn't doubt it."

Even though the occupation was over, Popov continued, the Russians were less popular than ever. At midnight the *Hausbesorger*, the superintendent, was not about to open the front door of the apartment house for anyone speaking German with a heavy Russian accent. When Maximenkov began shouting, the Austrian telephoned the police station a few hundred feet away. Minutes later, two uniformed Austrian police appeared. Not daunted, Maximenkov turned on the two *Schupos* with a stream of profanity.

During the ten years of occupation, Russians were not subject to Austrian police control or arrest. But now they were fair game, and most Austrian cops had had enough of drunken Russians. Without permitting Maximenkov to identify himself as a diplomat, they hustled him off to the police station. There, belligerent and screaming,

Maximenkov threw his wallet and diplomatic identity card at the police sergeant.

After the diplomat had been subdued and shunted into a waiting room, the desk sergeant telephoned the Soviet embassy. First Secretary Maximenkov was drunk and disorderly. He was not under arrest, but he would only be released when someone from the embassy came and assumed responsibility for him.

"It's a real damned mess," Popov said. "Maximenkov will be sent back to Moscow as soon as the thing cools off. But somewhere along the line he learned that I had been writing to Lyuba. The *rezident* cabled Moscow and now the center has asked what I know about it."

"But you had Ivanov's permission to write her," Domnin said.

"Sure, but I've written her from Berlin too. Ivanov doesn't know anything about that. Kriatov doesn't even know that I wrote her at all. It's a pretty good mess."

"Is that all there is to it?"

"Not exactly. In 1956 Lyuba apparently got upset about the Hungarian revolution. She may have sounded off about our intervention in Budapest to some party people. Now the security people suspect her of being on your side right from the beginning."

It was worse than Domnin had anticipated. If GRU counterintelligence suspected Lyuba of having been an anticommunist at the time Popov met her, it would be a serious reflection on his professional judgment to have recruited her, to have run her as an agent for four years, and to have embroiled her in an operation based in Germany. If they did suspect her, the security officers would check into Popov's relationship with her and use a microscope in going over the reports he had written on her political orientation and activity. Domnin had little doubt but what Popov had repeatedly vouched for and praised her.

"What do you think the chances are that she will say anything more about you?" Domnin asked.

Popov swirled the vodka in his glass and tossed it off in a gulp. "There's no chance she would do that. I don't know how Vienna knew I had written her, but she won't say anything about us to them. I'm sure of that."

Domnin could not be so sure. It was hard to see why Lyuba, a simple woman, would think there was anything wrong in telling someone posing as one of Popov's friends that she had been in correspondence with him. She might even have bragged about her relationship.

"Where does this leave it, what's the next step for you?"

"The first think I have to do is to tell Colonel Kriatov that I have written to Lyuba. He'll raise hell about it, I know that. But at least I can say that it was to help Ivanov in Schwerin and that he authorized me to do it. Then I'll probably have to write something to Moscow explaining it all. After that, they might even send some damned Chekist to investigate the whole story in Vienna."

"You're right, Petro, this is a pretty good mess," Domnin said.

Popov got up and walked to a table at the side of the room. Distracted, he shuffled through the pile of magazines until he found a copy of the *Farm Journal* and walked back to the chair across the coffee table from Domnin. As Popov began to thumb through the magazine, Domnin tried to fit the story together. Probably Popov had written to Lyuba more frequently than he had admitted. Possibly, Domnin reasoned, he had even invited her to visit him in Berlin. Ivanov's approval of the letter that the KGB knew about gave Popov a slight cover story. But unless Colonel Karlempegi and Kriatov were more tolerant than seemed possible, Popov would be in for a stiff reprimand. If there was, as Domnin suspected, more to the story than Popov admitted, it might be deemed so serious a breach of security discipline that Popov could be sent back to the Soviet Union. Nor could it be ruled out that Popov might be transferred from the GRU to some routine military assignment, troop duty in the back country far from Moscow.

Popov continued to study the magazine until Domnin interrupted him. "How much time will there be before you know how serious this is?" he asked.

"I don't know," Popov said listlessly. "I'd guess there will be a few weeks before they make any decisions."

Domnin remained quiet, watching Popov turn the pages of the magazine. He knew that any discussion of defection, of escaping from East Berlin, would upset the agent and add to the tension he suffered. Still, if he did not remind him that he could come across whenever he wanted to, Popov might take the silence to mean that he should stick it out, no matter how dangerous it was.

"You know, Pyotr Semyonovich, that you can come over any time you want to. You've done a lot, as much as anyone in your position could have done. If you want to come out with Gallina and the children all you have to do is say so. You won't have any trouble crossing over if you come on a Saturday or Sunday. There are always a lot of families crossing over for the day on weekends."

For a moment, Popov continued to stare at the magazine. Then he looked up at his case officer, his dark eyes watery. "I've thought about it. I'd like to do it, just once to live in a country where peasants are treated like human beings, can have their own land. But Gallina doesn't know anything about what I've been doing, or even what I think. As far as she knows, I'm just like the others, satisfied to have a good job and to be free of some of the shit that the other people, the ones who aren't in the service, have to take every day. I know she'd like it somewhere in the West, particularly if we could have a farm of our own. But her mother is alive—she still lives in Tula, in a little place like an *izba* on the outskirts of the city. Gallina would do what I say, but I don't think I can tell her to leave her mother behind."

"Even if you are in a real jam?" Domnin asked.

"If I had to run, she'd do it, but it wouldn't be fair. Anyway, that's not the most important thing. Why should we leave? We're Russians, maybe just peasants, but we're as good as anyone. Even better than those damned Chekists who are running everything. I know we could come out. And I know that sometime it might not be possible to get away. But that's not for me. I'm a Russian and it's my country, my land. It belongs to me just as much as it does to any of those damned party people. What I've done, it's all been for my own people, the peasants. How can I run, when they're all stuck there? My family, my brothers and sister—they're even worse off than under the czar. I haven't even heard from them since that time I went back to Solnechnaya. Sooner or later there'll be a war. If you win, the peasants win. The only way I can help is by working with you. I'm not a deserter like those guys during the war. I'm a Russian and I'll die a Russian, in Russia. I don't give a damn what they do to me."

It was almost midnight before Domnin dropped Popov off near the S-Bahn station.

In early April Popov was called to Lieutenant General Federenko's office in Karlshorst. Federenko, a former deputy chief of the GRU, was in command of the *Opergruppe* in East Berlin, and the most senior GRU officer serving outside the USSR. He upbraided Popov, reminding him that, as an *Opergruppe* officer, he had made a serious mistake writing to a former agent and trying to help Ivanov with the recruitment of the American sergeant while working as an illegals support officer under Kriatov's command. A case like that, Federenko roared, should have been handled by the Vienna *rezidentura* without resorting to the open mail. In future, the general said, Popov was not to make a move without clearing it with Kriatov, his section chief, and Colonel Karlempegi, the illegals support chief. For his indiscretion Popov would be given a written security reprimand. Colonel Ivanov would also be disciplined.

For a moment it seemed that Popov had weathered this storm and would remain in East Berlin. But, as a contingency against his sudden departure, CIA arranged for a contact man to meet Popov in Berlin. Huddled together with Domnin, Popov and the visitor picked sites for brush contacts in Moscow and chose dead drops from the selection the contact man brought to Berlin with him.

From East Berlin, Popov continued to cross into the Western sector to report to Domnin. His best intelligence reports were still in the military field, data he gleaned from the reserve officers' courses he regularly attended and information elicited from high-ranking officers stationed with the Soviet Central Group of Forces in East Germany. Bragging as they talked shop, these officers disclosed highly sensitive intelligence on Soviet weapons systems, data on missiles and guidance systems.

One report puzzled Domnin. A visiting colonel, awash in vodka at an officers' club, had boasted that the KGB had full technical details on a special high-altitude aircraft CIA had been flying over the USSR. Although the first U-2 had flown in 1955, the details of this revolutionary aircraft were very tightly held within the U.S. government. Only those directly involved in the project had any knowledge of it, and at the time no one in the Berlin office had been briefed on the U-2 project or the wealth of intelligence it was beginning to produce.

In Washington, Helms handed the U-2 report to Richard Bissell, chief of the directorate of operations and the man who had conceived and was directing the U-2 reconnaissance program. It was the first indication of a leak somewhere within the top-secret project.

Of less national importance than the military intelligence Popov was delivering, but of great interest were his reports on the work of the illegals support section. Never before had any Western intelligence service penetrated so deeply into the nerve center of Soviet secret operations. Popov's reports on illegal agents transiting East Berlin are still—twenty-two years after the fact—classified top secret within CIA, and no information on them has been, or is ever likely to be, approved for publication. Fortunately, none of this information is essential to the Popov story.

One writer* has quoted a CIA document that estimates the Defense Department saved more than half a billion dollars in research and development costs on the basis of Popov's military reporting. As difficult as it is to make even a tentative guess as to the dollar value of secret intelligence—if the reports showing the Japanese were going to make a sneak attack on Pearl Harbor had been properly interpreted and disseminated, what would they have been worth?—it is literally impossible to put a price tag on counterintelligence. Popov's reports on GRU illegal agents were unique; there was nothing they could be compared with. At the time, Popov's counterintelligence reports were assayed as being "priceless."

Although Popov should have been more at home in his role as a support officer, dealing with Russian-speaking illegal agents passing through East Berlin and free from the agonizing pressure of having to find and recruit agents on his own, the heavy—almost ostentatious—security precautions that governed every aspect of illegals work continued to fret him. Domnin understood this and sympathized with Popov's problem. Still, as seen from the outside, the GRU, for all its lip-service to the form of security, seemed to ignore an equally important problem—the illegals directorate of the GRU was almost as sloppy in its tradecraft as the Tactical Intelligence unit had been in the low-level operations Popov had reported on from Schwerin.

From what CIA had learned from the FBI about the Tairov couple in New York, it was difficult to see what function these two agents could possibly discharge that would repay the cost and time involved in infiltrating them into the United States. Neither had the personality to recruit American agents, or the intellectual, political, or social background that would make it possible for them even to assess Americans as possible agent candidates. The notion that either of the Tairovs might actually handle a valuable agent was dismissed as absurd.

When the FBI uncovered one apparent friend of the Tairovs, there was a momentary suspicion that the surveillance had at last led to another possible agent. But closer examination showed that this man, a sometime barber on the S. S. *United States*, was if anything even less competent or threatening than either of the Tairovs. The barber, a near-alcoholic, could hardly read. His occasional work on

*Harry Rositzke, *CIA's Secret Operations* (New York: Reader's Digest Press, 1977).

the liner might conceivably have qualified him as a courier, but the day when high-level intelligence reporting might have been entrusted to a semiliterate drunk had long passed. Intelligence reports went to Moscow via the diplomatic bag or clandestine radio or, after being reduced to microdots, were given to reliable, highly trained specialist couriers dispatched and controlled by the center in Moscow. Reluctantly, the FBI concluded that the barber was no more than a drinking companion of the Tairovs.

It was almost noon on 12 March 1958 when the FBI agents in the plant across from the Tairov apartment on West 105th Street saw Tairova, dressed as usual in a light coat and carrying her now familiar, small black handbag, leave the apartment and head downtown. This appeared to be part of a pattern she had followed for a month or more. After having a sandwich and coffee at a lunchroom, she would windowshop and browse through one or two department stores before going to a movie to kill time until about six o'clock. Then she would head for the McGuiness Sea Food Restaurant and bar where Tairov would meet her after finishing his day's work in the office on Thirty-eighth Street.

In the plant, the FBI agent made a note of her departure and called the surveillance team control center. After weeks of almost constant surveillance of the Tairovs, it had become apparent to the FBI that the couple had settled into a routine and that round-the-clock surveillance was not worth the risk of being detected. Now the form was random surveillance—three or four days a week, just enough coverage to confirm that, for the moment at least, neither of the Tairovs was engaged in anything even remotely operational.

As usual, the agent covering the Thirty-second Street door to the office building in which Tairov worked, noted that he left at five-fifteen, apparently headed for McGuiness's. A call to the control center alerted a surveillance team to pick up Tairov at the bar, where presumably he would be meeting Tairova.

It was seven-thirty before one of the Bucket Brigade telephoned the surveillance desk. Neither Tairov nor his wife had entered the bar. Had they been seen at the apartment? A quick call to the plant across from the apartment confirmed that neither of the Tairovs had been seen entering that building.

Within half an hour, surveillance agents fanned out across the city, checking each of the locations the Tairovs were known to have frequented. They were not sighted; nor did they return to 105th Street or to Tairova's room at the Broadway Towers that night. By noon on 29 March there could be no denying it—the Tairovs had vanished.

The following morning, two FBI agents crossed the roof of a building adjoining 70 West 105th Street and slipped down the fire escape at the back of the Tairovs' apartment. After prying open a window, they climbed in. The breakfast dishes had been washed and carefully stacked in the sink. The Tairovs' clothing—by now familiar to the Bucket Brigade—was hanging in the closet. On top of a dressing table was Tairova's cosmetics case. An inexpensive German camera and seven rolls of 35 mm film were in a dresser drawer along with Tairov's carefully folded shirts and underwear. In the closet, alongside Tairova's dresses, were two cheap men's suits. Tairov's neckties hung from a wire coat hanger. Tairova might not have made much of a spy, one of the agents mused, but she was nothing if not a neat housekeeper.

If the Tairovs had decamped, the two agents reported to headquarters, they had not even taken a change of underwear with them.

The FBI's final report on the Walter and Mary case noted that at no time during their stay in New York did either Tairov or his wife make any discernible countersurveillance moves. Nor, up to the moment they vanished, was there any sign that they had detected the surveillance. Although there was no indication as to why the Tairovs had been sent to New York City, the most reasonable explanation appeared to be that they were intended eventually to serve as support agents, possibly to handle the communications for an illegal *rezident* operating in New York City. An illegal *rezident*, a Russian living under nonofficial, or illegal, cover, directs the activity of a number of subordinate illegal agents and the spies they are handling. He is completely separated from the legal apparat in the embassy or consulate and has his own clandestine communications with the Moscow center. In effect, an illegal *rezident* functions like a chief of station. The most significant difference between an illegal *rezident* and his opposite number under diplomatic cover, is that the illegal is subject to arrest and interrogation. Until his arrest in June 1957 Colonel Rudolph Abel was a KGB illegal *rezident* in New York. Interestingly, it was Abel's communications man, an illegal named Reino Hayhanen, who defected and denounced Abel to CIA. Had the Tairov surveillance not been blown, the FBI might have uncovered a GRU agent as important as Abel.

After reading the FBI's final report on the case, one CIA officer remarked: "There's one thing you can say for the Tairovs—nothing in their operational life in the United States became them so much as their leaving of it. They simply dematerialized."

Popov accepted the news that the Tairovs had fled more philosophically than Domnin had anticipated. "I don't think there's too much to worry about," he said. "Tairova didn't want to go to New York anyway. Kriatov knew that, he even mentioned it to me. She probably took the first excuse she could to run back home."

Domnin was less sanguine. "It's important for you to let me know the minute you hear anything from Moscow," he told Popov. "If the Tairovs can convince Moscow that they were compromised, the GRU will have to check it out."

"Sure they will," Popov said. "But what can they find out? When something like this happens, they usually blame it on someone the agents got to know. Someone who became suspicious, who wouldn't believe the legend."

Domnin was not convinced.

"The one thing the center never worries about is the papers," Popov went on. "We can forge documents that are even better than the originals."

In a city like New York, filled with immigrants and tourists, Domnin wondered how bad an illegal's cover story would have to be before it attracted the attention of anyone.

It was almost three weeks before Popov came back to West Berlin.

"It's turned out worse than I thought," he told Domnin. "I don't know whether they jumped on their own or were told by the illegals support section to leave. But one thing is certain, that damned Tairova claims she was surveilled all the way from Tempelhof airport."

"That's crazy," Domnin said. "Nothing was done until she got to New York."

"That's great, I'm glad to hear it," Popov said. "But I don't think I can tell Kriatov that Colonel Grossman assured me that the surveillance began in New York." Popov managed a slight grin. "But perhaps he knows you as Scharnhorst here," he said, referring to the pseudonym Domnin used in Berlin.

"He doesn't know me at all—and neither does that KGB General Korotkov, or whatever he calls himself," Domnin said.

General Aleksandr Mikhailovich Korotkov was one of the KGB's German experts and the KGB *rezident* in East Germany.

In view of Popov's sanguine evaluation of his situation, Domnin decided to wait before again reminding Popov that he could defect with his family at any time. It would not be long before he would repeat the offer for the last time.

24
BERLIN EXIT

It was late in November when Popov reported that the Tairov matter had taken another, more serious, turn. He told Domnin that, from something Kriatov had said, it seemed certain that the GRU headquarters in Moscow had now accepted the Tairovs' story that Tairova had been set up the moment she stepped off the airplane in New York.

"This can only mean that the case will go to the KGB," Popov said. "The KGB has the final responsibility for any serious security problem anywhere in the Soviet Union. Much as the GRU would like to keep its problems within the GRU, they'll have no choice but to tell the KGB that Tairova was compromised. My guess is that the KGB will send its own investigators here to interrogate everyone who had anything to do with the case. They'll probably send someone to New York too. They're only too glad to make us look bad in front of the Central Committee."

Popov had not panicked, but he could not conceal his anxiety. He had weathered the first GRU investigation, but knew that the KGB interrogation would be more aggressive, more thorough.

Once more Domnin offered Popov the chance to leave with his family.

"You've done more than your share, Petro. If there's a real risk, you'd better come out now, while there's still a chance," he told the agent.

"I've come this far," Popov said. "I'm not going to quit now. There's no way they can prove anything against me, no matter how much fuss those two drunks make in Moscow."

A few days later, Domnin was surprised when Popov called for another meeting. Had things gone according to plan, he would have stayed in East Berlin for at least three weeks. As Popov stepped into the car and pulled his hat down over his eyes, Domnin noticed how drawn the agent looked and guessed the KGB had begun its investigation. In that circumstance, he would have preferred that Popov stay in East Berlin until the investigation had run its course. If the agent was under surveillance, his trip to West Berlin could be fatal.

"What's wrong, Pyotr Semyonovich?" he asked.

"Plenty—there's a big *papakha* here now, a KGB colonel from the center. He didn't say, but I think he's from the Second Chief Directorate." Popov stared ruefully at Domnin. "The only time one of those guys leaves Moscow is for an execution somewhere."

Domnin knew this wasn't entirely true, but Popov's hyperbole was another mark of his concern. The Second Chief Directorate is responsible for all counterintelligence and security matters in the Soviet Union. If the KGB was looking for a mole, the Second Chief Directorate would handle the case.

"What line did he take with you?"

"At first it was more of the same, almost exactly the questions the GRU guy asked. He wanted to know what I thought of Tairova, how nervous she was, how much she drank, if she really wanted to go to New York. He asked what could have gone wrong in Berlin, if there was any surveillance at Tempelhof. Stuff like that."

For once, Popov did not seem worried about the presence of Schubert, the case officer driver. It was Domnin who suggested postponing the discussion until they reached the safehouse and he could take notes.

As they settled down in the heavy overstuffed chairs facing each other across the coffee table, Domnin poured a stiff shot of vodka into Popov's glass. "Tell me more about the questioning," he said.

"This guy was tough, a real Chekist. Talking to him was like being in a vise. Everything I said seemed to make the pressure greater. Before it was over I couldn't make a statement on anything without him jumping all over me with more questions."

"Did he have anything new, any different line of questioning from what the GRU fellow asked?"

For a moment Popov was silent. Then, swirling the vodka in his glass, he said, "Not at first. It was the same old stuff. Did Tairova speak to anyone but her case officer, Kriatov and me? Did I think she was likely to have attracted attention by acting suspicious at the airport in New York? Would she have suspected surveillance when there wasn't any?"

Popov took a gulp of vodka. "The big difference was that he wanted to know minute by minute what I did while she was here. I'm sure the office was bugged, but he wrote down everything I said. He must have taken twenty pages of notes. Still, when we were finished—it took two days—he seemed satisfied."

"That doesn't sound too bad," Domnin said.

"But that's not all. He had the whole thing typed up, like a legal document. I had to read it and initial every page."

"That's customary in an important investigation, isn't it?" Domnin asked.

"I guess so. But it's the first time I ever had to do it. This guy really knew his business. I've never seen anyone with such a memory. Without even looking at his notes—he brought a sheaf of paper as thick as a Berlin telephone book with him from Moscow—he'd ask a dozen questions every time I said anything. Every question was clear, he never repeated himself or asked anything that wasn't right on the case."

"Is he still here?"

"No," Popov said. "He's gone back to Moscow. It was only when I thought we were all through that he really tossed something at me."

"Tell me," said Domnin, trying to keep the concern out of his voice.

"It was just after I had signed his papers that he dropped it on me, just as matter of fact as if he were saying hello. He said the KGB had confirmed from three separate sources in New York that the surveillance had started when Tairova got off the airplane in New York."

"What three sources?" Domnin asked, his voice rising.

"How do I know? Three sources, he said. Maybe in the police, the FBI, CIA—I don't know and I damned well wasn't going to try to pry into it. He's not the kind of guy who answers questions. He only asks."

"Three sources," Domnin said. "It's not possible. He was faking, trying to upset you."

"If that's all it was, it damned well worked. He scared the hell out of me."

"Did he talk to anyone else?"

"Sure. The day he got here he saw General Federenko and Nikolsky. After that he spent almost two days with Kriatov and Karlempegi.

I'm surprised he didn't talk to you," Popov added with a faint smile. "Incidentally," he added, "Nikolsky's been promoted. He's a general now."

"It can't be too serious if they promoted Nikolsky," Domnin said.

"He's General Federenko's chief of operations, but he's not in my line of command. It's Colonel Karlempegi and Kriatov who may be in trouble. He probably talked to Nikolsky because he knew me in Vienna too. Anyway, from what I hear Nikolsky is due for a transfer. He's got a big case somewhere up north, in Sweden maybe."*

For two hours Domnin and Popov threshed over the interrogation, making sure Domnin had all the details of the KGB questioning. At midnight, before getting into the car that would take Popov back to the U-Bahnhof, they agreed that he would not come back to West Berlin for at least three weeks. That would be enough time for Popov to determine if there was to be any follow-through by the KGB.

Eight days later Popov called and asked to be picked up at the Am See S-Bahnhof.

Popov began to speak even before he had settled back in the seat beside Domnin. "I probably shouldn't have come over tonight, but I wanted to see you before I leave," he said.

"Before you leave?"

"I've been ordered back to Moscow on a temporary duty trip. They want me to take back the files on that agent I've told you I'm trying to recruit."

Weeks earlier, Popov had told Domnin that he had been instructed to set up an approach to a possible support agent, a young West German who had been spotted by a case officer in another section of the *Opergruppe*. To fill the quota of agent recruitments imposed by the center on all field stations, the GRU routinely picked up agents of marginal value. The young German seemed to fall in this category,

---

*In June 1963 Swedish Air Force Colonel Stig Wennerstrom was arrested in Stockholm and charged with espionage. A few days later, Major General Vitaly Nikolsky, the Soviet military attaché, was declared *persona non grata* and expelled from Sweden. Wennerstrom, who had served as Swedish air attaché in Washington, had been recruited by the GRU in 1949. One of the most productive GRU agents, Wennerstrom compromised Swedish defense plans, reported regularly on sensitive NATO planning, and while in Washington, provided the GRU with complete details of the Bomarck and Falcon missile programs. For details see Thomas Whiteside's *An Agent in Place* (New York: Ballantine Books, 1983).

and Domnin wondered why the GRU could possibly think it was important enough to call Popov back to Moscow to discuss.

"I guess they're still jumpy after the Tairova case. Moscow wants to be sure there are no more squeals in the illegals section and wants to go over the file with me before agreeing to our recruitment proposal."

Domnin was less sure. To be on the safe side, they spent an hour reviewing the communications system the Moscow contact man had arranged with Popov—dead drops, telephone signals, and meeting places. He also checked to be sure that Popov had the concealment devices containing secret ink and miniaturized code pads he would need when he returned permanently to the USSR.

"Sure, I've got it all, but I'm not taking any of it with me—I'll only be gone a few days. I'm leaving all that stuff with my other things in the apartment. Gallina and the children will stay in Karlshorst while I'm away," Popov said.

"You know, Petro, it's not too late. If you're worried about the trip, you and the family can come out right now."

"I've said all I'm going to say about that. I'm not going to come over. There's one thing though," he added softly. "If I have a chance in Moscow, I'm going to ask for a different assignment. Illegals work is too touchy for me. I know it's good for you, but I don't think I can keep it up. Maybe after things cool off for a bit I'll get another job just as important. Right now, I've had enough of Kriatov and Karlempegi. They're going crazy about security. You can't make a move for all of the red tape they're tying around everything. I'm not the only one who's feeling the pressure. Everyone is. It's gotten so we scarcely even speak to one another."

Domnin nodded. "That's probably for the best. It's time to take it easy for a while, maybe coast for a bit."

Popov got up and walked across the room to a side table stacked with magazines. Rifling through the pile, he picked up a copy of the *American Farm Journal.* As he began to leaf through it, he turned to Domnin. "Maybe I am making a mistake. I'd sure like to see one of these farms and all of that equipment they are using."

With a lopsided grin, Popov added, "I'll be mad as hell if it turned out to be propaganda you've had printed just to fool a simple Russian *muzhik* like me."

"There's only one way to find out," Domnin said. "And you can do that any time you want to."

Popov continued to turn the pages.

"Will you need any money for the trip?" Domnin asked.

"No, money's the last thing I need. I've got plenty and it won't cost me much in Moscow. I'm leaving in such a rush, I haven't even got time to pick up any *blat*, presents for the poor bastards stuck on the desk back home."

The night had turned cold, but the air was crisp and clear by the time Larry pulled the car to the curb where Popov would be dropped. As they shook hands, Domnin put his left arm around Popov's shoulder and gave it a rough squeeze.

"Stop worrying," Popov said. "You're making me nervous. I'll call you as soon as I'm back. It'll only be a few days, I haven't got much to talk about."

When Popov opened the door and stepped into the darkness, Domnin remembered the first time he had shaken hands with Popov in Vienna. His hand was surprisingly big for a man his size and the grip iron-hard.

Through the back window of the car, Domnin caught a glimpse of the agent in the light reflected from a streetlamp.

Even after years of watching Popov hasten away from their rendezvous, Domnin was still intrigued by the contrast in his thickset torso and the quick, light steps he took when in a hurry. Domnin continued to watch until the agent disappeared in the shadows.

It was the last time he was ever to see Popov.

25
MOSCOW ENDGAME

When Popov returned to Moscow he was a senior and experienced GRU case officer. Aside from the time he had spent at GRU headquarters, he had more than three years' field experience in Vienna and some two years in Germany. This, and his diplomas from the Frunze Military Academy and the more senior Military Diplomatic Academy, qualified him theoretically at least for consideration for promotion to full colonel. But Popov had not been recalled to Moscow in connection with a possible promotion. Nor, contrary to what he had been told, had he been summoned to the center to discuss the routine recruitment of a German support agent. Popov had been directed to return to Moscow because he was suspected of high treason.

In Moscow there would be no possibility he might escape to the West, and in the cellars of the Lubyanka headquarters of the KGB, his interrogation could be conducted by the most skilled counterespionage officers in Soviet intelligence. They would have at hand all the means the KGB had developed for forced interrogation.

Whether Popov was arrested when the plane touched down at a military airport near Moscow or permitted to remain at liberty—under close surveillance—while undergoing an initially polite questioning is not known. Suffice it that even before he left East Berlin, Popov was under the deepest suspicion. The security investigation kindled by Tairova's report that she had been tailed from the moment she left Berlin had been exhaustive. The statement made by the KGB investigator that three KGB sources in New York had confirmed Tairova's suspicion, could, if true, only have intensified the investigation. Everyone who had any knowledge of the Tairov case had been subjected to the most extensive scrutiny. Whatever imperfections may have been uncovered in the background or work of his colleagues, Popov's case, as seen through the KGB microscope, could only have been egregious.

His performance in Vienna had been adequate, no more than that. Although no official record had been made at the time, there was probably some suspicion on the part of his friends that Popov's relationship with Lyuba Bielic had been more than professional. There was also the question of his correspondence with her from East Germany. Although Popov had covered himself by saying he had written only to locate the American sergeant whom the GRU in Schwerin hoped to recruit, KGB investigators might—through elicitation from Bielic or by questioning Popov's Vienna colleagues about his relationship with her—have learned that there was even more to the affair than a casual sexual contact between a case officer and agent. If Popov had been in more frequent correspondence with Bielic than he had admitted to Domnin, perhaps this was uncovered. If so, it alone could have been a sufficiently serious security violation to warrant Popov's dismissal from the GRU. If this was not enough, another even more serious hole had been burned in Popov's cover.

The most damning data in the KGB and GRU security dossiers had come from George Blake, the MI-6 case officer and long-term KGB mole in the British intelligence offices in Berlin. Late in the afternoon in 1956, when Blake had returned to his office at the British base and discovered a colleague laboriously translating six handwritten pages of Russian text, he asked what was up. His friend's thoughtless response that it looked "as if Bill Harvey has an important GRU case in the zone" must have sent the taciturn Blake's blood pressure rocketing. Blake was a KGB-controlled spy and had nothing to do with the GRU, but he had been in secret operations long enough to know what one bit of idle gossip could do to the best of cover. *Any* Western penetration of Soviet intelligence, KGB or GRU, was a threat to Blake's life. There is little doubt but that he passed this lethal nugget to the KGB within hours of having heard it.

As far as is known, Blake could not have learned any more about Popov. Once Harvey acknowledged that the letter was intended for CIA and that it was important, no further action would have been taken by British intelligence in Germany or elsewhere. And any British personnel—the translator, liaison officers, and base chief—would have protected the secret as if it had been their own.

Blake's brief report would have sparked a painstaking security investigation encompassing every GRU base in East Germany. Whatever suspicion may have fallen on other GRU personnel, there is nothing to suggest that Popov figured in it. At that time there were no security black marks in his file and, although not a particularly competent officer, he was known as a hard worker whose peasant humor and earthy manners made him well liked by his comrades. Proof that Popov successfully weathered this investigation would seem to be his transfer to the illegals section in Karlshorst. Had the slightest irregularity been perceived in any corner of Popov's background, he would never have been given this assignment.

When the Tairov case broke and the GRU—and subsequently the KGB—learned that the illegals operation had been compromised, the only officer who had been party to that operation and who had served in the Soviet zone in East Germany was Popov. It was inevitable that sooner or later the GRU and KGB investigators would put these two facts together. Earlier, another damning circumstance might have been unearthed. Any counterespionage officer brooding over Blake's report of the letter intended for delivery to CIA must have asked why an important CIA agent would *need* to hand such a devastatingly compromising document to a stranger, a British officer or not. The most obvious explanation could be that for some reason the spy's communications link with his case officer had been broken. There could be many reasons why a mole might have lost contact with his control, but one of the most likely could be that the agent had been in the Soviet Union for some time. The moment an investigator made this deduction, he would turn his attention to the GRU officers who had arrived in East Germany a few weeks, possibly even months, before Blake made his report. Although a few GRU officers were transferred to East Germany every month, an investigator would certainly have added Popov's name to the list. It would not have been a very long list—probably fewer than thirty officers had been posted to Germany in time to have plausibly made the contact with the liaison officer.

If this speculation is correct, by the time the Tairov case blew it should not have taken the counterespionage investigators long to determine that Popov was the only GRU case officer who knew the details of the Tairov case and who had arrived in East Germany at a time when he might have taken the foolhardy step of handing the letter to a stranger.

When Popov was ordered home on the pretext of discussing a routine recruitment operation, he was certainly already suspected of being the first Russian case officer to have been recruited in place by Western intelligence since before World War II. However suspect Popov was, it is clear that the KGB wished to protect the possibility of playing him back against CIA as a double agent. For this reason, considerable care was taken to convince CIA that, although Popov might have broken GRU security rules in maintaining his relationship with Bielic, there was no other suspicion attached to him. Hence the carefully staged departure of Popov's wife and two children.

For years, the KGB had known that the Soviet intelligence complex in Karlshorst, East Berlin, was a major counterintelligence target for the NATO espionage services. It was an obvious trove of secrets and a number of Western agents had been arrested in the Karlshorst area. But the KGB had much more information on Western activity than could be wrung from these prisoners. Heinz Felfe, a senior officer on the staff of the *Bundesnachrichtendienst* (BND), the West German intelligence service headed by General Reinhard Gehlen, had long been responsible for operations against Soviet intelligence in East Germany. Felfe had been insinuated into the BND by the KGB and was one of the most productive moles in West German intelligence. He had kept the KGB fully informed of Gehlen's operations in East Berlin and had passed along any snippets he might have been able to elicit from his liaison contacts in other Western intelligence services. If the captured agents and Felfe were not enough, the KGB had an even better source. As an MI-6 officer stationed in West Berlin, George Blake would have been perfectly placed to monitor British activity against Karlshorst.

Three weeks after Popov's departure, a report filtered through the mass of material forwarded by low-level observer agents in East Berlin. Among the Soviet military personnel and dependents boarding the Berlin-Moscow military train, a certain Gallina Popov and two children had been seen. Like other Russian dependents routinely leaving for Moscow, Gallina and the children had been seen off by several friends.

Whether the agent who reported on Gallina's departure from the East Berlin Bahnhof had been doubled against whatever service might have been controlling him—certainly other low-level observers of this sort had been played back against Western intelligence by the KGB—or was simply known to be an agent and was fed the report on Gallina, is moot. In the circumstances, the coincidence of a low-level observer remarking Gallina's apparently casual departure from East Berlin is too pat to be taken at face value. In an apparently clever way, the KGB might have hoped to encourage CIA to deduce that although Popov might be in trouble, it was not serious enough to warrant his wife and children being returned to the USSR under guard—as would certainly have been the case if he or any other Red Army officer was suspected of treason. Viewed with a bit of suspicion, and with the subsequent knowledge of Popov's plight, it would seem the KGB was actually advertising the "routine" aspect of the Popov family's departure.

As long as CIA assumed that Popov was in danger of being dismissed from the GRU because of his association with Lyuba Bielic, but not suspected of being a mole, the KGB would reason that the agency would remain in contact with him. Although he would not be nearly as valuable a source as he had been in Soviet intelligence, no espionage service would lightly drop contact with *any* field grade officer in the Soviet army. And, from the KGB's point of view, if Popov could be doubled and forced to cooperate with them against CIA, he could ostensibly be given a job with access to any subject on which the Russians wished to provide deceptive information. Still another, not negligible profit in running Popov as a double agent would be the insights the KGB might get into CIA *modus operandi* and operational facilities in the Soviet Union.

It was less than a month after Popov had returned to the Soviet Union for "a few days" when the world press trumpeted a story which, though mystifying at the time, can now be seen as the first clue in the public unraveling of the Popov case. On 9 December 1958 a Soviet press release announced bluntly that General Ivan Aleksandrovich Serov, chief of the KGB—his actual title was Chairman of the Committee for State Security—had been relieved of his post.

Serov was known as an unreconstructed Stalinist and one of the few of Beria's deputies to have weathered the storms that swept through the secret police after Beria's arrest and execution. Most observers credited Serov's survival, and his appointment as the first chief of the newly formed KGB, to his long-standing relationship

with Khrushchev as much as to his reputation for ruthless competence. Serov's association with Khrushchev began in 1938 when
Stalin sent Khrushchev to the Ukraine with orders to revive the economy, rebuild the Ukrainian Communist party apparatus, and to
"Russify" the recalcitrant Ukrainian separatists. It had taken a long
time, but Stalin had finally realized that the purges had reduced the
Ukraine to an economic shambles and blighted the rich farm areas.
Ukrainian nationalism, always a problem for Moscow, was on the
boil, and Stalin could not risk further civil disorder.

One of Khrushchev's first moves in his new job was the transfer of
A. I. Uspensky, the NKVD chief who had directed the purges in the
Ukraine, to Moscow. In place of the old Chekist, he chose Serov, a
young artillery officer who had been transferred to the NKVD from
the Frunze Military Academy. Serov had no experience in security
operations but, as his mentor had apparently sensed, he did have a
flair for the work. Later, Khrushchev was to write, "With [Serov's]
help, I was able to put the Ukraine back on its feet."* This help con-
sisted of mass arrests, wholesale deportations, and executions.

By 1941 Serov's talent for repression had spread and he was sent to
the Baltic states to subdue the recently "liberated" population. Hundreds of thousands were deported. Later, as the Soviet forces stumbled back from the German invaders, Serov's talents were put to
even broader use. He directed the deportation of the Volga Germans,
some six hundred thousand of whom were transported from the
Volga German Autonomous Republic to eastern Russia. As the German advance rolled on and panic developed behind the Soviet lines,
Serov directed the massacre of suspected dissidents, staged provocations—in one incident a troop of NKVD men in Nazi uniforms was
parachuted behind the Soviet lines and calmly executed villagers
who sympathized with their supposed deliverers—and deported entire ethnic groups from the Caucasus.

By the time he was appointed KGB chief, Serov had become almost
as well known to Westerners in Moscow as had Beria before his fall
from grace. A small, feisty man with piercing blue eyes and a reced-
ing hairline, he was frequently seen at diplomatic receptions. After a
hard day at the office, he emerged, at least in the eyes of his Kremlin
peer group, as "an amiable, kindly, and amusing companion."

---

*Strobe Talbott, ed. and trans., *Khrushchev Remembers* (New York: Little, Brown and Company, 1970).

Whether in uniform or civilian clothes, he favored the thick-soled shoes recognized in Moscow as a secret police trademark.

Serov also liked to travel and as KGB chief he rarely missed an opportunity to go abroad. In 1955 he accompanied Bulganin, then Soviet premier, and Khrushchev on their trips to India, Burma, and Afghanistan. Later that year he preceded them to England, ostensibly to check on the security precautions taken by Scotland Yard to protect the Soviet leaders. British reaction against Serov, whom the press described variously as a "grinning gunman," an "odious thug," and a "butcher," became so great that the aggrieved hangman left before the delegation had completed its visit. He had better luck in Hungary in 1956. After the revolution had been put down, he arrested General Pal Maleter and other leaders of the revolution and saw to their deportation and execution. Stalin would have had reason to be proud of his protégé.

Most comment on Serov's abrupt transfer from one of the most important jobs in the USSR speculated on the possibility that he had lost out—and perhaps been liquidated—in a Kremlin power struggle. Shrewder observers noted that the press release specified that Serov had been released from the KGB "in connection with his transfer to other duties." When this phrase is tacked onto such an announcement, it usually means that the subject has not been removed in disgrace. Serov's new assignment, however, remained a mystery. It was weeks before rumors circulated that he had been transferred to the GRU.

When Popov was graduated from the Military Diplomatic Academy and reported to GRU headquarters, Lieutenant General Mikhail Aleksyevich Shalin, an experienced and well-liked intelligence man, was commanding officer. Shalin remained GRU chief from 1951 until 1957 when he was shunted aside for Lieutenant General Sergei Shtemenko. Shtemenko was one of Stalin's favorites and although he had an outstanding military record, his identification with Stalin was so close that when his patron died, Shtemenko was demoted two grades and rusticated. Three years later he popped up again in Moscow and in 1957 took over the GRU. After a year, Shtemenko was reassigned and Shalin returned to his post as GRU chief. Why Shtemenko moved along after only a year is not clear, unless the GRU assignment was the first step in his rehabilitation. In the event, he was lucky to have shed the intelligence job when he did.

There is an ironic justice in the fact that Shalin, who had been Popov's ultimate boss throughout his intelligence career, came back and replaced Shtemenko in the GRU almost a year to the day before Popov was uncovered. Although he had probably never heard of Popov until he fell under suspicion, the fact that a CIA mole had been discovered in the GRU was Shalin's responsibility. Each of the officers in Popov's line of command was culpable to some degree, but it was Shalin who bore the ultimate responsibility.

When the enormity of Popov's agent activity was presented to Khrushchev by Shalin and Serov—probably no later than mid-November 1958—the irascible premier must have reacted violently. However much he may have wanted immediate action taken against everyone in the GRU whose "Bolshevik spy-consciousness" had failed him, someone—probably Serov rather than the discredited Shalin—had to impress Khrushchev with the need to weigh the counterespionage consequences before taking action. Serov must have moved adroitly in attempting to convince the short-tempered premier that only if Popov could be played back against CIA would Soviet intelligence recover even a fraction of what it had lost. If Popov was to be played back, Serov presumably argued, the government could take no action that might tip Western intelligence to the fact that the GRU was being shaken up. General Shalin was, of course, directly responsible for the security of the GRU and there could be no question but what he would have to leave in disgrace. His dismissal could not, however, be made public, nor could any reference be made to his successor.

It was soon to become apparent that Serov had been only partially successful in selling this approach to Khrushchev. When Khrushchev picked Serov to replace Shalin in the GRU, he indulged in such an obvious bit of overkill that Shalin's ouster could not be kept under wraps very long. Serov was too conspicuous a figure in the Soviet establishment simply to drop out of sight.

Serov could, of course, be counted on to repair any obvious security shortcomings in the GRU, but there were a dozen or more KGB officers who could have done an even better job of rebuilding Soviet military intelligence and whose transfer might have been concealed long enough to cloak any possible connection with Popov. But Khrushchev had more on his mind than straightening out Soviet military intelligence.

In the USSR the KGB has the ultimate responsibility for *all* security—in the armed forces, the party, and every government office. Although Shalin—and the GRU security and counterintelligence sections—bore the brunt of the criticism, the fact that the supposedly omniscient KGB had failed to detect the mole in the GRU was also a mark against Serov. The KGB lapse was not as serious as that of the GRU, but it could not be ignored. It may have been this that brought other considerations to Khrushchev's mind.

Two years after Serov took over the GRU, a CIA agent who knew him well described Serov as "not the most brilliant of men. He knows how to interrogate people, imprison them, and shoot them. In more sophisticated intelligence work he is not so skillful."* This opinion was shared by the most senior operations officers in the KGB, and Khrushchev was aware of it. But these two black marks—the failure to detect the GRU mole and an indifferent performance in intelligence—were not the most serious charges against Serov. Khrushchev had not forgotten the clamor Serov's presence in the delegation accompanying Bulganin and Khrushchev had raised in England in 1955. The presence of so noxious a secret policeman in the Soviet hierarchy detracted from the impression the shrewd premier wanted his government to project.

There was still another, rather subjective, consideration. Neither Khrushchev nor any of his immediate collaborators had forgotten the narrow squeak they had when Beria began maneuvering to assume Stalin's role as absolute dictator. Having outlived the master, the survivors were not about to have Stalin's star pupil grab the throne. Beria was cut down before he could make a definitive move. It was of course still essential that a strong KGB remain as "the sword and shield of the party," but the problem of Serov, the secret police chief who had studied under both Stalin and Beria, could not be ignored. If there is ever a palace revolution in the USSR, the secret police chief will almost certainly play a key role in it. Clearly, there was much to be said for ensuring that Serov, Beria's last remaining protégé, not become so powerful that he might be tempted to seize power.

The opportunity of replacing Serov, the outmoded secret policeman and weak intelligence chief, with a party man was too strong to resist. With one stroke Khrushchev could relieve his government of a

---

*Oleg Penkovskiy, *The Penkovskiy Papers,* trans. Peter Deriabin, introduction and commentary by Frank Gibney, forward by Edward Crankshaw (New York: Ballantine Books, 1982), p. 90.

political liability, ensure that GRU security was rebuilt, and make room for a Khrushchev man as KGB chief. Perhaps the irony of charging Serov with the task of cleaning up the GRU also appealed to the wily premier. Khrushchev then named Alexander Shelepin as KGB chairman. Shelepin was only forty and had made his career in the Komsomol and on the staff of the Central Committee.

If Western intelligence could piece together Khrushchev's logic and fathom the fact that Popov's arrest had triggered Serov's transfer, Khrushchev may have reasoned, it would be up to the intelligence services to sort out the counterespionage equities. It was not the first time intelligence had been shouldered aside by politics.

The fact that Serov's transfer was announced within a month of Popov's return to the USSR suggests that Popov was broken almost immediately after his arrest. Soviet counterintelligence practices had been honed for some forty years and interrogation techniques distilled from experience with tens of thousands of prisoners. Popov was a tough peasant but there seems little chance he could have withstood the pressure the KGB subjected him to. Even if he was at first able to withstand the interrogation, it is likely that the KGB uncovered hard evidence of his spying—subsequent Soviet press accounts refer to miniature code pads and secret writing materials, allegedly found in his luggage.

Various survivors of the treatment suffered by Popov had told strikingly similar stories. Judging by their published accounts, Popov would have been held incommunicado in the cellars of the Lubyanka prison, adjoining the rear of the KGB headquarters at Two Dzerzhinsky Square. The KGB's first objective in a forced interrogation—an interrogation in which the victim may be savaged at the whim of his questioners—is to reduce the prisoner to the lowest possible mental and physical condition. At the outset, Popov would have been beaten with professional skill, badly enough to convince him that resistance was impossible and that he was powerless in the hands of his jailers. To protect the possibility of playing Popov back against CIA as a double agent, care would be taken not to cripple him or to leave scars on his face or hands.

From the moment of his arrest Popov would have been kept in complete isolation and not allowed to speak to anyone but his interrogators; nor would the prison guards have been allowed to speak to

Popov. When not under interrogation he would be kept under constant surveillance in a small, windowless cell, barely wide enough to accommodate the heavy steel bed and skimpy blanket covering it. To ensure that the prisoner was completely disoriented, the time lapse between interrogation sessions and meals would be randomly separated. Popov would not have known whether it was day or night, nor would he have any idea how long he had been under interrogation. Food would consist of bread, a few scraps of meat or fish, and tepid water that passed for potato soup. The diet would be just sufficient to keep the prisoner from starving.

Popov's wife was presumably apprehended immediately upon her return from East Berlin. The moment the interrogators were convinced Popov was a spy, she would have been subjected to questioning and treatment almost as brutal as that inflicted on Popov. Only when the interrogators were convinced that she was completely ignorant of Popov's agent activity would this treatment be tempered. To increase pressure on Popov he may have been permitted to see his wife. Perhaps the abused and broken woman was allowed to plead with him to cooperate with her tormentors. The impact of Popov's appearance on his wife could only have added to her despair.

In these circumstances it is difficult to see how anyone, no matter how strong his motives, could have resisted making a full confession. Nor, as happened with the high-ranking old Bolsheviks who were led to make the most improbable public admissions during the purge trials of the thirties, does it seem likely that either of the prisoners could avoid making any statements the interrogators chose for them.

Once the initial phase of the interrogation was completed, and the outline of Popov's agent activity clearly established, a glimmer of hope would be introduced. By cooperating fully and without the least murmur of resistance, an interrogator would suggest, perhaps the prisoner's torment might be eased. He would be allowed a little more food and a slightly relaxed interrogation schedule. But the mere whisper of suspicion that the prisoner was not completely responsive would mean an immediate return to the intolerable regimen.

As the interrogators filled their dossiers, the details would be checked against the reports made by teams of experts questioning Popov's former colleagues, friends, and relatives. Other researchers would ransack the massive KGB and GRU files for collaborative data. Discreet investigations would be made in the field. A search would be initiated to identify "Grossman" and "Scharnhorst," the pseudonyms used by Domnin, from among the American intelligence officers who had been identified by the KGB through the years. The safe houses used by Popov in Vienna and West Berlin—but long since vacated—would be identified. Because it was important that CIA have no reason to suspect that Popov had been arrested, the field investigations would be done with the utmost circumspection.

It is difficult to judge how long it was before the counterespionage teams were satisfied that Popov had been completely broken and was no longer capable of offering resistance or withholding any scrap of information. Only then would the work of preparing him for a possible double-agent role begin. In exchange for complete cooperation he would have been told that his wife would be released and his relatives and in-laws freed of suspicion of having cooperated with him. Later, as the hundreds of details in his confession were confirmed in meticulous file searches, interrogations, and observations in the field, Popov might have been offered his life in return for his commitment to work as a double agent. Although Stalin's old comrades who were brought to make their fabricated confessions in open court were put to death, there is evidence that part of the suasion used against them was the promise of prison terms for themselves and freedom for their families. The few who had second thoughts and denied their confessions in court usually returned the next day to admit that their confessions had been correct and that no force had been used to make them confess.

Aside from suicide, a practical impossibility for a prisoner under constant observation in the Lubyanka prison, Popov would have had no alternative but to cooperate fully with the KGB. In these circumstances, the subsequent Soviet press boasts that Popov's final few meetings with his Moscow contact man were at the behest of the KGB may be taken at face value. It was October 1959, however, before the KGB chose to close the Popov case with a blast of publicity.

26
INCIDENT ON BUS LINE 107

Serov had not finished a year as GRU chief when there was another newsbreak datelined Moscow. As sensational as this story was, it would be another four years before Soviet publications linked the incident with the Popov case.

On 18 October 1959 a front-page story in the *New York Times* reported the seizure, detention, and attempted blackmail of an American diplomat in Moscow. Although released by the Russians in less than two hours, Russel A. Langelle, the chief security officer in the Moscow embassy, was charged with espionage, declared *persona non grata*, and ordered to leave the USSR within three days.

In another even more sensational disclosure, the story related how the attaché had, on 16 October, been "kidnapped by five unidentified Russians" who had then threatened him and his family and "had tried to blackmail and bribe him into becoming a Soviet espionage agent." Although several American diplomats had been expelled from the USSR, and a few charged with spying, the *New York Times* called this incident the most "melodramatic."

As reported by the *Times*, Langelle's story of what happened on 16 October began when he stepped off number 107 bus at the corner of Chaikovskovo and Vorovskovo streets, about a block from the chancery of the U.S. embassy in Moscow. There, three men in civilian clothes accosted him, pinned his arms, covered his mouth, and dragged him to a Zim automobile parked in a nearby alley. He was then driven to an unspecified address on Vorovskovo Street, pulled out of the car, and bustled into an apartment building.

As soon as he was in the apartment prepared for his interrogation, Langelle freed his arms, produced his diplomatic credentials, and asked to be allowed to telephone the embassy. At this point the "Soviet individuals laughed at the document and ignored" his request. When Langelle's topcoat was searched, "one of the men produced a notebook, which he said belonged to Mr. Langelle, but which, in fact, Mr. Langelle had never seen before."

Then one of the Russians took a bit of cotton batting from his pocket, dipped it in a solution, and wiped it across the pages of the notebook. To no one's surprise—except presumably Langelle's—this developed "supposedly concealed writing." One of the Russians then "identified the writing as referring to Soviet state secrets . . . [and] accused Mr. Langelle of engaging in espionage activities against the Soviet Union."

With the first act of the melodrama over, one of the men "attempted to interrogate Mr. Langelle about his duties in the embassy." When Langelle refused to enter any conversation, the Russians began to browbeat him. Asserting that his diplomatic immunity had been revoked and that he was therefore subject to imprisonment, the Russians threatened him with physical violence. They also attempted to cow him by threatening to take action against his wife and three children who resided with him in Moscow.

Since the KGB has used this technique dozens of times, and has schooled its satellite services in it, the embassy account rings true. The fact that the communist services continue to use it against Western diplomats suggests that in some instances it has worked. To Langelle's credit, he was not moved by the threats.

The *Times* also reported that when "Mr. Langelle continued to refuse to enter into conversation, the men then sought to enlist his cooperation in undertaking intelligence activities on behalf of the Soviet Union against the United States and promised him monetary reward." At this moment in the mad morality play, we may assume that one of the KGB heavies had been briefed to play the "good guy." It takes little imagination to see him sidling up to Langelle during a pause in the huggermugger and quietly suggesting that Langelle should be reasonable. Rather than having his career ruined by his expulsion from the USSR, Langelle could easily turn the incident to a profit, with no one the wiser. In KGB terms, being reasonable would mean signing on as a Soviet spy.

After an hour and forty-five minutes of threats, pushing, punches, and blandishments, the KGB apparently gave up. Three of the men escorted Langelle from the building and thrust him into the waiting automobile. He was then driven to Vostaniya Square and advised to forget the entire incident. If the KGB really expected the embassy to write off this episode as a bit of diplomatic bad manners, they were mistaken.

That afternoon Edward L. Freers, the embassy chargé d'affaires, handed a protest note to Sergei R. Striganov, acting chief of the American section of the Soviet foreign ministry. When Freers added a vehement oral protest to the diplomatic note on Langelle's kidnapping and the Soviet attempt to blackmail him, Striganov riposted with the allegation that Langelle had used his embassy position as a cover for spying on the USSR. Freers denied Striganov's charge.

Had the incident ended with this diplomatic stand-off, even experienced observers of Eastern Europe would have had trouble deducing what had really happened. Some might have thought that the KGB had found Langelle, the embassy security officer, to have been too effective in his work and had decided to create an incident that could, however implausibly, be used as grounds to expel him. More cynical observers might have assumed that, for reasons of its own, the KGB had decided that the diplomat might be susceptible to a recruitment or blackmail approach. When he rejected the recruitment and blackmail attempts, the KGB simply made good its threat and directed the obliging foreign ministry to declare him *persona non grata.* Others might have believed the Soviet story.

Then came the second phase of the incident. According to the *Times*'s Moscow sources, the USSR had told the embassy that it had no intention of publicizing the incident, allegedly lest it cast a pall over the spirit of mutual understanding Premier Khrushchev was trying to create. Not at all, said the State Department. Speaking for the department in Washington, Lincoln White stated flatly that the Soviet foreign ministry had said nothing whatsoever to the embassy on the question of giving publicity to the incident. Irrespective of who was lying, perhaps the American decision to publicize the event actually did move the Russians to publish their version of what had happened.

According to the story released by the foreign ministry to the Soviet press, passengers aboard the Moscow bus had noticed that during the Friday morning rush hour, two riders were exchanging packages, one of which "appeared to contain money." The passengers became suspicious and "detained" the two travelers until they could be turned over to "the authorities." Only then was it discovered that one package contained twenty thousand rubles. One of the persons detained by the sharp-eyed straphangers was a Soviet citizen and was alleged to have carried a letter "of espionage instructions showing that he was a spy." Along with this, he also carried "secret-ink materials." The other person—identified as Langelle—was accused of having in his possession a notebook containing secret data written in invisible ink. According to the Soviet press accounts, Langelle was released when he showed his diplomatic identification card.

In Washington a State Department spokesman said "there was no such person" as the alleged agent and denied that Langelle had paid anyone any money. As for the notebook allegedly in Langelle's possession when he was picked up: "in fact Mr. Langelle had never seen it before."

Langelle returned to the United States on 25 October and a day later appeared at a press conference in the State Department. Describing the incident, Langelle said that although he occasionally drove his car to the embassy, he often took the bus—a fifteen-minute ride. On the morning of 16 October he boarded the "rather crowded" bus at eight forty-five. Until the moment he got off, a block and a half from the embassy, Langelle had not noticed anything unusual. When he stepped off the bus, he was seized from behind, hustled into the Zim, and driven for five minutes to the "interrogation point."

An interesting part of this interview concerns the notebook—a palm-sized, spiral notebook of Russian manufacture. After Langelle described the KGB man rubbing a solution onto a blank page and watching as the writing appeared, reporters asked if Langelle could write or take notes in Russian. Langelle said that although he could speak Russian, he wrote the language very badly.

The following day, a *Times* editorial pointed out that the incident had a "nightmare quality reminiscent of Franz Kafka's most morbid writings," and asked perplexedly, "Why was this done?" Answering its own question, the editorial suggested that the incident might have been staged because Premier Khrushchev had become alarmed lest the atmosphere of good feeling he was spreading might have too great an effect on the Soviet people and that such an incident might help to re-create "the Stalinist spy mania" and restore "Bolshevik vigilance" in the USSR. If not this, the editorial continued, perhaps the event had been rigged by "important elements in the Soviet leadership" who felt Khrushchev had gone too far in his praise of President Eisenhower.

It says something for the temper of the *Times* that nowhere in the newspaper's coverage of the incident was there any discussion of the possibility that the diplomat might in fact have been engaged in espionage. On the basis of the press stories, a case might be made either way. A crowded bus *is* a likely place for a brush contact between a spy and a cutout. Twenty thousand rubles—five thousand dollars at the official rate—would have been a substantial payment for any agent. If Popov *was* involved, the payment would be very large in comparison with what amounted to expense money he had been given in the past. Even at the more realistic tourist rate, the payment would have come to two thousand dollars, still a sizable sum. But if contact with Popov, or some possible agent, were to be broken for some months, the payment would not have been unusual.

The rest of the story makes little sense. If a cutout were to hand a packet of money to a spy on a crowded bus, it is beyond imagination that it would be wrapped in a way that even the most curious observer could see that it was money. If we accept the notion that the "authorities" were called in only after the passengers became suspicious, we must wonder why they thought so quickly to develop the alleged secret writing. It is also remarkable that one of the authorities had cotton batting in his pocket. One other technical detail seems faulty. There is little reason why a spy would have a supply of secret ink *and* a bottle of developing solution on his person. If the diplomat had just given the alleged agent some secret writing equipment, how did it happen that there was already a secret writing message in the notebook? Perhaps the Russians wanted us to believe that the hardworking spy had used up his supply of ink and the diplomat was replenishing it—*and* paying him twenty thousand rubles *and* picking up a notebook *and* having a chat. If so, this would have been a rather busy brush contact.

The account of the secret ink poses other questions. The Soviet story mentions only that the "unidentified Russian" had secret writing material in his possession. Presumably it was this material that the "authorities" used to develop the secret messages in the notebook taken from the diplomat. But spies do not necessarily have—let alone carry around with them—the solution that will develop the messages they write to their case officer. Spies who get instructions in invisible ink must, of course, have a solution for the incoming messages. But there is no need for them to develop the letters that *they* write to their control.

Messages *from* spies are usually developed by technicians working in laboratory conditions. It is quite possible for the incoming messages to go through two or three stages of development. For security reasons and to avoid possible mistakes, agents working in the field are usually issued relatively simple, one-step systems for developing incoming messages.

On the basis of the evidence, some of it implausible, and the charges and denials, one is left with the impression that there might have been more to the incident on the 107 bus than was disclosed at the time. If the KGB had doubled the "Russian" who was arrested on the bus, they might have used the brush contact as an excuse to seize the contact man and attempt to recruit or blackmail him. This would account for the obvious preparations the KGB had made—the goon squad, the waiting car, the apartment, and the easily developed and presumably damning data in the notebook. When the intended victim of the set-up refused to cooperate, the KGB went to its fallback position and had him expelled. Possibly the KGB and foreign ministry hoped that the publicity attending the incident could be exploited to show the United States in yet another imperialist intrigue.

The story of the American attaché's Moscow experience was splashed across the front pages of the world press, but died almost as quickly as most such incidents. The allegation that diplomats sometimes double as contact men is not quite so startling as it used to be.

To follow the KGB's logic in releasing—*four years later*—a newspaper account that ties Popov to the incident, it is necessary to discuss another mole, Colonel Oleg Penkovsky, a senior GRU officer who was recruited jointly by CIA and the British secret intelligence service.

General Ivan Serov took command of the GRU in December 1958 with a mandate from Khrushchev to clean house and restore Soviet military intelligence to his former competence. Not the mildest mannered man, and nursing a soul-blistering grudge against the forces that tumbled him from his position in the KGB and Soviet hierarchy, he turned to his new task with surly vengeance. His first concern was the security of the GRU staff and operations. While reexamining the personnel and security files of all GRU employees, Serov began to streamline GRU organization and administration. These were tasks he understood and areas in which he was at home. Later, when he had identified the most gifted operators, he would begin to concentrate on raising the level of GRU operations—pruning unproductive cases, pushing his staff to make new recruitments.

Serov's deputy for operations was Major General Aleksandr Semenovich Rogov, a long-time GRU operative with many years of service abroad. He would remain in place, at least for the present. And so would Major General Khadzhi Mamsurov, the deputy for administrative matters. Serov was less sure of Admiral Bekrenev, chief of the First Directorate, responsible for all GRU illegals. As soon as an overseas assignment could be found, the admiral would be sent abroad.* Bekrenev might not have known Popov, but he had signed the order transferring him from Schwerin to the illegals section in East Berlin. Major General Aleksey Konovalov would remain as chief of the Second Directorate, responsible for operations in Europe. Even the KGB acknowledged that Konovalov was a competent operations man.

Ironically, one of Serov's favorites among the senior GRU staff officers was Colonel Oleg Penkovsky. He had first heard of Penkovsky in 1956 when the latter was deputy to Major General Savchenko, the GRU *rezident* in Turkey. As Penkovsky saw it, Savchenko was not only incompetent, but was deliberately disobeying orders from the Moscow center. In an extraordinary breach of GRU practice, Penkovsky took the bold step of drafting a cable detailing his chief's shortcomings and forwarded it to Moscow via KGB channels. As Penkovsky might have expected, he was immediately recalled to Moscow. There, Penkovsky was able to prove his case and Savchenko was eventually recalled and dismissed from the GRU. But in the Soviet system, subordinates do not lightly peach on their superiors, and if anyone in the GRU should be moved to do so he should not in any circumstance air the dirty linen in KGB cable channels.

Penkovsky was put on the shelf—in reserve status—and remained there until in 1958 he persuaded a friend, Chief Marshal Varentsov, to send him to guided missiles school. After finishing first in the nine-month course, Penkovsky expected to be assigned to a line military unit. But by this time Serov was in command of the GRU and, remembering the young officer from the Savchenko incident, refused to release him for troop duty.

Serov assigned Penkovsky to a cover position as deputy chief of the foreign section of the State Committee for Coordination of Scientific Research. "Coordination" is of course a euphemism. The committee was in fact a vehicle for the recruitment of foreign scientists and the procurement—openly or secretly—of scientific information from abroad. Data which could be adapted for military use was most

---

*Bekrenev was later assigned as Soviet naval attaché and GRU *rezident* in Washington.

sought after, but even such mundane intelligence as automobile-tire production figures was welcomed. All important positions were held by the KGB and GRU officers assigned to the committee. Penkovsky's chief was Dzherman Gvishiani, a Georgian KGB man distantly related to Stalin. Some sixty intelligence officers were assigned to the committee, which among its other responsibilities arranges for all visits to the USSR by foreign scientists and supervises the travel of Soviet scientific delegations.

Less than a year after Popov's arrest, Colonel Penkovsky, already one of Serov's favorites, attempted to make contact with the U.S. embassy through a tourist. Unfortunately, the embassy staff—too well indoctrinated against the perils of accepting gifts from strangers—did not follow up. It was almost twelve months later before Penkovsky made the contact that led MI-6 and CIA jointly to recruit him.

There is no evidence that Penkovsky knew Popov or had heard about his arrest. Popov never referred to Penkovsky and there is no mention of Popov in the *Penkovskiy Papers** or a book written by a Moscow contact man.† Still, it is difficult to believe that anyone as well connected as Penkovsky, and so close to Serov, would not have heard of the Popov case. If Serov did discuss Popov with Penkovsky, it may have been that Popov's story figured in Penkovsky's decision to break with the system he could no longer tolerate.

The uncanny similarities in the Popov and Penkovsky operations could only have added a measure to the panic that ripped through the Soviet security organs when Penkovsky was arrested some two years after Popov was uncovered. Both agents were graduates of the Frunze and Military Diplomatic academies. Both were senior GRU

---

*Frank Gibney, ed., *The Penkovskiy Papers*, trans. Peter Deriabin (New York: Ballantine Books, 1982). This book is based on material written by Penkovsky in Moscow and allegedly smuggled out of the USSR after his arrest. It was then given to Deriabin, who had lived in the U.S. since his defection from the KGB in Vienna in 1954. Questions have been raised about the provenance of these papers, but there can be no doubt that the material originated with Penkovsky. The book is rich in insights into the upper brackets of the Soviet establishment and details of GRU operational activity and organization. It is illustrated with photographs and documents that could only have come from Penkovsky. Incidentally, the transliteration used by Deriabin throughout the book accounts for the spelling of *Penkovskiy*.

†Greville Wynne, *Contact on Gorky Street* (New York: Atheneum, 1968). This book is unique for the view it gives of the handling of a Soviet mole in Moscow. Wynne was a contact man, operating without diplomatic immunity. When Penkovsky and Wynne were arrested, eight British and American diplomats were expelled from the USSR. Wynne was tried with Penkovsky and given an eight-year sentence. Wynne's interrogation gives clues to the more severe handling that Popov and Penkovsky suffered. After a year in prison, Wynne was exchanged for Gordon Lonsdale, a Soviet illegal arrested in England.

officers and both volunteered their services to Western intelligence. Neither agent was a mercenary, each understood the risks he was taking, and both had refused repeated offers of asylum.

Despite these parallels, the agents came from opposite ends of the Soviet spectrum. Penkovsky was as much a Soviet aristocrat as Popov was a peasant. Popov was moved to his secret war against the Soviet Union by his passionate concern for his own people, the Russian peasants. Penkovsky hated the Soviet system for what it was doing to *all* Russians and because he was convinced that Khrushchev and the Soviet high command were committed to a policy that could only lead to an atomic war. An idealist and a communist from his school days, he was appalled by the callous, self-serving attitude of the Soviet hierarchy he had come to know at first hand. Popov worked for some six years before he was uncovered and executed. Penkovsky, driven by his obsession to thwart Soviet policy, was arrested after a short sixteen months.

Penkovsky's family were middle-level civil servants of the czar. Popov's family were peasants from one of the poorest areas of the Soviet Union. Penkovsky's father was killed fighting as an officer against the Bolsheviks in 1919. Popov's parents were illiterate. Penkovsky spoke good English, liked posh restaurants, and when abroad indulged himself in nightclubs. Popov never lost his peasant tastes and could not master a foreign language. Both men loved their families, but Popov was hopelessly involved with a plain mistress and Penkovsky enjoyed casual flirtations. Penkovsky was an intimate of some of the most powerful men in the Soviet establishment; Popov had no friends at the top.

Unlike Popov, Penkovsky had a knack for making and exploiting contacts. In 1942, while working as a political commissar, Penkovsky met Major General Dimitri Gapanovich, a member of the Military Council and chief of the Political Directorate of the Moscow Military District. Gapanovich was one of the most senior political generals in the Red Army and a friend of Stalin. Three years later Penkovsky married Gapanovich's daughter, Vera. After service at the front—at one time Penkovsky commanded an artillery regiment in combat— Penkovsky was made an aide to Lieutenant General Sergei Varentsov, the Red Army artillery commander. His relationship with Varentsov became so close that the general referred to Penkovsky as his son and treated him as a protégé. At the time of Penkovsky's arrest, Varentsov was a chief marshal and head of the Soviet guided missiles program. Penkovsky's great-uncle was Lieutenant General Valentin

Penkovsky, commander of the Far East Military District. When Penkovsky returned to active GRU duty in 1960, he became one of Serov's favorites and an intimate of his family. Penkovsky guided Serov's wife and daughter on a tour of London.

Unlike Popov, Penkovsky was uniquely qualified to collect high-level intelligence. He was a well-trained artillery and guided missile officer and had a flair for science. As the son-in-law of a prominent political general, the protégé of a chief marshal, and a close friend of Serov, he had all bases covered—the party, the military establish-ment, and the intelligence services. In the sixteen months he worked as an agent, Penkovsky delivered thousands of pages of top-secret military, political, and intelligence data. Much of this was in docu-mentary form, but during the three trips he made abroad while working in place, he went through hours of interrogation by British and American experts. There may have been more important agents, but if one has been detected, his case has not been publicized. Until such an agent is identified, Penkovsky's reports will remain unique in modern intelligence history.

The first mention of Popov by name in the Soviet press came in *Red Star,* the Soviet defense ministry newspaper, on 20 December 1962. In an article marking the forty-fifth anniversary of the Soviet security services, Major General Anatoli Guskov noted that the KGB had re-cently unmasked an American intelligence agent, a "former military officer Popov." According to *Red Star,* "the Pentagon" had attempted to obtain information on Soviet rocket armaments and the location of of important military installations from Popov. Although a Reuters dispatch from Moscow summarized the story, it seems to have at-tracted no other press comment.

Three months later—and four years after Langelle was declared *persona non grata*—the KGB approved the publication of more data on the Popov case. When this release was made, it was not intended simply to inform Soviet readers who might have wondered what had happened to the Russian who was arrested on the 107 bus way back in October 1959, but to prepare the Soviet public for the sensational trial of another spy—Colonel Oleg Penkovsky. Penkovsky's trial would begin in less than two months.

"Duel in the Dark," a two-part article by George Berezko, was pub-lished in *Izvestya* on 12 and 13 March 1963. It concerned "Lieutenant Colonel P, a former officer in the Soviet army," who was known to

American intelligence as "Max," and Russel Langelle, an attaché of the American embassy in Moscow.

Berezko admits that there were no "factual reasons" not to have used the agent's name in the *Izvestya* account. Only after discussions with the KGB officers who briefed him on the operation was it decided that the use of a pseudonym would protect the spy's family, who were "absolutely not guilty" of any crime. The wife was working—at a job found for her by the KGB—and the spy's son would soon finish school. Berezko notes that "the comrades from [the KGB], who are far from sentimental"—an observation with which many of his Soviet readers might agree—concurred with this decision. It would be left to the mother "to tell her son everything that had happened when he was a little older."

According to Berezko, the story—"documented to the last detail"—began in 1956, "... perhaps even earlier." After a pious disclaimer that the article was not written for detective-story fans, but because it might be of some use "in the struggle for peace and humanity that people are now waging on our restless planet," he gets down to business.

In May 1958, he writes, Langelle and his family went on a picnic in the Lenin Hills, near a staircase leading to the Moscow River. When the picnic was over, Langelle ostensibly busied himself cleaning up, but in the process allegedly cached a small, waterproof package near the steps. The parcel "contained two thousand rubles, instructions for an agent typed in microscopic type on tiny sheets, and tablets used in cryptography." At this point Berezko states that the package was not for "Max" but for another agent, and adds that this "perhaps not so completely accidental find on Lenin Hills played a definite role in the uncovering of Max."

In mentioning that the surveillance of Langelle and his family was not accidental, the KGB seems to be telling CIA that the agent for whom the drop was intended had been detected and doubled. If there was any such agent, and if a cache was actually made, the story has remained in the secret archives. No further details have been released by the Russians. The KGB is also suggesting to CIA that when this agent pointed the finger at Langelle, the resulting surveillance led to "Lieutenant Colonel P."

At this point Berezko admits that as he studied the "P" file—presumably in a KGB office—he looked for an explanation of what might have led him to a "crime that can only be compared with fratricide" and wondered what "circumstances in his life or what somber spiritual 'kinks' had brought P to this terrible end. . . . Who was P and what moved his hand to strike out against the lives and well-being of his compatriots?"

After admitting that his researches had shown that P was "by no means a demonic figure," Berezko notes that he was "rather bashful" during the war and had clung to posts in the rear. After the war, when P served for a long time with "the troops abroad" his comrades claimed that he was an exemplary soldier, albeit without "manifesting any special talents." Although the crime P committed was "tremendous and could scarcely be expiated, he himself was a nonentity, a small-time scoundrel."

To prove this point, Berezko quotes from a passage allegedly taken from a "dispatch of P's that never reached its destination"—presumably a secret-ink message from P to his case officer. "I cordially thank you for your concern about my safety; it is for me a matter of vital importance. Thanks also for the money. It is possible that I may meet many acquaintances to gain information, and, apart from that, since I am now in reserve, every two months I get only the basic rate of pay according to rank—that is, one-third of the total pay. The move also demands supplemental expenses, so that I thank you once again very much."

It is almost inconceivable that any agent working in place in Moscow would write his case officer in open text. An agent operating in the Soviet capital—the most heavily policed city in this world—would probably encipher his messages and then commit them to secret ink. In the best of circumstances, enciphering is an excruciating task, one that would become even more complicated if the agent used "tiny" cipher pads like the ones allegedly cached near the stairway in the Lenin Hills. Transposing an enciphered message into secret ink is fussy work and, like enciphering, can only be done where there is no risk of observation. Penkovsky had a luxury flat by Moscow standards and enough privacy to prepare his messages without risk of interruption. It is doubtful that Popov had more than two rooms. Granted that he might have been able to do his enciphering at home, one thing is certain—facing these problems, even the most loquacious agent is likely to edit any unnecessary verbiage from his messages. The quotation attributed to P is apparently only one passage from a much longer message. In the circumstances, one may suspect that the KGB had a hand in preparing the letter shown to Berezko.

Whether or not P actually composed this letter, it seems to have convinced Berezko. "It is quite difficult," he wrote, "to find a term for all this. It is not even cynicism, it is horrifying baseness, self-enamored greed, emptiness of the soul. . . ."

He then notes that "on the whole, P's promotions were good. He was praised and had good certifications. To a certain extent he can perhaps be explained because he was unobtrusive, obliging, and tried not to be conspicuous. With people who liked their drink, he drank; with fishermen, he went fishing; and, with hunters, he went shooting. Even though he had no close friends, he kept up equally good relations with all his colleagues. In essence, however, P traded with their heads, not figuratively speaking, but literally. . . . In case of war the secrets sold by P would have led to heavy human losses if he had not been unmasked in time." As far as it goes, this is a fair picture of Popov. He was naturally unobtrusive and obliging and he was an enthusiastic hunter and fisherman.

It was, Berezko continued, the agent's "taciturn nature that helped him go unrecognized for a long time. Alas, one has to concede that P's colleagues, who had access to particularly important military and political information, were far too open with him. I will not err in saying that P's unmasking prevented very grave consequences from this impermissible sincerity." This is quite a concession for the ostensibly omnipotent KGB to have made. Since the Soviet press subsequently admitted that Popov had been at work as an agent since 1952, it had taken the KGB six years to forestall the "grave consequences."

Berezko then quotes from P's alleged confession. "I was drawn into collaboration with the Americans under the following circumstances. In the winter of 1956 I sent a letter to Austria to my mistress [Bielic]. . . .* Soon I received a letter from her in which she made an appointment in West Berlin where she intended to go for the Christmas holidays."

P arrived in East Berlin "on a mission" from his post in Schwerin, put on civilian clothes, and crossed into West Berlin. (Well-informed Soviet readers would have known that the only Russians stationed in East Germany who had access to civilian clothes were diplomats or intelligence officers.) Instead of finding Bielic at the rendezvous, he was met by two policemen in civilian clothes. They informed P that he was on the grounds of a secret installation and hustled him off to the American military police headquarters. There he was told that he had been caught red-handed on an intelligence mission and sub-

---

*Although Popov is only occasionally referred to by his true name in the Soviet press, whenever "Lyuba Bielic" is mentioned, her real name is used.

jected to a six-hour interrogation. When P refused to cooperate with his questioners, he was allegedly told that he would be flown to West Germany and that the press would be told he was a voluntary defector. Then, if he still refused to cooperate, he would be returned to the Soviet authorities. Faced with this threat, P allegedly lost heart and agreed to become an American agent.

At this point, according to the *Izvestya* story, "Lieutenant Colonel Scharnhorst (alias Harry Grossman) stepped into the act. He apologized for the bad manners of his colleagues and said that in future he would maintain contact with P through a 'liaison man.'" P was then allowed to return to Schwerin, where he was subsequently visited by "an elderly German." When "the old German returned from Schwerin to Lieutenant Colonel Scharnhorst with the first of P's dispatches, their cooperation had started." Early in 1957, P obtained a transfer to Berlin in order to meet Scharnhorst in person. "Every month P put on civilian clothes and made his way to West Berlin. He called Scharnhorst from a public telephone: 'Max calling.' They met in the street and the American drove to a secret apartment (No. 3 Litzensee Strasse)."

According to Berezko, P signed receipts for the monthly salary that was given him, rather delicately, in a plain envelope. Occasionally, presumably when he was hard up, Scharnhorst would pocket a portion of P's wages and fudge the receipt. This message, obviously intended for CIA, is standard KGB procedure—almost every time Soviet intelligence exposes a double agent, the spy will claim that his American case officer had been cheating him, forcing him to sign false receipts for wages he had not received. When a Soviet official defects, the KGB frequently charges that he skipped with a sizable amount of money embezzled from official funds or from his erstwhile comrades.

Later Berezko notes that the only thing Scharnhorst was generous with was praise. In an alleged letter to P, Scharnhorst cheered the agent along—"as I have often told you, our important people have always valued highly your political reports. The same is true of your reports on the army. That is why they are watching your career with great interest."

In April 1958, P is alleged to have testified, he was introduced to an American intelligence officer, code name "Daniel." "This was done in case I might be sent back to Moscow. Daniel gave me a telephone number in Moscow and two code sentences for arranging meetings."

The *Izvestya* article gives one indication of the information P allegedly was asked to supply. In a letter, P is told, "We are particularly interested in all details on the real Soviet intentions in Berlin and on any preparations for military actions. We are also interested in the precise number and location of launching sites for intercontinental missiles, the location and number of test launchings per month.... With a firm handshake from Scharnhorst, D." This, at least, has the authentic flavor of a letter to an agent.

When P was transferred to Moscow "at the end of 1958," he took with him a "hunting knife with a hollow handle and a dummy fishing reel, both containing code notebooks." P remained in Moscow until he "was transferred to the Urals." It was there, according to Berezko, that "his second job was finally discovered." From that time, P was "as if transfixed by a spotlight in the dark, he never left its beam again." And the information he transmitted was planted on him to lead the Americans astray.

Since it is clear that Popov was arrested immediately upon his return to the USSR in December 1958, the reference to his transfer to the Urals smells like a Soviet cover story. The KGB may have attempted to account for the period from Popov's arrest to the end of his interrogation by having him tell CIA—possibly in a message left in a prearranged letter drop—that because of his problems with Bielic, he had been disciplined and temporarily rusticated in the Urals. Once the interrogation was complete—this would have taken several weeks—and Popov was ready to act as a double agent, he could presumably signal his presence, meet with a contact man, and begin feeding CIA reports prepared by the KGB. Some of the Soviet accounts allege that Popov was in Moscow and in touch with a contact man in the months before the incident on the bus in October 1959. These reports make it clear that during this period Popov was acting as a double agent under KGB control.

If we discount the more obviously self-serving distortions the KGB made in the material given Berezko, the basic data clearly refers to Popov. He was a lieutenant colonel, he did serve in Austria, and Bielic was his mistress. Popov was also transferred to East Berlin from Schwerin. He used the pseudonym Max and knew Domnin as Grossman and later as Scharnhorst. And Popov did return to the USSR in December 1958. Along with these facts, three important changes were made. Since it would scarcely have served the KGB's purposes to describe Popov as an ideological dissident, it was best to portray him as a weak person who readily submitted to American blackmail. Although P was described as a former lieutenant colonel, no reference was made to his GRU assignment. The KGB has never shrunk from slanging the GRU to the Central Committee and the Kremlin, but obviously saw nothing to be gained by admitting to *Izvestya*'s readers that P was a military intelligence officer. It was bad enough to have to concede he was a military man. The USSR had never admitted that Popov, Penkovsky, or any of a dozen or more defectors from the KGB and GRU ever served in intelligence.

By suggesting that Popov was recruited in 1956, the KGB lopped four years from Popov's tenure as a penetration agent. Whether this was only a face-saving dodge concocted by a security service that did not want to admit that a mole had remained undetected for six years, or was intended to convince CIA that Popov had managed to conceal important parts of his story from his interrogators, cannot be known. Possibly the KGB had both objectives in mind. Later KGB-approved stories indicate Popov was recruited in 1952.

Berezko finished his article with alleged excerpts from P's final statement at his trial. "After I was arrested I felt that a mountain had fallen from me. What I lived through during my contacts with the Americans does not stand comparison with anything." Berezko then suggests that from the moment Popov began his work with American intelligence "... the traitor was dying hourly from fright. And this constant expectation of death could make death itself almost welcome."

In the end, P is quoted as saying, "I am ready for any punishment ... for the supreme penalty. I deserve it." To this Berezko adds, "There are crimes after which it is impossible to live. A bullet at the end of a contemptible life is not only a punishment but also an act of mercy."

Popov had accepted the possibility of death when he began his fight against the system he hated. But when he said that what he had lived through during his contacts with the Americans did not stand comparison with anything, he was telling the simple truth. Gregory Domnin was the only person with whom he could ever discuss his ideas and his dreams of a better life for his people, the Russian peasants. After months of brutal treatment, it took a strong man to speak with such ironic candor to his executioners.

The Soviet press has continued to refer to the Popov case. In 1965 *On the Front of the Secret War*, a book by Sergey Tsybov and Nikolay Chistyakov, was published in Moscow. After giving a brief account of the Penkovsky case, the authors add, "another American spy, a former military man, Popov, was shot for treason...a few years ago."

Another book, *The Hidden Front*, by Simion Tsvigun, published in Baku in 1966, makes more details of the Popov case known to Soviet readers. Although Popov has become "P" again, his history is more accurately recorded. The book states that after graduating from the Frunze Military Academy in 1951, "P" was sent to work in "the organs of the Soviet administration in Austria." (Actually, Popov was graduated from the Frunze Academy in 1947 and from the Military Diplomatic Academy in 1951.) Once in Austria, his "immoral life" attracted the attention of American intelligence. While he was in the American sector of Vienna, he was arrested, interrogated, and blackmailed into becoming an American agent. For a number of years "P passed ... intelligence information and state secrets to American intelligence." For this, a Soviet court "accorded him his just deserts."

In 1972 a book, *Empire within an Empire (U.S. Intelligence in the Service of Monopoly)*, by Fedor M. Sergeyev, also mentions Popov by name. In a chapter intended to warn Soviet citizens traveling abroad that American intelligence is out to recruit them, Sergeyev notes that several years previously, the Military Collegium of the Soviet Supreme Court sentenced a former officer, Lieutenant Colonel P. S. Popov, to be shot. According to Sergeyev, Popov had collaborated with American intelligence for some five years, meeting monthly with an American case officer. In this version of the operation, Popov was serving in Vienna in 1958 when Lyuba Bielic (her true name is used) became his mistress. (Sergeyev inadvertently comes close to admitting that Popov was an intelligence officer—there had been no Soviet troops in Austria since the occupation ended in 1955. In 1958 the only Soviet military personnel were in the military attaché's office. At that time, all members of any Soviet military attaché offices were GRU employees. Popov had, of course, left Austria in 1955.)

Sergeyev also refers to a scene in a Russian "documentary film," *Once Again on the Murky Path*, describing alleged espionage in the USSR. In full uniform, the actor playing Popov strides up to the Astoria Restaurant in Moscow and peeks in the window. Apparently unable to spot the person he is looking for, the officer paces back and forth in front of the restaurant until a foreign car drives up and a man and woman get out. The man goes directly to a telephone booth in the restaurant foyer. As soon as the foreigner puts down the telephone, the Soviet officer enters the restaurant and steps into the booth. A few minutes later, he leaves carrying a small box that the foreigner left for him. If a telephone booth were to be used for a drop—and it is a favorite Soviet site—the material cached would not be in a box that the spy could be seen carrying. Still, it is only fair to allow Soviet filmmakers as much license as that taken by American TV.

More recently a book, *The Military Chekists*, an account of military counterintelligence published in Moscow in 1979, refers to a certain "Petrov," unmistakably a pseudonym for Popov. This gives a slightly different version of Popov's recruitment in Vienna in 1952 and adds, rather illogically, that Petrov only became an active agent after his assignment to East Berlin in 1957. The most interesting admission in this book is that Petrov went from jail to the meetings with his Moscow contact man.

When Penkovsky was arrested in October 1962, the GRU bit the dust. Serov, the security expert who had been brought in to clear up the wreckage left by Popov, was dumped, demoted, and eventually expelled from the party. Some three hundred senior GRU officers were recalled from field assignments and a score of other officers was dismissed. Serov's replacement was another KGB man. Lieutenant General Petr Ivashutin. Had the Kremlin asked the Moscow Art Theater to cast an obese, vulgar, and brutal secret policeman, no better cliché could have been found than Ivashutin. To secure his flanks in this hostile territory, Ivashutin brought with him a cadre of senior KGB officers and installed them in key positions throughout the GRU's Moscow headquarters.

The GRU remains active and is indeed a more competent service than it was when Serov was sacked. But it is no longer an independent military intelligence organ of the Soviet General Staff. KGB officers supervise its every move, approve each projected recruitment, and evaluate and interpret the GRU's intelligence reporting. It is, in effect, an arm of the KGB.

EDITOR'S NOTE:

Since the above assessment was written, the GRU has pulled up its socks and has once again established itself as an effective, independent, military intelligence service. As might be expected, the GRU concentrates on collecting military information, and scientific and technical data.

27
AFTER-ACTION NOTES

When an agent is lost or an operation compromised, intelligence services scramble to cauterize any dangling operational ends. Safe houses used in the operation are closed, operations personnel who might have been identified and possibly subject to arrest or surveillance, go to ground or are transferred out of the area. Before the dust settles, counterintelligence analysts, like the bomb squad at the scene of a blast, begin to pick their way through the wreckage to see what went wrong.

In the Popov case, there were several obvious clues—which is not to say that *obvious* clues necessarily provide the best answers to counterintelligence problems. First, there was Popov's all but chronic lack of discipline. Because of his stubborn refusal to sever contact with Lyuba Bielic, the relationship had come to the attention of GRU security officers soon after his transfer from Schwerin to East Berlin. Later, the affair became known to GRU security officers and eventually to the KGB. This disregard for GRU security regulations—and the probability that he had initially lied to both the GRU and KGB investigators (as well as to Domnin) about the extent of their correspondence and his having invited Bielic to East Berlin—would not necessarily have been fatal, but would certainly have focused attention on him. The moment any other security problem arose in Popov's vicinity, he would be among the first to be subjected to further investigation. Once a counterintelligence searchlight is focused on an agent in place, chances are his cover will begin to melt.

When Popov handed the letter to the British liaison officer in East Germany, he broke compartmentation, a cardinal security rule. No one, certainly not the chief of the British service or Popov, could have known that George Blake was a KGB agent. (Blake's KGB activity was not uncovered by British counterintelligence until 1961, some three years after Popov's arrest. His treason was not known in 1958 and did not, of course, figure in the initial after-action analysis of the Popov case.) Nor could anyone reasonably have anticipated the fluke by which Blake learned about the letter. The probability remains that when Blake's report reached the KGB, it touched off an investigation that could eventually have led to Popov. Soviet counterintelligence would unhesitatingly have made a maximum effort to run down such a lead. Given Russian competence in counterespionage, Blake's report alone could have been enough to undo Popov.

The most obvious and direct reason for Popov's fall was the Tairov incident. His proximity to Tairova in East Berlin and the alleged KGB reports confirming her charge that she had been surveilled from the moment of her arrival in New York would have been sufficient reason to subject him to close investigation and interrogation. Even if Popov had deflected the initial questions, the eventual search of his personal effects might have produced the hard evidence necessary to break him. As described in the Soviet press, two of the concealment devices—the hollow handle of a hunting knife and the spool of a fishing reel—would have passed any customs or police search. But counterintelligence probes are more thorough. Soviet technicians are masters of concealment and can fashion hiding places in the most improbable articles. Being familiar with the high craftsmanship of their own specialists—and possibly aided in the search by these same technicians—Russian experts will systematically take apart and, in the process, destroy every artifact and article of clothing belonging to a suspect.

Some years ago, a low-level Soviet agent was apprehended and confessed that his ciphers were concealed in one of the two batteries of a flashlight he carried in the trunk of his car. The light worked, the two batteries were identical in appearance and exactly the same weight. But the bottom of the concealment battery had been threaded like a screw. When turned clockwise for five revolutions it came apart. (Screws in Soviet concealment devices are often made to turn in the opposite direction from normal. An effort to loosen such a threat merely tightens it.) Although the battery functioned, half of it had been hollowed out—leaving enough room to conceal the miniaturized cipher pads. If the agent had not admitted that the battery had been rigged, no external examination, not even X-ray photographs—the casing was lead—would have revealed the concealed material.

However convincing the obvious clues may be, in an important operation, counterespionage officers must also consider the "worst-case" possibilities. Could the agent have been uncovered by a different, more dangerous, source—possibly a leak from inside? Might there be a microphone or miniature radio transmitter undetected in an office or safe house? Could a cipher have been broken? Or might the agent have been betrayed by a mole? Analysts know that if the opposing service had any such sensitive sources, every effort would have been made to suggest that the agent's compromise had a more obvious origin—a simple failure of tradecraft or an unlucky accident.

The threat of audio penetration is so well recognized today that security technicians keep most military, diplomatic, and intelligence offices under what amounts to constant counteraudio surveillance. Safe houses, residences, and even operational vehicles are frequently tested for clandestine transmitters and microphones.

Broken ciphers have had more influence on history than is ever likely to be known, but modern cryptography has advanced to a point that it is now conventional wisdom that the cipher systems of the major powers cannot be broken. When intelligence officers recall the success British and American cryptoanalysts had against the "unbreakable" German and Japanese ciphers in World War II, the notion that any cipher is absolutely safe is likely to pale. Yet, the fact remains that today few governments hesitate to transmit their most secret data electronically. Certainly there has been no published evidence in recent years even suggesting that the sophisticated cryptographic systems of the world powers can be broken.

One last threat remains. It is as old as warfare, statecraft, and espionage. The traitor within the gate. In espionage, the mole.

The first substantive comment on Popov by name in the American press came in 1978 when *Legend: The Secret World of Lee Harvey Oswald*,* was published by Edward Jay Epstein. Epstein, who had already published a book on the Kennedy assassination and the shortcomings of the Warren Commission investigation of it, began his research on Oswald by trying to fill in the blanks in the thirty

*Reader's Digest Press, New York, 1978.

months Oswald had spent in the USSR. Unable to interview any sources in the USSR—the Soviet embassy turned down his request for a visa, saying that none of the people who had known Oswald when he lived in the USSR wanted to be interviewed—Epstein turned to Major Yuri Ivanovich Nosenko, a KGB officer who had defected to CIA in Geneva in 1964.

When Epstein did this, he pried open one of the most complex and controversial espionage affairs ever to be made public. One of the CIA studies of the Nosenko case is more than nine hundred pages long, another some four hundred pages. A third report falls short of three hundred pages. The documents supporting these studies fill forty file drawers and presumably run into thousands of pages.

In 1979 the House of Representatives Select Committee on Assassinations published some of the most comprehensive and best documented material on the Nosenko case. The Select Committee, established in 1976 to conduct investigations into the assassinations of President Kennedy and Martin Luther King, Jr., held hearings in 1978 and 1979 in which several retired CIA officers and two CIA men on active duty testified. Nosenko was also questioned by the committee.

The committee's findings and recommendations are included in House Report No. 95–1828, Part 2, dated 29 March 1979 and published by the Government Printing Office in Washington. The testimony of Mr. John Hart, a special representative of Admiral Turner, then CIA director, is included in *Hearings Before the Select Committee on Assassinations,* Volume II, dated March 1979, GPO, Washington. Volume IV of the committee includes the testimony of Richard Helms, retired CIA director. Volume XII, appendix to the hearings, covers the committee's questioning of Nosenko; Mr. David E. Murphy, former chief of CIA's Soviet operations division; Murphy's former deputy; and Mr. Bruce Solie, the CIA officer who conducted the investigation that resulted in CIA's determination of Nosenko's bona fides.

In 1980 David C. Martin, a Washington-based journalist, published *Wilderness of Mirrors,* with extensive comments on the Nosenko affair.*

The well-documented Nosenko affair began in June 1962 when a man identifying himself as Yuri Nosenko, a KGB officer on temporary duty with a Soviet delegation in Geneva, approached CIA with

---

*David C. Martin, *Wilderness of Mirrors* (New York: Harper & Row, 1980; paperback, Ballantine Books, 1981).

an offer to sell information—he allegedly needed money to replace official funds he had spent on a binge in Geneva. Nosenko did not want to defect—he had a wife and family in Moscow—and did not wish to communicate with CIA from the Soviet Union. He would, however, meet CIA officers whenever he came abroad. Nosenko, who was born in 1927, had joined Soviet naval intelligence in 1949. In 1953 he transferred to the KGB and was assigned to the Second Chief Directorate, the KGB arm responsible for counterintelligence and security within the USSR. Nosenko claimed to have spent most of his KGB career in the American department and at various times to have been involved in operations against American tourists, journalists, military attachés, and, most important, the U.S. embassy in Moscow.

After disclosing enough details of several KGB operations against American and NATO targets to establish, at least initially, his credibility, Nosenko hurried back to Moscow with the disarmament delegation. On the basis of the data he had given his case officers, Nosenko seemed to be an exceptionally important walk-in.

According to Epstein and Martin, one of the inside stories Nosenko told CIA in Geneva concerned Popov. The agent was allegedly uncovered when a KGB surveillance squad tailing an American diplomat found he had dropped a letter addressed to Popov into a Moscow mailbox. According to Nosenko, the diplomat had taken all the necessary countersurveillance precautions and had every reason to believe that he was not under observation. Unfortunately, he fell foul of a new KGB technique. A maid had coated his shoes with a chemical substance that permitted the KGB surveillants—possibly assisted by a well-trained dog—to pick up the track long after the diplomat was out of sight. This may smack of James Bond gadgetry, but it is scarcely beyond the competence of a service ingenious enough to construct a radio transmitter that could be hidden in the heel of a diplomat's shoe.*

Nosenko's report on Popov seemed plausible enough. As a KGB officer working in the American department, he might presumably have heard about Popov's arrest. Alas, it was not to be that simple.

By the time the case officers had returned from Geneva, some of the analysts in Washington had begun to suspect that Nosenko might not be a bona fide source, but could well have been sent by the KGB in a complex deception operation.

*John Barron, *KGB* (New York: Reader's Digest Press, 1974). The device was uncovered in Bucharest, but in view of the Rumanian service's limited technical capability, was probably developed in Moscow by the KGB.

As the analysts pored over Nosenko's reports, some of the most interesting data was found to touch on information reported by another KGB officer. Anatoli Golitsin, a major in the First Chief Directorate, the KGB component responsible for espionage abroad, had defected six months before Nosenko appeared in Geneva. Some of Nosenko's information seemed to parallel what Golitsin had told his interrogators—with one important difference. Golitsin had allegedly asserted that the KGB had recruited "an agent within the highest echelons of United States intelligence." In the eyes of some counterintelligence officers, Nosenko's reports seemed calculated to convince CIA that although the KGB had recruited agents on the periphery of American intelligence, there had been no penetration of any important CIA office.* If this analysis was correct, it was another example of the tactic of deflecting attention from a well-placed source by blowing less important agents. In Germany the KGB was suspected of having taken the heat off Felfe, a senior West German intelligence officer and KGB agent, by deliberately exposing another, less important, spy.

As tantalizing as these discrepancies were, CIA could only wait until Nosenko signaled his return to the West to question him further. It was not until eighteen months later—in January 1964—that Nosenko returned to Geneva, again the security officer of a disarmament delegation. Moments after slipping into a safe house, and before the case officers could turn to the pages of questions prepared for him, Nosenko announced that, contrary to his previous position, he now wanted to defect at once. He had fallen under suspicion and was about to be recalled to Moscow—in the circumstance, he had no choice but to escape and to make a new life for himself in the West. Before the case officer could react to this, Nosenko dropped another bomb. As a KGB officer, Nosenko had "personally superintended" the KGB file on Lee Harvey Oswald while he was in the Soviet

---

*In October 1980 David H. Barnett, a former CIA officer, was convicted of espionage and admitted having received ninety-two thousand dollars from the KGB. Barnett worked for CIA from 1958 to 1970, when he resigned. In 1976 when he was living in Indonesia, Barnett encountered financial trouble and offered his services to the KGB—CIA is not the only beneficiary of the walk-in trade. After recruitment Barnett made a trip to Vienna where he was given training in a KGB safe house by case officers he knew only as "Mike," "Aleksi," and "Pavel." Although he was rehired by CIA in 1979, apparently as a training officer, Barnett's long-range mission seems to have been to get a job on the Senate Select Committee on Intelligence or the White House Oversight Board. Barnett is the most senior CIA man known to have been recruited by the KGB but, on the basis of the press accounts, was at a far remove from the "highest echelons" of U.S. intelligence when he was detected.

Union. This statement, made less than two months after Oswald assassinated Kennedy, exploded in CIA headquarters. No time was lost whisking Nosenko out of Switzerland and to the United States.

If Nosenko was bona fide, his knowledge of the KGB relationship with Oswald would be vitally important. If he was a dispatched agent, he had been sent by the Soviet government to deliver a message, presumably a deceptive one.

In Washington the first questions put to Nosenko concerned Lee Harvey Oswald.

Oswald was seventeen when he joined the Marine Corps in 1956. After training as a radar operator he was assigned to the Naval Air Facility at Atsugi, Japan. As Epstein discovered, Atsugi was one of the airfields used by the U-2 aircraft developed by CIA for secret photographic reconnaissance over the USSR. The marine radar operators at the base knew the plane operated at ninety thousand feet—an altitude then well over the world record for any aircraft—and that it was involved in secret work.

As much a misfit in the marines as he had been in civilian life, Oswald returned to the United States in November 1958. He was discharged in September 1959 and a few days later left for Europe by ship. On 15 October he entered the USSR on a six-day tourist visa. In Moscow, Oswald informed his Intourist guide that he wanted to renounce his American citizenship and remain in the Soviet Union.

This brought about an interview with a Soviet official who, perhaps understandably, could scarcely credit Oswald's intent. A few days later he was informed that his request was refused and that he would have to leave the Soviet Union when his visa expired. The following afternoon Oswald was discovered unconscious in his hotel room, his wrist slashed. By the time he was released from hospital, Soviet authorities had a change of heart and he was given permission to remain in the USSR.

Oswald then visited the consular section of the U.S. embassy in Moscow with the intention of renouncing his citizenship. In a discussion with a consul who gently attempted to dissuade him, Oswald admitted that he had already agreed to furnish Soviet authorities "with such knowledge as he had acquired while in the Marine Corps concerning his specialty." He also suggested that he had information that would be of special interest to the Russians. The process of renouncing his citizenship may have proved too time-consuming for Oswald—he did not return to the consulate to complete the procedure.

Soviet authorities refused Oswald's request to study at Moscow University, but arranged a job for him in an electronics factory in Minsk. The Soviet "Red Cross" granted him a seven-hundred-ruble monthly stipend and he was given a comfortable, all but rent-free apartment. Despite these considerable benefits, Oswald soon began to sour on life in Minsk. Not only were there no nightclubs or bowling alleys but, in addition to his factory job, he was expected to do an occasional turn picking potatoes on a collective farm. Some eighteen months after his defection, Oswald wrote the embassy asking for his passport so that he could return to the United States.

Before the drawn-out negotiations were complete, Oswald had married Marina Prusakova, the niece of Colonel Ilya Prusakov, a Ministry of State Security (the MVD, parent organization of the KGB) official stationed in Minsk. Not only was Colonel Prusakov Marina's uncle, he was also her surrogate father—Marina lived with the Prusakov family in Minsk. Before the travel arrangements were complete, Oswald was the father of a daughter, June Lee. After lengthy negotiations with the American bureaucracy and relatively little trouble with Soviet officialdom—notoriously reluctant to permit the emigration of Soviet citizens married to foreigners—the Oswald family left the Soviet Union. They arrived in the United States in June 1962. Seventeen months later, Oswald murdered John F. Kennedy.

Under interrogation Nosenko allegedly stated flatly that the KGB had never heard of Oswald until he arrived in the USSR and during the thirty months he had spent there had no contact whatsoever with him. Under repeated questioning Nosenko elaborated a bit on his answer, but stuck to the basic point—the KGB had not so much as interviewed Oswald in the USSR. The notion that the KGB would not bother to question a recently discharged marine who had defected to the USSR and been given a residence permit, a good salary, an apartment, and a handsome monthly allowance from the Soviet Red Cross, struck Nosenko's interrogators as bizarre. This carefree approach to security did not jibe with what was known about the treatment given other military defectors to the Soviet Union. Nor did it square with Oswald's statement to the consul that he had already volunteered to inform Soviet authorities on his "military specialty."

Nosenko admitted that, had the KGB known Oswald had information on the U-2, he would have been interrogated. But, he said, since this was not known, Oswald was not questioned. This was not a convincing argument: one reason intelligence services interrogate defectors is, of course, to find out what they may have to offer. For all the

KGB knew, Oswald might have been an expert on military cipher machines—a topic of even greater interest than the U-2. Then, too, as a Soviet sympathizer from the age of fourteen, Oswald might well have known others who would respond to a KGB approach.

Had Nosenko, who served in Soviet naval intelligence before joining the KGB, asserted that Soviet navigators worked on the assumption that the earth was flat, it would not have been less convincing than his account of Oswald in the USSR.

Taken in context with Nosenko's other disclosures, it seemed to the interrogators that the KGB might have intended to make sure that the CIA—and the Warren Commission—would have no reason to think that Oswald was a KGB agent or that the Soviet Union was in any way involved in the Kennedy assassination. As one witness testifying before the House Select Committee suggested, the KGB would scarcely go to the trouble—and risk— of dispatching a false defector to tell such a tale unless they had something to hide.

If Oswald had been handled in the USSR as other defectors are known to have been, the story would be quite different. As a defector, Oswald would have been thoroughly interrogated by the KGB and GRU before he was granted a residence permit and the other perquisites. His knowledge of radar and the details of his Marine Corps service would have been carefully recorded. In view of his statement to the consular officer that he had something of special interest to give to the Russians, Oswald may have realized that his information on the U-2 would be valuable. If he had not raised the subject, the interrogators should have uncovered it. Oswald would also have been asked about any former buddies—possible Soviet sympathizers, chronic debtors, alcoholics, homosexuals—who might be susceptible to recruitment. Because the Marine Corps provides the guard force at most U.S. embassies, the KGB and GRU carefully index operational data on enlisted Marine personnel against the day that a potential recruit may appear as an embassy guard.

In the course of the interrogation a case officer would have assessed Oswald's potential as an agent. If, as seems likely, Oswald had not shown the discipline and stability necessary for undercover work—and his suicide attempt would have been a mark against him—he might still have been considered for possible wartime work. In the event of war, a stable of native Americans trained, for example, as saboteurs, could be committed with little or no security risk.

To continue this speculation, it seems possible that whatever work might have been considered for Oswald would have been put aside once his intellectual shortcomings and emotional instability had started to show. When Oswald's disenchantment with the USSR had become obvious, making him a public relations liability in Minsk, the KGB could have been glad to be rid of him. And if his departure was contingent on that of his wife, it is possible that she would not have been considered such a loss either. If, after deciding to quit the Soviet Union, Oswald had volunteered his future services to the KGB as a "sleeper" or standby agent in the United States, one can even imagine a case officer saying, "Don't call us, we'll call you."

In that case, when, almost a year and a half later, the KGB learned that Oswald had killed Kennedy, someone would have had to go to Khrushchev and admit that, although the KGB contact with Oswald had been relatively innocent, it might be misinterpreted once the United States found out about it. (Had the KGB wanted to assassinate Kennedy it seems unlikely they would have chosen Oswald, a crackpot who could not even be counted on to keep cover before the deed, much less to resist interrogation if taken alive. The KGB might also have been expected to avoid a candidate who had paraded his communist sympathies in the U.S. Marine Corps and who was known to have spent thirty months in the USSR.)

But, the supposition continues, like the sculptor who, having finished a marble bust, decides to give the nose one last tap, the KGB went too far. Few with the slightest knowledge of Soviet intelligence could swallow Nosenko's story that the KGB had *never* bothered to speak to Oswald. As one witness before the House committee put it, if the KGB found that a defector from the Marine Corps knew nothing else, they would question him on close order drill.

After two months of polite questioning, during which time Nosenko is alleged to have ducked and parried questions intended to clarify his bona fides, CIA took off the gloves. Nosenko was put under what amounted to house arrest. From April 1964 to December 1968, when the conditions of his detention were moderated, he was held in solitary confinement and subjected to extensive interrogation. Despite pressure, Nosenko stuck to his story, adamantly denying that he had been sent by the KGB. In December 1968 the results of an independent review of the entire Nosenko case by an officer who had not participated in the earlier interrogation led the agency to conclude that Nosenko was a bona fide defector and that his observations on Oswald had been made in good faith.

In September 1978 CIA responded to a series of questions posed by the House Select Committee. Asked for "... CIA's position today on the question of whether Nosenko is bona fide?" the agency's response was measured and clear. "The point is that CIA, per se, did not reach an agreed position on Mr. Nosenko until late 1968. Various persons within CIA entertained serious doubts about his bona fides, believing in fact that he was a dispatched agent. Had the Agency, as distinguished from those employees, so concluded he could simply have been turned back. The final conclusion was that he is a bona fide defector, a judgement that has been reinforced convincingly by 14 years accumulated evidence."

The persons who "entertained serious doubts" included most of the senior counterintelligence officers and Soviet operations experts who had handled the case from the outset.

This is not the place to debate the Nosenko case. That can only be done by those with access to the complete file and the most current intelligence bearing on it. If Nosenko is on the level, then the allegation reported by Epstein and Martin that Popov was uncovered when the KGB found the letter addressed to him, is presumably correct. If Nosenko was dispatched, then the possibility remains that this tidbit is meant to conceal something of importance—conceivably even the identity of the agent—another defector allegedly reported to be in the "highest echelons of American intelligence."

From the evidence unearthed in preparing this book, there are several obvious clues suggesting why the KGB might have come to suspect Popov—the Bielic relationship, Blake's report from Berlin, and the Tairova incident in New York are more than enough to have focused security attention on Popov. Even if he withstood interrogation, it could only have been a matter of time before the investigators found the espionage gear concealed in his fishing reel and hunting knife.

But obvious clues are rarely the best explanation of counterintelligence problems. Even without tapping secret files, there is enough information in the published record to indicate what appears to be a significant discrepancy in Nosenko's alleged version of the Popov arrest. In reading this account, it should be remembered that it is based only on the published record. If the secret archive offers a different version, it has not been made public.

Soviet accounts of the Popov case agree that Popov returned to Moscow late in December 1958. On 9 December 1958 General Ivan

Serov, who had commanded the KGB since its inception, was abruptly transferred to "other duties." Later it was learned that General Serov had been seconded to the GRU to replace General Shalin, the long-time chief of Soviet military intelligence. John Barron's comment is pertinent: "But the real eclipse of the GRU's independence began in 1958, when the KGB discovered that GRU Lieutenant Colonel Yuri [sic] Popov was a CIA spy. Khrushchev ordered KGB chairman Ivan Serov to take personal charge of the GRU and clean it up."[*]

Khrushchev obviously was informed of the Popov case in time for him to order the significant transfer of Serov from the KGB to the lesser post of GRU chief. His decision to remove Serov from the KGB does not seem to have been based entirely on the need to tidy up the GRU—he quite likely welcomed the opportunity to rid his government of a notorious secret policeman and name a party official, and Khrushchev man, as KGB chief. However complex Khrushchev's motives were, Serov's transfer was an important move that could not have been taken lightly.

The timing of the move—December 1958—suggests that Khrushchev acted at about the time Popov returned to Moscow from Germany. If so, how could Popov have been detected—as Nosenko allegedly reported—when the KGB tracked an embassy official to a letterbox and discovered a letter addressed to Popov? Popov had ostensibly returned to Moscow on temporary duty and expected to be back in East Berlin within a few days. In such circumstances, it is unlikely that an intelligence service could have had any reason to risk posting a letter to him in Moscow, or would even have had an address at which they could be certain of reaching him.

Could Barron have been wrong in his reason for the transfer of Serov from the KGB to the GRU? Hardly, it would seem, in view of what happened to Serov three years later. In 1962 the KGB discovered that GRU Colonel Oleg Penkovsky had been recruited by British and American intelligence. Not long after that, the news leaked that Serov had been summarily relieved of his GRU post, stripped of several decorations and demoted. If the Central Committee was prepared to fire Serov, once one of the most powerful men in the USSR, because a subordinate had been discovered to be a CIA agent, surely they would not have jibbed at sacking General Shalin, a much lesser figure, when his subordinate was found out. There can be little doubt

*Barron, *KGB*, p. 344.

that General Shalin's termination was directly related to Popov's discovery and arrest.

Various Soviet publications mention that Popov was sent to his Moscow rendezvous with the CIA contact man from jail—that is, after his arrest and while he was operating as a double agent under KGB control. It seems highly unlikely that the abrupt transfer of a man as conspicuous in the Soviet hierarchy as General Serov would have been publicized before Popov, the cause of all the trouble, was safely in the Lubyanka cellars. Thus, Popov must have been under arrest by 9 December, the day Serov's transfer was announced. Again, one must ask when the letter-mailing incident could have occurred.

According to Epstein and Martin, Nosenko was not the only source to attribute Popov's unmasking to the diplomat who was trailed to the mailbox. In October 1963, over a year after Nosenko made his first approach to CIA in Geneva and reported on how Popov had been detected, a furtive stranger handed a packet of papers to an American tourist and asked him to take them to the American embassy. The tourist delivered the documents but, after photographing them, the embassy allegedly decided to return them to Soviet authorities. Apparently some faint-hearted person in authority was concerned lest the mere receipt of such a gift would somehow upset international relations.

The documents were allegedly the gift of a KGB officer named Cherepanov who professed to be a member of the American embassy section of the KGB, the unit in which Nosenko had claimed to work. One of the documents described the new KGB technique of coating the shoes of diplomats the KGB wished to keep under surveillance— and mentioned that this had led to the arrest and execution of Popov. On the face of it, Cherepanov's documents seemed to be a fortuitous confirmation of one aspect of Nosenko's story.

In January 1964, according to Epstein, when Nosenko appeared in Geneva for the second time, and signaled his intention to defect, he had among his papers a travel order authorizing him to travel to Gorki. Nosenko allegedly explained that he had been issued this document when assigned to help in the search for a colleague—none other than Lieutenant Colonel Cherepanov. Now the circle was complete—Cherepanov's notes and Nosenko's documented travel dovetailed perfectly.

Alas, as often happens in counterespionage cases, things became more complicated as the investigation continued. Nosenko went on to claim that Cherepanov had been transferred from the First Chief Directorate—espionage abroad—to the Second Chief Directorate—counterintelligence—when he was suspected of having attempted to make contact with a Western intelligence service in Yugoslavia. This baffled the interrogators. Why would the hyper-security-conscious KGB dismiss a man suspected of attempted treason from one directorate only to assign him to another, equally sensitive unit? What first appeared to be a comforting confirmation of Nosenko's version of Popov's arrest now seemed to be just another piece of KGB deception.

If Nosenko *was* a dispatched KGB agent, then it followed that the Cherepanov reports were intended—in part at least—to convince CIA that Nosenko was on the level and that his accounts of Oswald's activity in the USSR and of Popov's arrest were valid. Aside from the identical reports on how Popov was detected, there were allegedly other parallels in the ostensibly independent reports from Nosenko and Cherepanov.

As speculation continued, according to Epstein, counterintelligence experts turned again to Golitsin's allegation that there was a KGB mole in the "highest echelons" of American intelligence. If such a source had blown Popov, then it would have been in the KGB interest to make sure that CIA had no reason to suspect how Popov had been betrayed.

This logic seems sound enough, but the fact remains that there were at least three obvious ways in which Popov might have been tripped up—Bielic, Blake, and Tairova. In the circumstances, why would the KGB have gone to such lengths to provide CIA with a story that not only did not hang together but which, when tested against overt data on Serov's transfer, made no sense at all?

One line of speculation suggests that when Oswald shot Kennedy, the KGB might have been put under heavy pressure, presumably from the Central Committee or Khrushchev, to convince CIA and the Warren Commission that the Soviet Union had not been involved in any way with Oswald. What if the KGB had been preparing Nosenko for a long-range deception scheme that did not involve his defection (he had said he did not want to defect at his first session with CIA in Geneva) and then had been forced to make a sudden change of plans and instruct the ill-prepared Nosenko to defect before his mission had been thoroughly thought through?

For all of this speculation it must be remembered that as recently as September 1978 CIA assured the House Select Committee that Nosenko was a bona fide defector and stated that his information on Oswald had been reported in good faith.

There remains another loose end. When Popov was first questioned about the Tairov case in East Berlin, his interrogator alleged—or seemed to let slip—the news that "three KGB sources" had confirmed Tairova's story that she had been surveilled from the moment she arrived in New York. The fact that a senior KGB officer had told a reliable source—Popov—that the Russians had three sources in a position to report on an operation handled on a maximum security basis by the FBI and CIA is more than enough to cause an implosion in both services. If the KGB man's allegation was correct, the confirmation of Tairova's report probably could only have come from a mole or a technical penetration—a hidden microphone or a compromised communication system.

But before rushing to the conclusion that there was a troika of moles buried in the inner circles of the FBI and CIA, counterintelligence experts would first examine the report itself. Could it be that a counterintelligence officer, experienced and senior enough to be sent from Moscow to East Berlin to investigate the compromise of the Tairovs, would *inadvertently* blow the fact that the KGB had three such well-placed sources in New York? Any *one* such source would be a treasure, something to be protected at all costs. On form, no Russian officer would be so foolhardy as to deliberately expose the existence of these sources to anyone, least of all in an attempt to intimidate one of the persons under investigation.

Still, the possibility of penetration always exists and no oncologist on the trail of a malignant cell would be more diligent than a counterintelligence officer tracking down such a lead.

In 1979 a curious allegation, possibly pertinent to the Tairov incident, surfaced. This story began in 1971 when a long-smoldering feud between J. Edgar Hoover and William C. Sullivan, then the number-three man in the FBI, burst into flames. When this happened, Hoover demanded Sullivan's resignation. Sullivan, a thirty-year FBI veteran, counterattacked by sending Hoover a scorching indictment of Hoover's performance. Furious at this *lèse majesté*, Hoover had Sullivan locked out of his office. Taking his boss's point, Sullivan retired to New Hampshire.

In 1975, with the help of Bill Brown, a New York TV producer and member of the NBC news staff, Sullivan began working on a book giving his side of the story. By 1977, when the book was ready to be put into final form, Sullivan was shot dead, the victim of a hunting accident. Although TASS, the Soviet press agency, released a bulletin suggesting that Sullivan had been the victim of a joint FBI/CIA plot, New Hampshire officials, Brown, and other responsible authorities agreed that Sullivan's death was accidental. Brown completed the book, which was published in 1979.*

It is a vindictive book and some of the judgments seem distorted by Sullivan's hatred of the man for whom he had worked so assiduously for so many years. One part of the angry account might possibly bear on the Tairov story.

At an unspecified time, Sullivan became convinced that the FBI's New York office was penetrated by the KGB. When Sullivan raised his suspicions, Hoover, quite correctly, asked him to prove his case. Sullivan could not do so to Hoover's satisfaction. The evidence cited in the book—the alleged drying up of an FBI operational program and the collapse of a double agent case Sullivan ran against the KGB—is much too fragmentary for analysis. But Sullivan apparently remained convinced. He closed the pages on this subject with the comment, "At the time I left the FBI in 1971, the Russians still had a man in our office and none of us knew who he was."

Whatever the validity of Sullivan's observations—and one may assume that the allegations have long since been run to ground—he was right in being suspicious. Any intelligence officer who assumes his service is penetration-proof is ignorant of intelligence history. Sullivan was a keen student of spying and some of the documented Soviet activity in World War II may have fanned his suspicions.

When German troops were within sight of Moscow and the USSR was fighting for its existence, Soviet intelligence found the time and was able to devote the sophisticated skills of senior operatives to handling penetration agents within the top echelon of at least one of its most important *allies.* Anthony Blunt, allegedly a Soviet agent since 1933, had dug so deeply into the British government that by the end of the war he was one of a handful of the most senior officers in MI-5, the British security service. Throughout the war he was in a position to keep his Soviet case officers intimately informed of much of

---

*William C. Sullivan with Bill Brown, *The Bureau: My Thirty Years in Hoover's FBI* (New York: W. W. Norton & Company, 1979), pp. 188–191.

British counterespionage and security activity as well as to forward inside comments from his peers in the diplomatic and military establishments. Kim Philby, less highly placed in MI-6 than the patrician "Blunty" in MI-5, nevertheless mustered sufficient cunning to pass along MI-6's secrets to his Soviet comrades.

Operations at this level against an ally are intricate and, if compromised, have a spectacular potential for rattling diplomatic relations. Only the most adroit case officers can be trusted to keep such penetration agents happy, maintain security, and generate the maximum of information. But for all the guile and dexterity Soviet intelligence devoted to its allies, it cannot be said to have neglected similar operations against Nazi Germany.

In 1943 General Viktor Abakumov, then chief of Soviet military counterintelligence (SMERSH), struck directly at the Nazi jugular. After a SMERSH operative recruited a high-ranking Gestapo officer in Danzig, Abakumov supervised the maneuvering of the agent into a position where he could sound out, and subsequently recruit *Obergruppenfuehrer* Heinrich Mueller. Mueller was not just any SS general, he was chief of the Gestapo. Ostensibly, Mueller was a more savage anticommunist than his boss, Heinrich Himmler. Abakumov must have had remarkable insights into the Nazi high command to realize that Mueller could be convinced that the millennial Reich was doomed and that he was enough of an opportunist to make a deal.

Mueller disappeared in the last days of the Berlin fighting. At first thought to be dead, his presence in the USSR was mentioned in several unverified reports. In 1945 an American war crimes investigator sent a formal request to the Soviet war crimes authorities for information on the whereabouts of SS *Obergruppenfuehrer* Mueller, one of the most notorious Nazi war criminals. Weeks later, the Soviets responded. Noting that there were many Muellers in East Germany, the Russians asked for the lieutenant general's first name. Pawky humor is not an exclusively Anglo-Saxon taste.

Sullivan's suspicions notwithstanding, there is at least one relatively innocent and highly plausible explanation for the allegation that the KGB had three confirmations of Tairova's suspicions.

It was not long after the Tairovs' flight that Western intelligence tumbled to the fact that KGB was making strenuous efforts to monitor the radio frequencies used by security services in surveillance operations against Soviet intelligence officers. The extent of the monitoring done with powerful receivers and directional antennas from the roofs of Soviet diplomatic installations throughout the world has continued to increase. In 1980 press reports noted that the Soviet embassy in Washington was intercepting telephone calls of U.S. government officials in the Washington area by monitoring the microwave transmissions that have replaced old-fashioned telephone wires. Given the right equipment, this sort of operation can be done with complete immunity from within any diplomatic building.

Anyone doubting the commitment the Russians have made to monitoring need only look at the antennas on the roof of the Soviet embassy in Washington. There are so many masts and spars supporting the antennas that, given a force-five breeze and enough canvas, an experienced skipper could *sail* the embassy down Sixteenth Street and into the Potomac River. (Since the publicity given Soviet monitoring activity, many of the antennas have been masked or dropped below the line of sight from the street, but enough are still visible to give a good indication of what is going on.)

Because there are dozens of surveillance radios on the air on any given day—police, FBI, narcotics, private investigators, and security services—the KGB presumably has a difficult time sorting them all out. The fact that the interrogator mentioned three sources might mean that a back check showed three different occasions when monitoring reports could have been tied to Tairova's known movements—on arrival, at the meeting in Yonkers, and perhaps after the Tairovs' escape. Knowing these specific dates and times, analysts in Moscow might have checked the intercept logs and determined that there was a flurry of radio activity at these times.

If the KGB's three sources were in fact intercepted surveillance messages, then the sources have long since dried up. For years now, Western security services have masked the radio activity of their surveillance squads. The fact that the KGB probably knew that this intercept activity had run its course, may have prompted the interrogator to attempt to cow Popov by mentioning the alleged three confirmations of Tairova's story.

The first of the many writers to liken espionage to chess coined one of the least apt analogies in literature. However fetching the notion that opposing intelligence chiefs are like chess masters—pondering the black and white pieces and plotting tactics a dozen moves ahead—it is absurd. Worse, it ignores the real fascination of espionage.

On the chessboard each piece is clearly visible and moves in a prescribed fashion. In victory and defeat, the white men remain indelibly white, the black resolutely black. There are no traitor pieces, no false knights, and even pawns never defect.

Spy, counter-spy; agent, double agent; traitor, hero—the Gestapo chief, *Obergruppenfuehrer* Mueller; heir apparent chief of British intelligence, Kim Philby; the Keeper of the Queen's Pictures, Sir Anthony Blunt; Colonel Penkovsky and Lieutenant Colonel Pyotr Semyonovich Popov of the GRU—spying is life turned all around.

Was Popov betrayed or did the KGB uncover him? It seems likely that the KGB found him out, but perhaps it is fitting to end a spy story with a question.

ABOUT THE AUTHOR

William Hood was born in Maine and attended school there. He served in the OSS in England, France, and Switzerland during WWII and retired from the CIA in 1975. When asked about his major accomplishments, he responded, "Such as they may have been, they are all classified." He currently divides his time between Portland, Maine, New York City, and Amagansett, Long Island.